The

Great Railway
Conspiracy

The British Railways passenger system in approximately
1959, before the Beeching cuts. British Railways map.

The
Great Railway
Conspiracy

The fall and rise of Britain's railways since the 1950s

By David Henshaw

With a foreword by

Stan Abbott

Leading Edge
press and publishing

This book is dedicated to the railwaymen and women who kept the system running through all the years of turmoil.

The Great Railway Conspiracy
Published by Leading Edge Press & Publishing
The Old Chapel
Burtersett
Hawes
North Yorkshire
DL8 3PB
☎ (0969) 667566

ISBN 0-948135-28-X (cased)
      0-948135-30-1 (paperback)

A CIP Catalogue record for this book is available from the British Library.

Editing and design: Stan Abbott
Cover design: Ruth Abbott
Cartoons: Bill Lehan
Maps: David Henshaw
Indexing: Midge Whitelegg
Type: Leading Edge Press & Publishing
Colour reprographics: Impression, Leeds
Printed and bound in Great Britain by Bath Press, Avon

Title page picture shows an ex-Great Western Railway railcar at the overgrown platform at Easton Court station on the Woofferton Junction to Tenbury line, north of Hereford, just before its closure in August 1962. The GWR had pioneered the use of railcars between the wars but, in 1962, British Railways was saddled with a legacy of uneconomic steam trains. W F Finch.

Contents

7 Publisher's foreword

11 Author's introduction

13 Chapter 1. The Railway Revolution, 1825-1945

A summary of the railways' origins and their development through the periods of railway mania. How the foundations were laid for the national system through the pre-war groupings of the old private companies.

34 Chapter 2. State control, 1947-1951

The nationalisation of the railways under the post-war Labour administration. How the dream rapidly began to turn sour.

57 Chapter 3. The closures begin, 1951-1954

The return of Winston Churchill and the Tories to power saw the ideological pendulum swing away from the railways and notions of an integrated transport system.

87 Chapter 4. You've never had it so good, 1955-1959

The premiership of Harold Macmillan saw the car become God as the railways' financial state became ever more parlous.

116 Chapter 5. The Marples-Beeching axis, 1960-1963

Ernest Marples' appointment as Minister of Transport marks the road industry's zenith. Dr Richard Beeching gets the job of scything the rail network down to size.

145 Chapter 6. The Beeching Report

Dr Beeching's "Reshaping" report envisaged major cuts to the network. But flaws in his analysis meant the savings he expected to achieve never materialised.

171 Chapter 7. The axe falls, 1964-1969

The Beeching cuts begin to bite — and continue apace, despite the election of a Labour Government which has pledged to halt closures and dismisses Beeching.

199 Chapter 8. The energy crisis, 1970-1990

After the loss of trunk routes such as the Waverley line, the closures finally begin to slow down as the Arab oil embargo changes the transport agenda overnight.

227 Chapter 9. Retrospective

The Beeching years in context. The way forward.

238 Appendices

i) Summary of lines for reopening

ii) The case for reopening

iii) Comparison with Europe

248 Bibliography

248 Glossary of terms

250 Index

v

The British Rail passenger network in 1990, including a modest number of lines reopened during the previous 20 years. British Railways map.

Foreword

THERE exists in any society built on the principles of free speech a desire constantly to reappraise historic events the better to understand our present.

Part of this process has seen the portrayal of popular anti-heroes in a less demeaning light, the passage of time being permitted to dim less favourable memories of those whom historians and biographers may wish to rehabilitate.

The question in the case of one such anti-hero, Dr Richard Beeching, is whether or not he was justifiably the object of public anger for his role in the demise of Britain's once extensive railway network during the 1960s. As the tide of public derision has ebbed with the years, more writers have begun to brave the waters to swim against it.

Chief among them have been the author Richard Hardy, Beeching's biographer, and Nicholas Faith, journalist and author of *The World the Railways Made*. Hardy's central message is that Beeching was a sensitive and courageous man who, in failing to understand people's attachment to their railways, was himself sadly misunderstood and branded, unjustifiably, a soulless axeman or butcher. Faith, in a tribute to Beeching in the *Independent* magazine's *Heroes and Villains* column, goes onto the offensive, condemning those who dare criticise Beeching policies as "emotionally retarded adolescents" intent on running the country's railways as "a gigantic toy train set" with no thought for the community at large. Beeching, on the other hand, was "the only man since the War with the vision and management and intellectual equipment to provide Britain with an efficient railway system attuned to the country's social and economic needs".

Beeching did, undoubtedly, have his good side: before his day, the management of Britain's railways was a total shambles, and it is telling that it was, ultimately, the road transport lobby which prevented Beeching (after his departure from the railway helm)from carrying out a wide-ranging review of the nation's transport policy because it felt he might unduly favour rail over road.

Yet — in heaping excess praise on the man for his positive achievements — Beeching's posthumous friends risk obscuring the issues behind those turbulent years for Britain's railways and those who rode, or would have liked to ride, on them. It is rather like praising Hitler for helping create the VW Beetle while conveniently forgetting his other notorious deeds.

No-one need question Beeching's integrity, his belief in fair play or his conviction that the logic behind the statistical test he applied to rural railways and some trunk lines was a sound one.

In this book, however, David Henshaw analyses the economic and political developments that preceded Beeching's appointment. The extent to which the railways were victims of a conspiracy — in the primary sense of its participants hatching plots in dimly lit rooms — remains the subject of debate. But the author's researches do put considerably more flesh on the bones of the plot that has long been suspected in informed circles.

The book began life with the title, *The Beeching Years*, but it became apparent that Beeching himself was only one more participant, albeit a significant one, in a complex game. A game in which — by cock-up or conspiracy — the road transport side, backed by a partisan government, was ready to run riot against a railway opposition with both hands tied behind its back.

Into this uneven contest stepped Dr Beeching, secure in his conviction that the policy of radical pruning of the network was both essential to its future and backed by irrefutable logic.

Beeching applied himself as effective arbiter of the future of individual railways.But what he failed to grasp was that the game he refereed was governed by a set of rules that would not have been out of place at the Mad Hatter's tea party.

The rule book was cooked — the economic merits of road transport could be judged against all kinds of measures of vague social benefits, such as drivers' time, while the railways were judged on strictly financial criteria. Yet, as David Henshaw describes, the basis of even these financial criteria was seriously flawed.

The result was the grievous loss to the country of its strategic transport network with — thanks to Beeching's failure properly to address the more serious problem of over-staffing — virtually no financial benefit to the railways themselves.

Today we are increasingly paying the price for that bitter legacy and can only regret the wasted post-War years — before and during Beeching's reign — when bold investment combined with sensible trimming should have transformed Britain's railways into a system fit to lead the country to prosperity.

I am pleased, as publisher, to enable David Henshaw to tell the story and thereby put the record straight on Dr Beeching and all the others who played a part in the demise of the railways, and to endorse the work of such organisations as the Railway Development Society which strive to undo some of the worst aspects of the Beeching Years.

Stan Abbott, Wensleydale, September 1991

Introduction

IN THE western suburbs of London, where the leafy villas of Richmond lean gently towards the River Thames, there stands an extraordinary edifice. Low, mean and vaguely threatening, this concrete carbuncle of a building is not, as it appears to be, the embassy of some totalitarian regime, or a rather superior multi-storey car park, but the Public Records Office, where official documents wait in air-conditioned seclusion for public perusal. It was here that much of the research for this book was carried out.

Railway records are not, strictly speaking, government records at all, but the British railway system has become so intimately entwined with government affairs since the war that railway files are disclosed only under the same rules as documents relating to political affairs, defence matters, and other state secrets: those that are considered suitable for eventual public scrutiny are mostly held for 30 or more years before release to the Public Records Office.

But what, one might ask, becomes of the documents that are too embarrassing for release even after 30 years? The official line is that they are carefully sifted to preserve a balanced and accurate cross-section of material."But why," I asked, "are comparatively innocuous records (such as railway track-costs, railbus economics, and branch line closure papers) held for 30 years?"

"Because no-one made a decision that they should not be...."

Whether there really has been a conspiracy to withhold information — either at the then Ministry of Transport or the Railways Board — is hard to judge. But the fact remains that the records dating from prior to the late 1950s do,indeed, provide a detailed account of railway affairs, but those from later years (and all the records up to, and including,1960 should now be open) are distinctly lacking in candour.

That the movements of Royal trains should remain secret for 30 years is perhaps understandable, but are railway reports, statistics, and records of committee meetings really state secrets? And who actually decides which documents relating to those turbulent years should be withheld, released, or destroyed? We may never know, and it will be a number of years before it is possible even to judge which records remain, for files are held for 30 years from the date on which they were originally closed: many files were held open at the Railways Board and the Ministry for a decade or more. The only records currently open from the 1960s relate to such harmless matters as holiday guides, railway horses(!) and locomotive head-codes. Of the affairs surrounding the massive closure programme overseen by Dr Beeching, the Public Records Office has just one file — a box of press-cuttings.

Thus, although the first and last chapters of this book are based upon information form a wide variety of sources, and Chapter 4 leans heavily on public records, Chapters 5 and 6 are constructed around what little written evidence exists, together with interviews with railway managers and others. In Chapter 5, in particular, some broad assumptions have necessarily been made. Nevertheless, a picture has emerged that goes some way towards explaining the near collapse of Britain's railways: a picture of incompetence, political skullduggery and a final, and all-enveloping, official silence.

Needless to say, this book could not have been written without the kind assistance of those within and without the industry who were willing to be interviewed or provide information. Perhaps understandably, many were not, and one or two must remain anonymous, but particular thanks must go to staff of the Public Records Office; to Owen Prosser, founder of the Railway Development Association, who provided unlimited access to his extensive archives; and to Trevor Garrod, General Secretary of the Railway Development Society, who gave every assistance.

***

The seeds of *The Great Railway Conspiracy* were sown long ago... The decades that followed the second world war saw many far-reaching political and social changes in Britain: industrial concerns, some of which had seen precious few changes in more than a century, were brought kicking and screaming into the 20th century overnight, but none were to suffer as much as the railways. And in no case would their strife cause quite the same heartfelt public concern and heated Parliamentary debates as that of the railway industry.

Britain, it seemed, had retained a system of parliamentary patronage from a previous more gentlemanly age, but it was a system that was bound to fail under the intense commercial pressures of the late 20th century. The road transport pressure groups — the car manufacturers, the road builders, the oil companies and ancillary industries, and the bus operators (who were later to change sides) — were ranged against a nationalised, yet virtually powerless, railway industry. Aided by the Ministry of Transport, they succeeded, by the late 1960s, in bringing the railway system to its knees.

Eventually, governments of all political shades might have been happier had the entire railway network, with its associated staffing and infrastructure problems, been swallowed up overnight. Such divine intervention never arrived and, by the early 1970s, there did not appear to be a need for the last vestige of the railway in any shape or form. The question was no longer "How large a railway system do we need?", but "Is any sort of railway system actually necessary?" It was not until the Arab-inspired oil crisis of 1973 that the mood changed, and by then much of the railway system had been lost.

By and large then, the railways were perceived as a hangover from Britain's gloomy industrial past. In Harold Wilson's technological revolution their place would be taken by the bus, the private car and the short-haul aircraft.

That such a situation never arose was due largely to the work of a handful of far-sighted private individuals and a small, but dedicated, group of MPs. This is their story.

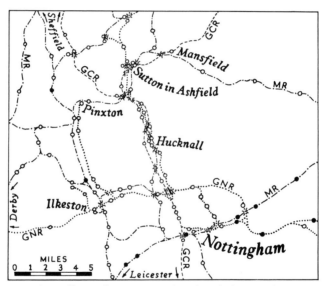

The extensive railway closures associated with the Beeching era were frequently justified on the grounds that competition between the original railway companies in the pre-grouping days. The map illustrates the most notorious example, in the area north of Nottingham, where the Midland (MR), Great Northern (GNR) and Great Central (GCR) fought for supremacy. The maze of competing facilities remained until well after nationalisation, but such excesses were few and occurred within a very limited area. Under Beeching, however, for most communities, three stations became none. Only the stations marked in black remain open today. See also map, over page.

The Waverley route between Carlisle and Edinburgh proved to be the last major railway closure in Britain — on the grounds that it duplicated the main West Coast route via Carstairs. Nothing could have been further from the truth, as the line served a higher intermediate population than either the West Coast line or the East Coast route, north of Newcastle. Indeed, the Waverley exhibited almost every quality to justify continued rail services, serving the commuter and broader travel needs of a large, if remote, population in wild region with immense tourism potential. Its retention would have brought significant extra revenue to the new, fast West Coast services and its closure was an unforgivable tragedy.

12

1.
The Railway Revolution
1825-1945

...in evolutionary law we come to an instinct to tear down and smash up all the old and put up the new... A savage man obeys his instincts.

Lord Strange, speaking in the House of Lords, May 1965

There is machinery for preserving ancient monuments, but I doubt whether it should be applied to the railway service.

Reply from Lord Silkin

ALTHOUGH the origins of the railways are popularly assumed to lie with the Stockton & Darlington in 1825, the concept of running wagons on a fixed trackway originated much further back in time. There are well recorded examples from the Middle Ages, and even earlier, of mineral wagons running on wooden or stone plate-ways, and no doubt the first railway passed by without attracting any publicity at all, as some nameless haulier noted with satisfaction that his wagon ran more easily when guided on a resilient channelled surface. Certainly many Roman roads, worn over the years by wagons of a standard width, took on the appearance of railways, necessitating the standardisation of wheel gauge for Imperial traffic.

It was not until the appearance of cheap and plentiful iron towards the end of the 18th century that railways (of an industrial nature at least) became commonplace. At a time when the condition of even the best roads varied with the seasons between poor and downright atrocious, colliery owners and others gladly adopted the new technology and benefited from a leap in productivity as a result. Even the crudest of wagonways showed considerable benefits over road haulage by the simple expedient of keeping the wagon wheels clear of the ground, and it was soon realised that an iron wheel running on an iron rail proceeded on its way with the minimum of friction. The horse that previously laboured to pull a single wagon could now handle half a dozen, and even the most simple minded of colliery owners could understand that sort of message.

By 1800, industrial wagonways were well established. And as the volume of freight increased, so too did the sophistication of the tramways. Efficiency had been improved dramatically by adopting rails; it was further improved with the adoption of a relatively level "permanent" way. A single horse could now handle tens of empty wagons, and if the line was built with a downward gradient from pit-head to destination, the train would actually propel itself, with the horse taking a ride on the outward journey, and pulling back the empties.

Amid these crude beginnings were sown the seeds that would create the most important technological advance of the 19th century. It was by chance that a new wagonway between Stockton and Darlington achieved the next great advance: for, in its meanderings from colliery to shipping wharf, the line linked two sizeable towns.

The origins of the line were somewhat confused. The intention, as early as 1768, had been to build a canal, but nothing much came of the scheme and, in 1810, a committee was formed to investigate whether a railway might not prove of greater benefit. Eventually, in 1818, a proposal for a combined canal and tramway was rushed before Parliament, only to be thrown out. The result was a firm decision to opt for a tramway in future proposals and, with the arrival on the scene of George Stephenson in the early 1820s, the stage was set for construction to begin.

Provisions to allow for the carriage of passengers, and for the haulage of trains by steam locomotives, were included in the Parliamentary Bill as no more than a sideline, for the Stockton & Darlington company was expecting to make its money by hauling coal in the traditional manner.

Early steam engines were expensive and unreliable, with a marked propensity for demolishing the fragile colliery wagonways. But under the guidance of George Stephenson, the technology began to advance, and by the opening of the Stockton & Darlington, steam engines were considered more or less financially viable, although not yet superior to horse traction.

The official opening of the line on September 27, 1825 was to change the course of history, however, for a rudimentary steam locomotive was provided to haul the first train — something that it proceeded to do with consummate ease. Indeed, although only 300 tickets had been issued, around 600 people actually clambered aboard, indicating that passenger services were a distinct possibility, and that a single steam engine was more than a match for even a team of horses.

On October 7, 1825, the company received a licence to carry passengers and three days later an experimental service was instigated between Stockton and Darlington. Not surprisingly, the first vehicles looked and performed in a similar manner to a contemporary stage-coach, the horse-drawn vehicle taking a leisurely two hours for the 12-mile trip. It wasn't a particularly lucrative operation either, for after a few months the company let the contract to one Richard Pickersgill who promptly slashed the journey time to 75 minutes and reduced the fare for outside passengers from 12d (5p) to 9d. This sort of

The opening of the Stockton and Darlingon Railway on September 27, 1825, marked the start of a revolution. Sketch by A R Brown, Trustees of the Science Museum.

arrangement was by no means unusual, for the Stockton & Darlington simply followed the practice of contemporary turnpike companies and opened its tramroad to all comers.

There was, however, a gradual appreciation that something entirely new was at work on the Stockton & Darlington. Most traffic was horse-drawn at first, and the line a single track with passing loops at intervals, but as fights for right of way became increasingly commonplace, the decision was taken to lay a second track. This was a crucial advance — two dedicated trackways, one for each direction of travel, a rudimentary signalling system to keep trainloads apart and, eventually, a single operator: the Stockton & Darlington company itself.

It soon became apparent that horse-drawn traffic was holding back the more sprightly steam locomotives. Steam traction was expensive, but a steam locomotive could haul more wagons, and it could haul them faster. In a typical working day the expensive steam engine handled a good deal more coal than the economical horse. In the end, it was a matter of simple economics, and as steam engines became more reliable, horse traction was gradually abandoned.

In September 1833, traffic levels really began to take off, and the company bought back the passenger carriage rights and instigated its own steam-hauled service. It had invented the first railway, and within a few short years had also discovered the most suitable method of operating it. But by increasing the speed and sophistication of its service, the company had learned the first lessons as well: for September 7, 1833 was to go down in history as the date of the first railway passenger service closure, when the horse-coach was taken off the Yarm branch. It was easier, from an operational point of view, for Yarm passengers to join trains at Yarm Branch End Station on the main line. And so it was that, 130 years before Dr Beeching, the first railway company rationalised a branch line service in order to speed traffic on the main line!

The Stockton & Darlington proved a phenomenal success. In the first nine months the railway carried a modest 42,983 tons of coal, but by 1860 it was carrying more than 2 million tons a year. Receipts rose accordingly — from £9,194 in the first full year, to almost £500,000 in 1863. Engineers arrived from all over the world to study the new methods, but it was George Stephenson who carried the word with the most vigour, being instrumental in the construction of the Liverpool & Manchester Railway, completed in 1830.

This line was built on an altogether different scale, for the earthworks, the strength and durability of the track, and (thanks largely to a single technological advance) the size and speed of the locomotives, left the little Stockton & Darlington out of the limelight. The technique of utilising a "forced draught" (whereby the exhaust steam from the operating cylinders of the locomotive drew air through the firebox) was first successfully demonstrated by Robert Stephenson on the Liverpool & Manchester. It was a crucial breakthrough that made previous machines obsolete overnight, for the power-to-weight ratio of steam locomotives was suddenly limited by technology alone and, thanks to the vision of the Stephensons and their contemporaries, technology was set to advance at an astonishing pace.

Within a decade of its conception, the railway had evolved into its final form — traffic would be handled (in most cases) by a single operator, and both passengers and freight carried in train-loads of hitherto undreamed of size, hauled along a dedicated trackway by a single powerful locomotive. These working practices — at once highly efficient and dangerously inflexible — were to prove both the saviour and the near downfall of the railways when more flexible modes of transportation arrived on the scene a century later.

* * *

The early optimism of the Liverpool & Manchester company proved well-founded, for traffic exceeded all forecasts. The line carried 460,000 passengers in its first year of operation— four times the total stage-coach traffic between the two towns in the previous year. Clearly the new railways had done more than just leach away the road traffic: they had actually generated new business by tapping into an unsatisfied demand for travel. It was a lesson that was not to be forgotten and, in the years that followed, investors clamoured to climb aboard.

In 1830 the Charleston line opened in South Carolina USA; 1832 saw the first French railway, at Lyon; and, by 1842, Britain could boast a network of more than 2,000 miles, linking all the major cities and turning over about £4 million a year. It might conceivably have stopped there, or soon after, but the profits of the pioneer lines were so tempting to investors (the Stockton & Darlington paying a handsome 15 per cent dividend) that there followed a renewed outbreak of speculation that culminated in the "railway mania" of 1844 to 1847.

By January 1846, no fewer than 815 schemes had been laid before Parliament, involving an estimated capital outlay of about £350 million, or six times the Gross National Product of the day. Perhaps fortunately, only a minority of these schemes were actually authorised, but the result was 8,600 miles of new track and a link to every major port and city in the land.

The problem was knowing where to stop. If a railway could bring prosperity and growth to a city — and the early lines undoubtedly did — then what might a railway line do for a town, or even a village? The railways were on the cutting edge of a rapidly growing economy, and the authorities were generally unable to persuade the citizens of a particular district that their poor and underpopulated region did not actually warrant the construction of a line, particularly if other similar areas were enjoying the advantages of a railway.

There was, of course, another reason for Parliamentary reluctance to turn down fresh railway schemes. The railways had almost destroyed the coaching trade and the canal operators, creating for themselves a near monopoly. As the roads and waterways were unable to compete, it was felt that the answer lay in the construction of competing railway lines. Thus, amid growing nervousness at the power of the railway companies, Parliament sanctioned the construction of many lines simply to tame the capitalist zeal of the others. It is important to note though, that in only a minority of cases did competing lines actually follow the same route — they were usually constructed well apart, serving quite different regions along their routes to a common destination. When, a century later, the authorities were to try and prove that "duplicate" lines were wasteful and unnecessary, they were wrong in many of their assumptions.

The all-encompassing solution of bringing the railways into national ownership had been considered as early as 1844, and the idea was raised at regular intervals thereafter. A possible alternative to full state ownership would be to transfer responsibility for fixed assets, such as track and signalling, to the Government, and to lease the operating side to private enterprise. Had such a scheme been instigated, there is no doubt that the railways would have developed differently in the years that followed. Railway services would presumably have been leased to the highest bidder, while those lines that failed to receive a satisfactory bid would have become the responsibility of the State. More importantly, investment in new construction, or disinvestment by way of closure and retraction, would all have become the Government's responsibility. Despite various problems, however, the private enterprise system proved fairly successful, and calls for national ownership were never taken very seriously.

By the 1860s, railway technology had advanced considerably, both figuratively and geographically. The first railway carriages had been constructed along stage-coach principles, first as a single stage on railway wheels, then as two or three units joined as one. Seating arrangements followed exactly the same principles, with inside accommodation for a lucky minority and open coaches for the rest. After the Gladstone Act of 1844, the railways were obliged to provide "Parliamentary Trains" for the lower orders, enabling the impecunious to travel at no more than a penny a mile — often, it should be added, in atrocious conditions. But travel they did nonetheless. The railway companies were far from happy with the arrangement, but the Parliamentary Trains were to prove a blessing in disguise, for they so widened the general appeal of travel that a whole new class of passenger was to appear. A penny per mile was still expensive to the working classes, but the new freedom proved so attractive that by 1860 receipts from Third Class travellers were exceeding all others.

One of the most innovative companies, the Midland, introduced Third Class carriages on expresses from 1872, and abolished Second Class two years later, thus effectively upgrading the rudimentary Third Class accommodation to Second Class standard. Such moves were popular with the public, but in operating terms they proved expensive. The 1870s had seen the arrival of eight-wheeled double-bogie carriages, together with toilets, sleeping and dining cars, which all increased the size and weight of trains and necessitated an increase in the size and weight of the locomotives. Heavier trains and higher operating speeds brought further requirements: powerful brakes, more complex signalling and generally improved standards of engineering. After a few well-publicised and spectacular accidents, the writing was on the wall, and by the end of the 19th century the activities of the railway companies were restrained by safety legislation which increased costs still further.

Increasing sophistication, although very welcome, did not come cheaply — in the 1860s, working expenses had absorbed a reasonable 48 per cent of railway income, but by 1900 the figure had risen to 63 per cent. Nevertheless, the railway system continued to expand, although the impetus of this expansion began to slow towards the end of the century.

By the 1880s most cities were linked to the railway network, and some by two or three competing routes, with beneficial results to the customers who were free to choose the most advantageous service. The railway companies, on the other hand, were beginning to realise that growth, in terms of mileage and profits, would not be infinite. Only a few new lines were authorised in the last years of the century — mostly small concerns to connect communities missed by the more prestigious projects of earlier years. Legislation, in the form of the Light Railways Act, did much to assist the construction of such low technology, low cost railway lines, by easing the signalling and maintenance requirements in exchange for certain limitations as to the speed and weight of traffic.

And there were still a few trunk lines to be built. Some made good economic sense, such as the Great Western Railway cut-offs bypassing Bristol and Bath to speed traffic to the West of England and Wales, but other schemes were based on stonier economic ground. The last great trunk line was destined to be the Great Central London Extension from Nottingham to Aylesbury at the turn of the century. The Great Central extension would probably never have been built at all were it not for the enthusiasm of Sir Edward Watkin, Chairman of the Manchester, Sheffield and Lincolnshire Railway. Although operating a sizeable network of lines in the North, he dreamed of joining the big league — adding "Great" to his railway's title and driving southwards to London and beyond. Quite a way beyond as it transpired, for Watkin became heavily involved in a Channel Tunnel scheme which — had it borne fruit — would have assured the future of the Manchester, Sheffield and Lincolnshire for ever more.

As it was, the tunnel scheme was put on ice after protestations from the military, but Watkin, ever hopeful, went ahead with the London extension. The MS&L renamed itself the Great Central (as most of the points of the compass had by this time been claimed by other companies) and cut a line to the south, building to the wide European loading gauge at enormous expense. Unfortunately, the tunnel was never built — or at least not in the lifetime of the Great Central — and with a trunk route that duplicated at least one other for most of its long journey south, the line was destined never to pay a dividend.

By the turn of the century, the railways of the British Isles were acknowledged to be the very best in the world; the expresses were faster, they included more Third Class accommodation (93 per cent against 27 per cent in France, for example) and, by and large, the vast system was efficiently run. That is not to say, however, that the railways were universally admired. Traders had long complained about freight charges, which contained many strange anomalies and more than a few sharp practices. Passengers, who generally found it easier to transfer their custom to a competing line if they weren't satisfied, were better looked after. All the same, the British people and, more particularly, the governments of the day, were highly suspicious of the monopoly position of the railways.

Nevertheless, the railway monopoly had, by the turn of the century, become a fact of life, mainly because the nation's traders show a marked preference for railway transportation:

...for the general object of developing the country he thought railways so far outstripped canals in efficiency that the latter really had no chance. By the side of the Kennet & Avon Canal there were large works belonging to a gentleman who was an enthusiast on the subject of canals; yet he sent more than half his goods by railway, although the station was more than one and a half miles away. Obviously that gentleman would not use the railways unless it suited the conditions of his business better than the canal...

Colonel J A Saner presenting the thoughts of a GWR engineer in a paper to the Institute of Civil Engineers

By 1913, after some 80 years of development, the railway system had more or less reached its zenith, extending to more than 20,000 miles. Had conditions remained locked in that long glorious Edwardian era, the system would probably have proved quite satisfactory, but there were some worrying trends even then: 20,000 miles of railway line represented a network of unsurpassed density on an island measuring barely 600 by 300 miles. Yet a quarter of the network, including many of the smaller and more vulnerable lines, had been constructed since the early 1880s.

The smallest and most vulnerable of all, including many of the so-called light railways, had never paid a dividend and were never likely to. A few had so exhausted their reserves in the construction phase that they were unable to purchase locomotives, and were immediately snapped up by acquisitive neighbours. Generally, this was a beneficial process, for the larger companies were wealthy enough to carry the losses of a few small concerns and more than willing to provide a local service in exchange for a little extra revenue to their networks.

In the same way that the Stockton & Darlington had discovered the basic principles of railway operation, so it was that the companies within the fully developed system gradually discovered the benefits of "contributory revenue". Even before the companies were grouped together into larger concerns, it became clear that the entire system functioned more in the manner of a single giant organism than as a collection of isolated entities. Fast expresses roared between the major cities, connecting with stopping services to towns and wayside stations, and at junctions with branch line trains to remote villages and hamlets.

If a branch line carried 1,000 passengers a week, each paying a fare of a shilling, the contribution from the branch to the railway network would be £50 per week — a sum that might or might not have covered the operating expenses of the branch. If, however, the 1,000 passengers continued their journey on a main line connecting with the branch, paying a total fare of 2 shillings, the basic revenue from the branch would still be £50, but the total effective income would amount to £100, the additional £50 raised being passed to the main line in the form of contributory revenue.

If the branch line were suddenly and mysteriously to close, many passengers would find alternative means of travelling to the main line (not very easy at the turn of the century) and then continue their journey by rail. Others would abandon rail travel altogether and reach their destination by other means, and no doubt a few would cease travelling entirely. Thus the loss to the system would not be £50 a week, but somewhere between £50 and £100, the true figure being quite impossible to calculate with any degree of accuracy.

Every mile of track had a part to play; the branches fed traffic to the secondary lines, and they in turn fed the trunk routes. Many minor branches would, in isolation, have proved quite unprofitable, but as part of a unified system they performed an invaluable role.

In many cases, the contributory revenue of a branch line was higher than the earnings along the branch itself. A good example was the short link between the main line of the North British Company and the town of North Berwick, east of Edinburgh. The branch was just four and half miles long, but most passengers continued their journey for almost 20 miles along the main line to Edinburgh. Thus, earnings on the branch itself were minimal, but the contributory revenue was disproportionately large.

Taking the theory a little further, five branches each carrying 1,000 passengers a week might disgorge 5,000 passengers onto a secondary line, and five such secondary lines might feed 25,000 passengers, via a trunk route, into a city centre. In reality the situation was never as simple as that, but the theory was perfectly sound. A branch line closure policy might have the effect of putting the secondary lines at risk, and closure of the secondary lines would threaten the whole system.

The railway companies were well aware of the theory and practice of contributory revenue, and it was this principle that later kept many minor branch lines alive. Their individual worth was marginal, but their contributory value could not be ignored.

The theory could also be applied to trunk lines by introducing a linear stream of stopping, semi-fast and express services interconnecting at towns and cities along the same route, the stopping services contributing revenue to the semi-fast and express trains.

The innovative Great Western Railway went a stage further and provided buses to contribute traffic from outlying villages without a rail connection. Its neighbour, the Southern, introduced the Atlantic Coast Express that served the West Country by physically releasing branch line carriages at various junctions along the route from London, thus removing the necessity to change trains, and providing a graphic illustration of the benefits of contributory revenue. Had the branch lines closed, the express would literally have ceased to exist. Sadly, this is exactly what did occur many years later.

In this manner the branches, not necessarily profitable in themselves, contributed revenue to the rest of the system. And in a situation of near monopoly it worked very well. There were a few closures in the early years, but by and large the railways, untroubled by road competition, ran a large and complex system very efficiently.

The onset of the First World War was to change Western civilisation forever. For the British railway system, it marked the end of a heady era of growth and development, for from 1913 onwards the story was to be one of retraction and decline.

The railway managers were brought together into a Railway Executive Committee for the duration of the war, and the railways were effectively taken into government control as a single unified system. All war traffic was carried free of charge but, by way of exchange, the Government guaranteed revenue to the companies at 1913 levels. The results of such national organisation were spectacular, and in just eight days, 334 trains were run through to Southampton for the military. Altogether 69,000 men were moved to the south coast, together with 22,000 horses and 2,500 guns. In the far north, the long and tenuous lines to Kyle of Lochalsh and Thurso carried some 400 trains in six months to assemble the Northern Barrage Minefield between the Orkney Isles and Norway. Notwithstanding their military commitments, many lines continued to operate a reasonable civilian service as well, although some of the smaller branches closed, and a few were actually dismantled to assist the war effort. Not surprisingly, by the end of the war the railways were in a less than satisfactory condition.

After the armistice had been declared, the railways remained under state control, and there were calls for national ownership to be put on a more formal and permanent basis. Having seen the generally beneficial effects of state ownership during the war, even Winston Churchill had been won over to the cause of nationalisation:

> Railways in private hands must be used for immediate direct profit, but it might pay the State to run the railways at a loss to develop industries and agriculture.

The circumstances in peacetime were, however, very different to those that prevailed during a state of conflict. Three years later, after the Government had made a disastrous job of running the railways and had handed the system back into private hands, Churchill changed his mind.

There were economic problems aplenty after the war. The promise to guarantee income at 1913 levels had turned out to be fairly worthless, for inflation had been particularly severe. Inflationary pressures were behind a series of pay rises that saw the railway wage bill increase threefold between 1913 and 1920. There were political problems too: in 1919, when events in

Russia caused a general uprising of industrial militancy that began to look ominous, the Government placated striking railwaymen with a sizeable pay award. Further industrial troubles in 1921 led to a coal strike, and the loss of trade that followed caused the railways to plunge £60 million into the red.

Combined with a slow release of Government aid and continuing high inflation, the industrial problems precipitated a financial crisis. Fares had risen by 50 per cent in 1917 and by another 25 per cent after the war, but freight charges had remained fixed since 1913, and were soon left far behind, despite the general increase in costs. Some of the weakest railways, stripped of their track and locomotives during the war years, were never to reopen, for conditions had changed so dramatically in seven years that it was no longer worth the trouble.

The post-war coalition Government led by Lloyd George created a Ministry of Transport and proceeded to look into the railway issue. The first Transport Minister, Sir Eric Geddes, decided against nationalisation, but chose instead to amalgamate some 120 independent concerns into four regionally based companies. It was a neat solution and, many would claim, long overdue. By creating four large statutory companies, obliged by law to carry on their trade in a prescribed manner, the Government had sidestepped the enormous problems that would have been created under a full-blown nationalisation scheme, but succeeded in tightening its grip over the railways.

Strangely enough, the most vociferous opponents of railway nationalisation had been the road transport pressure groups of the day. Although motoring was in its infancy, the "road lobby" was fairly well organised by the end of the First World War. The chief proponents of road transport were the two motoring groups — the Automobile Association and the rather more conservative Royal Automobile Club — the all-encompassing Society of Motor Manufacturers and Traders, and special interest groups, such as the London General Omnibus Company. Their chief concern was that the new Ministry of Transport would inevitably be given something of a pro-rail bias should the railways be put under state control. But, with the railways effectively excluded, the opposite occurred, and from its very beginnings the Ministry of Transport developed a distinct bias towards road matters.

All the same, the railways remained enormously powerful institutions, and it was felt that adequate safeguards would be needed to prevent the four new companies from abusing their monopoly position. This general fear was exploited very effectively by the road lobby. The British Road Federation, for instance, was established "to combat the sinister and distorted propaganda of the railways in their efforts to enslave British industry". No-one provided an adequate explanation as to why the railways should want to destroy their own customer base but, nevertheless, the 1921 Transport Act contained a variety of provisions aimed at limiting their power and influence.

According to Eric Geddes, the railway amalgamation would provide numerous benefits to the community at large, and more than a few to the railway companies themselves. It was estimated that as much as £20 million a year could be saved by rationalising the railway management, and considerably more if wasteful competition could be avoided:

> **The state must harmonise the operation of the different agencies of transport as between themselves in the interests of the community as a whole. Under a system of competition not only did one railway or one dock strive to divert traffic from another, but trams sought to wrest traffic from the railways, railways to wrest traffic from canals, coastal services to wrest traffic from both, and so on and on.**
>
> **In future our effort will be to encourage each agency of transport to undertake that part of the total work which it, owing to its own special qualities, can most efficiently and economically perform.**
>
> *Eric Geddes, first Minister of Transport*

It was certainly a radical idea, but although the Railways Act was successfully implemented, Geddes's wider vision of a fully integrated transport system met with considerable opposition, and after two years of planning he resigned in disgust.

The railway companies were not over-enamoured with the new legislation either, but being unable even to voice an opinion, they were effectively powerless. After release from Government control in August 1921, the old order was to survive only until the new Railways Act came into force on January 1, 1923.

Perhaps the most controversial provision of the Act was to create a Railway Rates Tribunal to standardise freight and other charges, the objective being to freeze revenue at the elusive 1913 levels. The railways were now obliged by law to carry any load, however uneconomic, and to publish their rates. To prevent the railway companies showing undue preference to one trader at the expense of another, rates for the carriage of particular commodities were fixed, irrespective of the actual costs involved, and hours of work, wages, and conditions of service were all fixed by central and national wages boards.

The Government's intention was to maximise the social and commercial benefits that a unified railway system could offer the nation. For instance, rates for the carriage of raw materials were set on the low side, while those for finished products were generally higher — a policy that assisted the all-important manufacturing industries.

This was all very reasonable as a means of controlling a monopoly carrier, but within a few years of the Act's implementation the railways were faced with competition from private road transport concerns that did not need to publish

rates, could pick and choose the most lucrative traffic, and obtained it by undercutting the railways, which were powerless to intervene. Between 1919 and 1921, as ex-army lorries came onto the market and were bought by potential profiteers, the number of goods lorries doubled. By 1926, they had doubled again. The forces of the state had moved painfully slowly to control the railway companies' monopoly and, by the time they did, circumstances were already changing so as to make the legislation an unnecessary burden.

Inevitably there were problems with the amalgamation proposals, for there had been little or no consultation, and the complex legal tangle that the various companies had created over the preceding century or so meant all manner of legal and financial difficulties. Reorganisation also brought quite a few strange geographical and strategic anomalies. Some railway companies, such as the Great Western, had built up a comparatively compact and unified territory. The Great Western subsequently emerged almost unscathed from the amalgamation, even retaining its full title, but other companies caused a few problems.

For strategic reasons of its own, the Midland had driven tentacles (mostly under joint operating agreements with other concerns) into almost every corner of the land. The Great Central, which arrived on the scene too late to carve a clear-cut territory, crossed several regions and duplicated more than a few facilities. It was absorbed into the London & North Eastern Railway, a massive (though relatively satisfactory) combine, formed of the old Great Northern, the Great Eastern, and others, controlling the whole east side of the country north of London.

The west coast saw an unhappier amalgamation, for the new London Midland & Scottish Railway had absorbed sworn enemies: the London & North

Western Railway and the Midland. Scottish railway companies were divided up between the two massive English concerns, those on the west coast coming under jurisdiction of the LMS and those to the east falling to the LNER.

The most successful alliance was probably that of the new Southern Railway, composed of three former companies (notably the London & South Western Railway) whose territories were generally complementary.

Despite the considerable upheaval entailed, the amalgamation process was to have beneficial results, as Geddes had predicted. Once the new organisations had settled down, many economies were realised by way of standardisation and centralised control, yet the companies were not so large as to lose touch with regional demands. And although the new companies adopted very different styles of management, they remained flexible enough to learn from each other's experience, even sharing research and development, and other expenses, on a few occasions.

Because of continuing economic difficulties, investment was no more than piecemeal, and largely confined to the Southern Railway. Under Sir Herbert Walker, of the London and South Western Railway, the Southern continued the process of electrification that Sir Herbert's company had pioneered, utilising the "third rail" current collection technique that was well suited to the strategic conditions and compact geography of the South-East.

The North Eastern Railway, too, used the third rail system on its Tyneside suburban network, which was electrified as early as 1904 and continued to give good service until the mid-1960s, when diesels were deemed cheaper to run. Within a few years, the system had been re-electrified with overhead wires and converted into the Tyne and Wear Metro.

By 1926, electrification on the Southern Railway had been completed outwards from London to Guildford, Sutton, Coulsdon, Orpington and Dartford, and in 1930 work began on the Southern's most important line — the trunk route between London and Brighton — the electrification of which was completed in 1932. Despite the untimely arrival of the depression, the electrification schemes continued, and by 1937 almost a quarter of the company's network had been converted. By 1939 most of the major lines east of Portsmouth were utilising electric traction, and electric trains accounted for more than half of all the passenger service mileage on the Southern Railway.

The impact of these swiftly executed and cost-effective investments by the Southern were of particular importance, for they proved to be the principal modernisation achievement of the railways in the first half of the century. The newly electrified lines offered a fast and frequent service to and from London and, besides improving railway efficiency, they actually encouraged the creation of whole new communities based around suburban railway stations. As a direct result, passenger traffic on the Southern Railway increased by a quarter between 1923 and 1939.

Investment that made a lot of sense in the South-East did not, however, necessarily point the way for the rest of the country. Across the Thames, the LNER received Government aid to electrify the line from its Liverpool Street terminus out into the northern suburbs of the capital, and the company also began work on a major project to convert the former Great Central trans-Pennine route between Manchester and Sheffield to electric traction. But both schemes were undertaken rather grudgingly by the company, and it was to be many years before either was brought to fruition.

There were a variety of reasons for this lack of enthusiasm for modern technology. Cash was painfully short between the Wars (and some investment plans appeared to show little in the way of return), the lack of an effective national electricity grid more or less ruled out widespread electrification, and the railway companies saw no reason to invest in diesel locomotives requiring relatively expensive imported oil, when steam engines operated satisfactorily on home-produced coal.

Steam traction was still relatively efficient for long-distance passenger and freight services, but for stopping and branch line trains it had always proved costly and inefficient. All the same, new technology arrived very slowly where the minor services were concerned. In the early years of the century, several companies had experimented with the "railmotor" — a carriage grafted to a small steam engine that promised to cut costs on lightly used services. The railmotors could be driven from either end, and they were cheap to operate, but in terms of passenger comfort they were the cause of considerable distress:

Its power and flexibility, its acceleration and de-acceleration [*sic*] were all that could be desired. It fulfilled its duty efficiently... and very uncomfortably. Vibration on the locomotive footplate has come to be recognised as part of the day's work for the driver and fireman. Its transference to the seats of the passengers was not accepted by them as a part of their daily journey, and the experiment was not a success.

E Kitson Clark

Although the railmotor proved something of a failure, experiments continued with more sophisticated machines. In 1923, the Sentinel company introduced a steam railcar — more or less a passenger carriage powered by a small steam motor — that seemed to point the way to the future. The LNER acquired 22 of the new vehicles between 1927 and 1928, and by 1931 it had introduced another 50 constructed to a more advanced design. Steam was not really a suitable medium for powering railcars, however, and it was only in 1933, when the GWR began tentatively to introduce diesel machines, that such vehicles truly came of age. Although the company had introduced no more than a handful of diesel railcars by the outbreak of the Second World War, they proved outstandingly

27

Steam railmotors were a cause of some distress to passengers...

successful, and more or less unique in British practice. Diesel engines proved suitable for all manner of railway operations, and the LMS discovered the merits of diesel-powered shunting locomotives, introducing about 50 before war intervened.

Generally, the investment picture remained fairly bleak. The railway companies had emerged from the First World War in an impoverished and broken state only to be subjected to the turmoil of reorganisation. No sooner had they drawn breath after amalgamation than they were hit by the General Strike in 1926, followed by the Great Depression of 1929. It was a double blow from which they were never fully to recover. And the companies did nothing to help themselves, by spending what little money was available buying into road-haulage firms, bus companies, and even the fledgling airlines. To a limited extent these acquisitions were useful, feeding traffic to the railways, but generally speaking, such attempts at diversification were ill-timed and inappropriate.

With little cash left for investment purposes, the railway system largely stagnated during the 1930s. Productivity rose by a meagre 1.2 per cent per annum, and the tight financial controls of the 1921 Railways Act proved a major burden — the intention had been to fix net revenue at around £51 million from 1928 onwards, but in 1929 earnings barely reached £41 million, falling remorselessly thereafter to £28 million in 1938.

Despite various measures aimed at tightening control over road transport in the early 1930s, the railways experienced a continuing loss of traffic to the roads. By the end of the decade, car production had reached levels undreamed of 20 years before, and most of the growth had been in smaller, cheaper vehicles that brought personal transport within reach of the masses. Pressure from the road lobby encouraged abolition of the 20mph speed limit in 1930, causing a

Above: Indicative of the lack of investment that dogged the railway system after the war is the enduring presence of inefficient steam push-pull units, such as the one pictured here at Dudley in 1951. At the same platform is an ex-GWR railcar, also pre-war. Owen Prosser.

Below: The LNER took the railmotor concept further and bought more than 70 Sentinel steam railcars in the late 20s and early 30s. This one is pictured at Ripon in 1938. N E Stead.

dramatic increase in the number of road accidents, the casualties reaching an horrendous peak in 1934, when 7,343 people were killed. With the exception of the wartime black-out years, that figure would not be exceeded until 1964 when increased car ownership, coupled with the closure of many railways, coincided with a run of high accident figures which only turned down again with the arrival of the oil crisis in 1973.

The urgent imposition of compulsory driving tests and a 30mph speed limit in urban areas went some way towards reducing the pre-war accident toll, but did nothing to slow the spectacular growth of the motor industry. Where freight traffic was concerned, road transport continued to attract a measure of business from the railways, which were caught in a stranglehold by tight Government control over rates and fares and were unable to respond. The road lobby began to press for wider, faster roads and, finding few Government supporters in Britain, they looked abroad and discovered an unlikely ally in the form of Adolf Hitler.

In Europe, the mighty forces of fascism were working miracles on the transport front. While Mussolini struggled to make the trains run on time in Italy, Hitler announced the "people's car", and a network of *autobahns*, or motorways, in Germany. To the British Road Federation it was all too good to be true, and in 1934 it invited Ministry of Transport officials on a tour of the Fatherland. Fortunately, the Ministry representatives declined. Ignoring the snub, Hitler pressed ahead with a policy of motorway construction, completing the first *autobahn* in 1935 and opening almost another 2,000 kilometres the following year.

In 1937, as the clouds of war gathered menacingly on the horizon, the road lobby sent a sizeable delegation to Germany. It was a major propaganda coup for Hitler (for the delegation included 58 British MPs), and an opportunity for the road groups to press for motorway construction at home, although the Ministry remained critical of motorway techniques, preferring instead a measured policy of road-widening.

The following year there were signs that the Minister of Transport, Leslie Burgin, was beginning to come around to the idea, although his suggestion of an experimental motorway was firmly quashed by the Treasury which was, by this time, overwhelmed by demands on the defence budget. The road lobby replied by suggesting the defence budget be reallocated towards road construction. Had common sense not prevailed, Hitler might have found little opposition from the RAF, and a convenient network of motorways to aid the progress of his motorised divisions across southern England...

Thus, the primary aim of the road lobbyists was frustrated, but they had succeeded in severely denting the profitability of the railway companies, for railway dividends never came anywhere near the levels of 1913. Even the

Southern paid only 0.5 per cent in 1938, and the LNER failed to pay a single ordinary dividend between 1925 and 1938. The GWR dividend fell from a satisfactory 7.5 per cent in 1929, to three per cent in 1931, and thereafter was maintained at around that figure, mainly by drawing on capital reserves.

By 1938, the dividend was cut to 0.5 per cent, which was rather fortunate, for by this time £8 million had been drawn from the modernisation fund and general reserves. It was something that provided wonderful ammunition for Labour MPs in later years, when a Conservative government blocked railway investment proposals, for among the GWR directors was none other than Harold Macmillan, a future Conservative Prime Minister. Nevertheless, the big four private companies had survived all manner of upheavals between 1923 and 1939 without once returning a loss. It was a remarkable achievement. And as a lobby group, the railways were still a force to be reckoned with for, in 1938, no fewer than 24 railway directors sat in the House of Lords, and 11 in the Commons.

Throughout the inter-war years there were few attempts to close unremunerative services, just 240 miles of unprofitable or duplicate route being

Below: A pre-War Great Western railcar pictured in the 1950s at Ledbury Town halt, near Hereford. Owen Prosser.

closed outright, and a further 1,000 miles closed to passenger trains. This was partly due to the railway companies' healthy regard for the contributory value of branch services, but it was also a side-effect of having no clear idea where profits were actually being made — or money lost. Without a doubt, many of the minor lines could have been closed and replaced by bus services in the gloomy depression years, but hardly anything was done in this direction, presumably because the railway companies had a degree of faith in the future.

This faith in their own enterprise emerged briefly with magnificent results towards the end of the 1930s for, despite serious financial problems, the two largest companies introduced a series of high-speed express trains that put Britain back into the forefront of railway technology. In 1935, the hard pressed LNER introduced the Silver Jubilee, running between London and Newcastle in four hours. In 1937, the express services were extended to Edinburgh and, in the same year, the LMS responded by slashing the express time on its own route to Scotland from seven and a half to six and a half hours. Finally, in 1938, the LNER took the world speed record for a steam locomotive at 126mph. It was a sign of things to come that the record was destined to stand for all time — the Americans, the French and, most notably, the Germans, were pouring investment into high-speed diesel and electric traction.

The record speeds of the 1930s were to stand unconquered in Britain too, for by this time war in Europe had become inevitable, and the Second World War was due to deal the railways a far more serious blow than had the First.

In an effort to put their financial affairs back in order, the big four railway companies belatedly launched a "square deal" campaign aimed at rectifying the imbalance between road and rail transport legislation. They intended to persuade the Government to relax financial controls, giving the railways freedom to tender for suitable traffic at a price that reflected the ability of the market to pay.

The "preferential charges" legislation had already been challenged when one of the railway companies offered to introduce a flat-rate contract with a particular trader that took no account of the Railway Rates Tribunal fees structure. After the affair had been brought to court, the Government agreed to loosen the rates restrictions to allow similar schemes, but such "agreed charges" still needed to be settled in open court, and other traders had the right to object and demand identical treatment. It was far from being a free and open charges policy, and the square deal campaign was launched to remove, or relax, the remaining controls.

Just as the campaign was approaching a successful conclusion, events in Europe took a turn for the worse, culminating in Britain's declaration of war in September 1939. The railways were put back under state control, leaving the question of rates and charges unsettled.

Once again, a Railway Executive Committee was formed to take control of the system, and compensatory income was set to pre-war levels. Fortunately, not to those of 1938, which had been a particularly gloomy year, but to an average of the revenues between 1935 and 1937.

As before, the railways gave sterling service during the war, although this time the demands on the network were markedly more severe. Almost immediately after the declaration of war, 1.3 million parents and children were successfully evacuated (mostly from London and the South-East) aboard 4,000 trains. And, as in 1914-18, an expeditionary force was carried to the south coast. This time the troops were all also brought home again unceremoniously after the evacuation of Dunkirk — an operation involving 620 train movements, carrying 319,000 men.

Throughout the darkest days of the war, when Britain stood alone and the might of the German army waited across the channel in preparation for an invasion that never came, the railways received a merciless pounding. Nine hundred staff and passengers were killed and 4,000 carriages and wagons destroyed in no fewer than 9,000 "incidents". Yet, strangely enough, only eight locomotives were put out of action. It was, perhaps, fortunate that the railway companies had had neither the capital nor the imagination to invest heavily in fragile and temperamental diesel and electric locomotives.

The real pressure came during the build-up to the D-Day landings in 1944. This was an operation of unprecedented size and complexity in which the role of the railways was paramount. Altogether, 524,000 trains were operated on behalf of the State during the war; railway factories were handed over for tank, aircraft and munitions construction; and many locomotives were sent abroad to assist the war effort elsewhere.

After five and half years of war, the railways were in a sorry plight for, with the exception of a few improvements to speed the flow of military traffic, investment had virtually ceased, leaving track and equipment close to collapse. A system that had once provided the finest trains on the densest network in the world had fallen almost into ruin.

The railways were primarily a heavy industry, and heavy equipment could survive without maintenance for a considerable period; track renewals had been suspended and steam locomotives had continued to function more or less adequately without heavy repair, but the backlog, when it came to be considered, was immense. By the end of the conflict, the authorities owed the railway system a vast sum in war reparations.

That was the situation in 1945 as the nation awaited the results of the first post-war election.

2.
State control
1947-1951

I am not unmindful of the fact that nationalisation does not give the workers control of the industry. But each and every locoman sincerely hopes that the first is the biggest stepping-stone to the second... Was I wrong to look for an indication that we shall not be "supervised" by incompetent position-seekers? Was it wrong to believe that with nationalisation would come a clear-out of the old school tie and the "wizard show" clique?

Railwayman E J Doody in a letter to the Locomotive Journal (ASLEF magazine)

WITHIN months of VE Day, Britain had returned a radical socialist Government. The election had been held as early as July 5, 1945 but, with many servicemen still overseas, it was several weeks before all the proxy votes had been counted, and a result declared.

Labour achieved an overwhelming victory... the new Prime Minister Clement Attlee found himself holding 393 seats in the House of Commons against the Tories' 213 and the Liberals' 12. No fewer than 13 cabinet rank Tories had been defeated, leaving Churchill with just a handful of suitable Shadow Cabinet appointees. The upset surprised almost everyone, for Churchill had been a popular wartime leader and, during the election campaign, he had been welcomed as a hero throughout the land. One interesting explanation was that the people had lived so long under a "national" administration, they fully believed it would be possible to vote Labour yet keep Churchill as Prime Minister. Whatever the reason, it was, according to Mrs Churchill, a blessing in disguise. "It seems quite effectively disguised," replied the great man.

The radical new Government rapidly implemented a policy of nationalisation, and on January 1, 1948, the railways were absorbed into a vast national undertaking, the British Transport Commission, charged with integrating and rationalising the entire system of inland transport. Under state ownership, a policy of branch line closures was implemented, for the Transport Commission had investments in companies operating competing buses, and was generally in favour of road transport for minor services. There was to be no more than a trickle of successfully implemented closures though, for the Commission discovered that the process was fraught with legal and social difficulties. Meanwhile, the Railway Executive had begun to introduce a range of standardised *steam locomotives for main line services, completely ignoring well proven technology that might have improved the viability of the branches.*

The introduction of new equipment came painfully slowly, the financial compensation paid to former railway shareholders proved more of a burden than had been expected, and road freight-haulage concerns fought long and hard to frustrate the policy of integration.

* * *

The House of Commons reopened in August, 1945 amid some extraordinary scenes. The Tories rallied around Churchill, singing *For he's a jolly good fellow!*, while the Labour ranks replied with a massed rendition of *The Red Flag*. The Speaker, Colonel Clifton Brown, later remarked: "I wondered whether I was going to be Speaker or director of a musical show!"

The new Government was determined to do more than voice socialist rhetoric in the House of Commons, however. After sitting largely on the political sidelines for almost half a century, the Labour Party had at last been given an overwhelming mandate to press ahead with socialist policies, and it wasted little time in preparing legislation for wide scale public ownership (or nationalisation), and a variety of prestigious public works.

Germany had established a world lead in the construction of motorways and, in 1945, the British Road Federation and the Society of Motor Manufacturers & Traders sent another committee to Germany to investigate. Predictably enough, the Committee's report to the Ministry of Transport and Civil Aviation was strongly in favour of motorway construction:

The results of this enquiry show that the construction of motorways is more than justified solely on economic grounds, apart from any considerations of safety, convenience and amenity.

In fact, the BRF had already decided to press for 1,000 miles of motorway — all that remained was to persuade the Government to do something about it. In May 1946, the Minister of War Transport, Alfred Barnes, announced a motorway programme to be completed within ten years, and extending to some 800 miles. The primary routes were remarkably similar to the elements of the basic motorway network completed 30 years later:

London-Cardiff (later to become the M4)

London-Carlisle via Birmingham (the M6)

Bristol-Leeds (partly M5 and M1)

Warrington-Hull (the M62)

The various motorway construction plans culminated in the Special Roads Act of 1949 which legalised the construction and use of motorways. Such a massive investment programme was, however, little short of make-believe in

35

the 1940s, for Britain was on the verge of financial collapse. A loan from America of almost $4,000 million had served to stave off bankruptcy after the war, but by September 1947 it was almost exhausted, and being depleted at the rate of almost $500 million a month.

Britain was unable to pay for even the most essential imports and, faced with a mounting financial crisis, the Government introduced a round of austerity measures. With no prospect of a relaxation in fuel rationing, motorway construction plans were put on ice. Indeed, the total spending on roads was destined to run to no more than £35 million in the following six years, and it was not until 1955 that a rather more modest programme of 147 miles of motorway was once again under active consideration. For the railways, this should have provided a vital breathing space and a chance to put together a viable modern network, but events were to prove otherwise.

Nationalisation was rather more easily achieved than grand capital-intensive projects, and during the early post-war years the nationalisation policy was advanced with enthusiasm. State control of health brought the National Health Service — a generally popular move. The fall of the Bank of England was accepted with less enthusiasm in some quarters, however, as was state control of the civil aviation industry, but, on December 18, 1946, Parliament voted in favour of a larger, and more controversial, proposal — national ownership of the entire transport industry.

Amid wild scenes, and renewed outbreaks of revolutionary refrains from the crowded Labour benches, the House of Commons voted to bring the railways, the road haulage industry, the waterways and the ports under state control. A fortnight later, on January 1, 1947, the coal industry was nationalised and state control of heavy industry became a reality. Almost unnoticed among the mountain of colliery assets was a small passenger railway in South Shields that passed into history as the first nationalised passenger line in Great Britain.

In the months since the arrival of the Labour Government, the four statutory railway companies had been more or less biding their time, for nationalisation of the railway industry had been on the agenda from the beginning, and with compulsory purchase just around the corner, the companies were content to assume a caretaker role. Just a few years before, the situation had been very different.

During the war the big four companies had studied every public, private and quasi-public railway network in the world, and had come (perhaps inevitably) to the conclusion that private ownership was the most satisfactory system. The private companies had experienced problems before the war owing to the overwhelming burden of legislation, particularly where rates and charges were concerned, but they felt that if the legislation could be adjusted, and they were granted a reasonable sum by way of war reparations, the financial position would be satisfactory. They had even considered the question of uneconomic branch lines, and had reasoned that a future government would probably be prepared to grant cash assistance to cover losses where the services maintained a social function.

The Labour Party was not the slightest bit interested in the suggestions, and the proposals of the private companies were ignored. In retaliation, the boards of the various railway companies declined to offer any assistance with the long-winded and complex nationalisation procedure. A few men stayed, notably Sir Eustace Missenden of the Southern Railway, but many of the best managers and administrators left the service, including a few with unique knowledge, such as Sir James Milne of the Great Western Railway, who had assumed the role of Deputy Chairman of the Railway Executive during the war. Lord Portal, also of the Great Western, declined to stay and refused an offer of financial compensation. But he did force a remarkable concession from the railway's new masters, insisting that former Great Western directors should retain their travel passes! Generally speaking, the railway company directors began to lose interest in the day-to-day operations of their companies and concentrated instead on fighting for favourable compensation.

The railway system had emerged from the war in a terrible state. Traffic had been exceptionally heavy for six years, and the system had survived with minimal maintenance. It was estimated that as many as 1,400 miles of track needed immediate replacement, and a considerable mileage was in need of urgent repair. Speed restrictions, which had stood at 90mph in the late 1930s, had been reduced to 60mph or even lower. Coal was of such inferior quality that few locomotives could exceed the new limits anyway.

The railways needed five years of sustained investment but, as a direct result of the impending upheaval of nationalisation, the management lost interest and the system stagnated instead. The immediate post-war years should have seen frantic reconstruction and forward planning, but they were largely wasted.

To add to the confusion, the small body of Conservatives under Winston Churchill had done all within their power to fight the nationalisation proposals during the Bill's slow passage through the Commons. In all, some 800 amendments were tabled by the opposition, some of them serious, others implemented merely as blocking manoeuvres to hold up the legislation, but the majority fell by the wayside.

Amid mounting controversy, Labour responded by introducing a guillotine — if discussion of an amendment ran beyond a prescribed time limit it was simply abandoned. All the same, some more radical proposals were lost at the Committee stage, including a provision to restrict all lorries, even those carrying a trader's own goods, to within a 40-mile radius of their depot. No Western country had yet attempted to place all transport undertakings under state control, and public interest proved so intense that the 1947 Transport Act became an overnight best-seller, running to more than 30,000 copies.

At midnight on December 31, 1947, the railway system came under state control. A month later, as the financial crisis took hold of the country, the recently nationalised coal industry announced losses of more than £5 million for the last quarter of 1947. It was not a very encouraging omen.

The Government had chosen to put all of the transport undertakings under the control of a comparatively small organisation to be known as the British Transport Commission. According to the Transport Act, the role of the Commission would be:

> ...mainly concerned with questions of policy, including general financial control, the preparation of schemes relating to fares, rates and charges, supervision of research and development, and arrangement for the co-ordination of inland transport.

The powers of the British Transport Commission were wide-ranging — an almost total monopoly in the carriage of passengers and goods by rail and inland waterway; and provisions to create a similar monopoly for road transport, shipping services, port and inland waterway facilities, hotels, hostels, and even places of refreshment. In the light of future events, there were two provisions in the Transport Act that were to have a particular significance. The first outlined the duty of the Commission:

> It shall be the general duty of the Commission so to exercise their [sic] powers... as to provide, or secure, or promote the provision of, an efficient, adequate, economical and properly integrated system of public inland transport... for passengers and goods... in such manner as to provide most efficiently and conveniently for the needs of the public, agriculture, commerce and industry.

Another gave guidance on the disposal of surplus equipment:

> The Commission may dispose... of any part of their undertaking or any property which in their opinion is not required by them for the discharge of their duties under this Act.

Transport Act 1947 Part 1, Subsection 2, Provision 4

The Commission had been empowered to co-ordinate and integrate public transport so as to produce an "efficient" and "adequate" system — a very commendable aim. Unfortunately, many of the road, rail and shipping interests that had fallen into its hands had previously been operating in competition with each other, most notably the rural railway lines and country bus services. Competition, of course, had little to do with integration, leaving the Commission with the difficult task of deciding which services should be earmarked for development and which might have to go.

In theory, the BTC was to assume central control of the entire transport industry, and almost anything would be possible for, by juggling fares and charges one against another, it would have the power to alter the balance of transport economics. Traffic would be guided to the most efficient carrier, not through force or legislation, but by a subtle adjustment to the charging structure. As the Commission was bound by law to produce neither a profit nor a loss overall, it would also be possible to cross-subsidise loss-making services with profits from more lucrative areas.

It appeared logical then, that the strategy of the new Commission would be to concentrate resources on the most efficient and effective carriers, withdraw the least competitive services, and balance the books at the end of the day — without drawing a penny in profit.

There were, however, a few rather fundamental flaws to the legislation, for the 1947 Act had maintained the freedom of traders to move freely between carriers, implying that the BTC would be expected to retain a broad range of services. And the Commission had only two weapons with which to alter the balance between the various modes of transport — price and quality. Price was not really an option, for rates and charges were to be tightly controlled by a Transport Tribunal, equivalent to the old Railway Rates Tribunal. Ultimately, the only means by which the supposedly all-powerful Commission was able to effect the removal of traffic from one carrier to another was by altering the quality of one or other of the services. With capital investment severely restricted, the only real option was to reduce the quality of the service the Commission intended to run down. It was a policy that was to be used to devastating effect in later years.

The BTC was also constrained by rather vague social obligations. The Labour Party had been determined to beat the capitalists at their own game, but it sometimes found difficulty in reconciling socialist doctrine with the demands of the market. The resulting policy directives were skilfully worded so as to mean virtually nothing, leaving the Commission to make its own judgment as to whether to provide a social service or to succumb to commercial realities. Typical was the following Labour Party policy statement issued during the war: "In the case of real conflict between public desires and sound commercial practice it does not necessarily follow that the latter should prevail."

To keep the vast transport monolith in touch with consumer and business demands, the Transport Act made allowance for the establishment of Transport Users' Consultative Committees to liaise between the Commission and the public. It was a radical and egalitarian solution to a difficult problem — there was little point in state ownership if the people had no opportunity to communicate their desires and grievances to the transport concern over which they held nominal ownership.

Nine regional English Committees were established, together with a single body covering Wales and Monmouthshire, and another overseeing the whole of Scotland. Each local committee comprised an independent chairman and a wide selection of members representing various sections of the community, such as agriculture, commerce, industry, labour and local authorities. All were chosen at the discretion of the Minister of Transport. Less reasonable was the provision that other members would be appointed by the Transport Commission itself and, rather ominously, the regional TUCCs (with the exception, after 1953, of the Scottish and Welsh bodies) were to report the views of the public to a Central Transport Consultative Committee funded by, and partially staffed by, the BTC. The central body would report, in turn, to the Minister of Transport.

Timetables, quality of service, even complete loss of service: any matters relating to BTC operations would be discussed at local TUCC level and recommendations passed up to the Transport Commission via the Central Committee. Where services were to be withdrawn, the proposal would be discussed at the local TUCC level and a report forwarded to the central body. The committees later became synonymous with the railway closure procedure, although they performed many less notorious tasks as well.

The Transport Users' Consultative Committees had no real teeth however, for rates and charges were already firmly in the hands of the Transport Tribunal. In fact, the TUCCs were unable to force the BTC to accept any proposal. All the same, they provided a forum for limited discussion on transport affairs, and they did allow ordinary people to get their views across, although — as TUCC reports were never released to the public — it was impossible to tell whether a grievance had got as far as the central body, let alone reached the heights of the Transport Commission itself. And the Commission was by no means the end of the chain of communication, for the actual day-to-day operation of the various transport concerns was placed in the hands of the Executive Committees.

Initially, four Executives were created — Docks & Inland Waterways, London Transport, Road Transport, and Railways. The shipping and hotel interests of the former private railway companies remained for the time being under the control of the Railway Executive.

From the very beginning it was unclear who was actually in charge — the BTC or the Executives. According to the Transport Act, the Executives were merely agents, to "assist the Commission in the discharge of their duties". The British Transport Commission, under the Chairmanship of Sir Cyril (later Lord) Hurcomb, had initially empowered the Railway Executive to function broadly as the former statutory railway companies had done, with the proviso that it was bound to obey any directives that might be passed down from the Commission. This was where the conflicts arose, for to enable a policy of transport integration to be developed, the Commission (overseen by the Transport Tribunal) retained the power to fix railway rates and charges. Furthermore, the Executives had no power to borrow money, and they were obliged to carry all of the rights, powers, obligations and liabilities of the BTC.

Thus, as far as the Commission was concerned, the Executives were merely employers of staff with control over day-to-day operations, and they were obliged to follow the general policy of the Commission. As employers, the Executives initially undertook to negotiate with the unions over wage claims, but the BTC later assumed this role for itself.

Some Executive appointees interpreted their role as being a primary one, while others considered themselves no more than agents of the Commission. Sir Eustace Missenden, the first Railway Executive Chairman, subscribed to the former view and did his best to look down upon the British Transport Commission from his imposing headquarters at 222, Marylebone Road. To make matters worse, company loyalties caused regional managers to adopt a similar attitude with regard to Sir Eustace and his Railway Executive. The result was a long-running and sometimes bitter war of attrition between the regions, the Executive and the Transport Commission.

Sir Cyril Hurcomb, as a former Permanent Secretary at the Ministry of Transport and a life-long civil servant, had interpreted the rules along suitable civil service lines and decided that the Commission should assume the role of a policy-making body to liaise between the Government (which wanted rapid integration of public transport) and the Executives (which, by and large, did not). The British art for compromise and fair play had more or less succeeded in neutralising the radical socialist legislation, transforming it (in the best traditions of the Civil Service) into an extra tier of bureaucracy. But the relative independence of the various Executives did nothing to assist the policy of transport integration, for there was little consultation between the new organisations. For example, the bus and road-haulage operators acquired by the private railway companies had achieved a measure of integration with the railways before the war, but they were handed to the "competing" Road Transport Executive after nationalisation.

When the dust had settled, the BTC found itself in control of a vast empire. The Railway Executive alone had inherited between 632,000 and 649,000 staff (no-one seemed quite sure of the exact figure), together with 20,000 steam locomotives, 1,223,000 wagons (half of which had been inherited from private owners), 56,000 coaches, 19,414 miles of track... and 7,000 horses. Surprisingly, horse traction outlived many of the steam locomotives, for the last animals were not retired until March 1964.

According to the Labour Chancellor, Dr Hugh Dalton, a man renowned for his outspoken and indiscreet manner, the nation had got hold of a "poor bag of assets". This off-the-cuff remark caused widespread resentment within the industry, although there was a certain amount of truth to it. For, besides the

Southern electrics, a collection of state-of-the-art express steam locomotives and a handful of diesel railcars, the nation had acquired very little in the way of modern technology.

The LNER had produced an electric locomotive for the still-born Manchester to Sheffield electrification scheme as early as 1939. For the duration of the war the locomotive gathered dust and eventually, in September 1947, the company had generously lent it to the Dutch railways. The LMS, on the other hand, had preferred to put its money on the express diesel locomotive, although it was not until two weeks after nationalisation, on January 14, 1948, that Britain's first main line diesel-electric locomotive began operational trials. It soon proved underpowered for fast main line duties, but by September 1948 it was joined by a sister locomotive, and the two went on to give sterling service.

Ex-LMS diesel, No. 10000 — one of a pair being constructed at the time of nationalisation — pictured in 1948 at St Pancras, backing on to a Manchester train. Owen Prosser collection.

The BTC had been obliged to acquire a vast assortment of good, bad and indifferent private railway wagons, as private owners were henceforth to be banned from the network. Something of the nature of the wagon problem can be deduced from the sliding scale of compensation paid to private owners: it was agreed that £16 10s would be paid to owners of eight-ton wagons built before 1902 — and almost half the private wagons were of that vintage! At the other end of the scale, a large modern wagon was valued at £430. Unfortunately, the large modern wagons were few and far between, while the antiquated Victorian variety emerged to be counted from overgrown sidings the length and breadth

of the railway system.

Nationalisation also created some extraordinarily difficult legal and financial complications, for it emerged that several ancient railway companies had remained technically independent, thanks to the rather untidy corporate affairs of the railways over the preceding century or so. In total, it was found necessary to absorb no fewer than 60 railway companies and 17 canal companies, some of which were inextricably linked with railway concerns. A further 28 railways, mostly derelict or pitifully unremunerative narrow-gauge concerns, were deemed worthless and allowed to escape the net. However, a few delightfully ramshackle but equally worthless Light Railways, such as the Kent & East Sussex, the East Kent and the Shropshire & Montgomeryshire, had survived in nominally independent form, and they were all absorbed into the nationalised railway system, together with a handful of little known independents, such as the Easton & Church Hope Railway Company, in Dorset.

Initially, the railway system was divided into six regions that more or less mirrored the territories of the former private companies:

London Midland Region — largely LMSR

Western Region — largely GWR

Southern Region — largely SR

Eastern Region — Southern area of the LNER (Doncaster to London)

North Eastern Region — North East of LNER (Doncaster to Berwick)

Scottish Region — LMS and LNER territory in Scotland

The national financial situation was so serious that an outright purchase of

43

the various railway companies proved out of the question. Instead, it was decided to compensate former railway and canal shareholders by exchanging their shares for a continued holding in the Transport Commission in the form of British Transport Stock. No less than £1,150 million worth of Stock was issued for this purpose.

Rather than yielding an annual dividend based on trading performance, the Transport Stock would pay a fixed rate of interest for a set period, thus compensating former shareholders from BTC income. The nation would, in effect, purchase the assets over a period of time by paying a small surcharge on transport costs. The value of individual shares was set with regard to the Stock Exchange standing of the various companies on a particular date, chosen as November 1946. Interestingly, the financial state of the Southern, Great Western and London Passenger Transport Board were quite healthy at the time of the take-over, although the others were less buoyant.

The scheme went badly wrong right from the start. The market value of the companies was particularly high in 1946, for the considerable volume of traffic carried during the war, allied to restrictions on road transport, had combined to make their financial position look much rosier than it was. And although the railway shares were valued in relation to a low 2.5 per cent gilt-edged interest rate, the return on Transport Stock was not fixed until later, when rates had risen. As a result, the value of railway assets was fixed far too high, and the burden of interest payable to former shareholders emerged at four per cent — on stock that was to be redeemed over 90 years.

This disastrous valuation was to saddle the railways with a terrible debt in future years for, whereas a private company would have paid little or no dividend in lean years, the return on British Transport Stock was guaranteed. The Commission was later to claim that a payment of just two per cent would have been more suitable, even in the best trading years. Yet the railways were obliged to pay a fixed sum of around £40 million a year — even when they were making substantial losses.

The nationalisation legislation, formulated to take the railways out of private hands, had the unfortunate effect of providing a decent dividend to former shareholders. Obviously, the system would have been fairer if the interest rate had been allowed to float with the fortunes of the Commission, but no-one considered this necessary, for no-one had expected the BTC to fail.

Road transport presented more of a problem, being something of a moving target, for it would have been quite impractical to nationalise every delivery van and every one-man haulage firm. The solution was found by nationalising all lorries working on journeys of more than 40 miles which also extended for more than 25 miles from the vehicles' "operating centre". Excluded were traders' own vehicles which remained outside the legislation.

Nearly 3,800 road haulage concerns eventually became involved, and the BTC found itself holding all manner of dubious operations. Sometimes the lease on premises or equipment was on the point of expiry, and occasionally a fly-by-night operator flew, leaving the Commission empty-handed. An operation that had been accomplished with remarkable speed in respect of the much larger railway concerns, dragged on interminably for road transport and, two years later, many firms remained in private hands. This was partly due to the success of the British Road Federation and other lobby groups, who fought a long and bitter campaign against national ownership.

It was not until 1951 that road haulage was finally dragged kicking and screaming into the public domain, and by then the opportunities for integration had largely passed. A unified system of road charges, which would have treated road transport in the same manner as the railways, was never established.

As compensation was fixed at the value of the assets at the time of transfer, implementing the legislation proved an administrative nightmare, and there were plenty of loopholes that enabled the shady operator to make a bob or two at the Government's expense. If he wanted to keep his vehicles, he had only to prove that they were used for local deliveries. If he wanted to dispose of a clapped-out lorry, he might send it out on a long-distance job the day before the Ministry inspector arrived to guarantee compensation. It was this sort of flexibility that made the whole nationalisation procedure unfair towards the railways, for the road hauliers could always set up again with new vehicles should the political wind change — something that the monolithic railway companies would be unlikely to accomplish.

The winter of 1948 provided the first opportunity for the BTC to manipulate the transport system on a large scale. The previous winter had produced blizzards and frosts of almost unmatched severity, and it was decided to mobilise the forces of the State to guard against a repeat performance. So the Commission formed a Winter Executive Committee, which came to the somewhat quixotic conclusion that certain freight traffics should be transferred from the railways to the roads for the duration of the winter. Unfortunately, when the Commission came to wind up the scheme in March, it was unable to steer the traffic back to the railways, for traders were unwilling to go through the upheaval of another change. It was a rather unsatisfactory introduction to state control as far the Railway Executive was concerned.

All in all, the railways were in a sorry condition. In March, the Railway Executive completed an appraisal of the system and informed the BTC that arrears of maintenance totalled approximately £179 million, but finance was short, and nothing was done to alleviate the situation.

The Executive was, however, busy investigating the capital investment position and, after holding a number of inter-regional trials in 1948, it was decided to introduce a range of standard steam locomotives to replace the vast array that had fallen into public ownership from the old companies.

In April 1948, Sir Cyril Hurcomb, of the Transport Commission, suggested that the Railway Executive should investigate other forms of motive power (notably diesel and electric) but such was the inertia engendered by the complex BTC/Railway Executive relationship, that it was not until the end of the year that a Railway Motive Power Committee was formed.

But while the committee deliberated, the plan to construct a range of new steam locomotives was already being implemented, and the Executive was busy cancelling experimental diesels ordered by the former private companies. It was not until 1951 that the Committee prepared a report in favour of the tentative investigation of diesel traction — by which time the Executive had invested a considerable sum in steam power. Meanwhile, other railways both in Europe and the United States were withdrawing steam locomotives and investing heavily in diesel and electric traction.

Much has been written about the failure of the Railway Executive to invest at this critical time. The problem stemmed partly from lack of funds: steam locomotives were well understood, relatively cheap (diesels costing two to three times as much) and, although steam was comparatively expensive in manpower terms, labour was still fairly cheap in the 1940s. Another dampener on investment came from the restrictive charging structure imposed on the railways, for the Executive saw little point in investing large sums in, say, an electrification project, when it would not be possible to capitalise on the improved service by raising fares.

New investment was not the only divisive issue in the late 1940s, for it was already clear that a considerable railway mileage would have to close as part of the Commission's integration policy. Some commentators put the mileage as high as 30 per cent and, within weeks of nationalisation, the first lines were earmarked for closure. The quaint and largely semi-derelict Light Railways had survived all manner of vicissitudes between the wars but, in the new era of state control, their days were numbered.

A handful of dedicated enthusiasts set off to explore the remote corners of the network before the Transport Commission could set to work implementing the closure programme. Late in 1947, Owen Humberstone Prosser, a young ex-serviceman, discovered a run-down Kent & East Sussex Light Railway:

> We did not stop at Salehurst, the first halt, the platform at which seemed as much overgrown as is the track along most of the route. We stopped at Junction Road Halt at 11.50 and ten minutes later reached Bodiam, where No. 4 shunted for some time with passenger coaches attached. This all had to be done over the level crossing, at which pedestrians and vehicles impatiently waited. I found that the other five people who had come from Robertsbridge had alighted, and

The Kent & East Sussex was typical of the doomed minor railways encountered by Owen Prosser on his travels. I L Wright.

for the rest of the journey to Rolvenden I was the only passenger...

It was a situation that could not continue for very long, and on May 1, 1949 closure of the nearby East Kent Light Railway was announced, and subsequently implemented, under the Transport Users' Consultative Committee procedure. Writing some years later, when closures had become commonplace, the Committee Chairman, Sir Egbert Cadbury, looked back rather wistfully on the process he had unwittingly set in motion:

I am in favour of closing really derelict lines, but not some of the lines which I think could add to the railways being a little more efficient, and where — by improving the lines rather than, to my mind, using every possible device to make the service uncomfortable and inconvenient to passengers — the public could be encouraged to use them.

The closure of a handful of unremunerative lines did little to satisfy the Transport Commission, which could see its goal of efficient transport integration receding into the next century or beyond. To accelerate the programme, a shadowy Branchline (later to become the Unremunerative Railway) Committee was established, at the behest of Sir Cyril Hurcomb, in March 1949. Composed of representatives from the regions as well as the Railway Executive, the new committee was charged with the unsavoury task of seeking out and destroying uneconomic branch lines, and a team of full-time officers set to work, putting forward a steady stream of loss-making, and generally unopposed, closure proposals.

It was hardly surprising that these early closures were largely unopposed for, although 86 lines had been wholly or partially eradicated by October 1950, many of them had lost their passenger services years earlier, and a handful had been derelict since before the war. Under the stewardship of the Branchline Committee, however, the programme began to gather pace, and 152 proposals were put forward for consideration during 1951. In the event, nothing like that number of lines was actually closed, and by June 1951 the total had been revised downward to 146. Fewer than 100 proposals were actually investigated that year, and the remainder were put aside for consideration at a later date.

The problem stemmed not so much from public opposition, but from legal objections, for all manner of legal obligations remained in force from the previous century to slow the railway closure process. When, for example, the Branchline Committee investigated the Yealmpton branch in Devon, it found it was obliged under a Statute of 1899 to maintain Billacombe Station in perpetuity for the convenience of the Duke of Bedford and his heirs. It was noted, however, that regular passenger services had been withdrawn 20 years previously, and the Duke had failed to object! A similar situation arose at Plodder Lane Station in Lancashire, where the BTC discovered to its chagrin that an Act of 1871 empowered the then railway company to maintain the station for the Earl of Bradford. As the said Earl had long since expired, it was left with the choice of closing the line and hoping for the best, or tracing the whereabouts of his heir...

In west Wales, a closure proposal brought an objection from a Captain Lewes, who claimed that his grandmother had sold land to the railway company at £25 below the market value, on the provision that she was given a station. Lengthy research proved the claim to be perfectly legitimate, leaving the Executive liable to the tune of £25.

Occasionally, railway travellers took advantage of the ancient legislation to force the Executive to reinstate a service. A few years later, the authorities innocently withdrew passenger services between East Grinstead and Lewes, including the stretch that was later to achieve fame as the first standard gauge preserved passenger railway — the Bluebell line. According to one railway-man, it had never been a particularly lucrative operation:

> **What they call the Bluebell line? We never done nothing much. Well we used to take the goods up there and that. It must have made some money or they'd have closed it down, wouldn't they?**

Sensing that even the staff were aware that profitability was not what it might have been, they did exactly that, but a wily passenger invoked an Act of 1878 requiring the former London, Brighton & South Coast Railway to run at least four trains per day in perpetuity. The authorities had no choice but to comply, and it took another 18 months, and an Act of Parliament, before the service could finally be laid to rest.

Despite the various legal difficulties, the minor closure proposals were generally unopposed by the travelling public, for even the most significant of the closures affected only a handful of regular travellers. But as the net tightened, and the Branchline Committee looked further afield for candidates, public concern began to mount. As a result, several over-optimistic closure plans involving busy branch lines, such as those to Swanage and Hayling Island, met with considerable opposition and were rapidly shelved. But it was clearly just a matter of time before the Railway Executive found itself in confrontation with railway travellers.

Elsewhere on the system, a very limited degree of modernisation was taking place. In November 1949 the Minister of Transport, the Rt Hon Alfred Barnes, officially opened the electrification scheme between Liverpool Street and Shenfield, originally instigated by the LNER before the war. The project proved an immediate success, and the number of passengers increased by almost 50 per cent — a fact that should have come to the notice of the Motive Power Committee which was still closeted away at 222 Marylebone Road considering the ins and outs of modern traction equipment.

Far away, in the corridors of power, the winds of political change were beginning to blow. In November 1949 it was revealed that the Labour Party, unnerved by public criticism of the nationalisation schemes, was busy diluting socialism for the forthcoming election campaign. The results of the BTC's first trading year did little to assist the embattled Labour administration, for the Commission returned an overall loss of some £4.7 million. And, in January 1950, it was announced in the House of Commons that the railways were due to return a loss of around £20 million. Sure enough (despite increasing its share of the vote), Labour's majority of 166 seats was demolished at the general election the following month, leaving the party hanging onto power by a thread, with a majority of just six seats. It was really the end of the socialist experiment, for the reduced majority left the Government effectively powerless.

The Transport Commission, however, was still engaged in the unequal task of implementing the 1947 Transport Act and, as late as 1950, it believed the elusive goal of full integration might still be attainable:

> The Road Haulage Executive will employ the Railway Executive's rail services for direct trunk haulage of long distance "smalls" and wagon-load traffic where the Railway Executive can make available suitable terminal accommodation, containers and train services. The Railway Executive will employ the Road Haulage Executive's road services for trunk haulage of cross-country traffic and wherever use of road services will reduce staging and transit time, and facilitate rail movements in direct train loads between main centres... Where branch lines are wholly or partially closed to freight traffic, the Road Haulage Executive will provide a substitute service where this can be justified.

It was quite clear that the BTC had decided to withdraw many railway services. Steam-hauled branch line trains were horrendously expensive to operate and, to a Commission which also controlled a network of fast, modern and economical road buses, the answer seemed clear-cut. Thus, while the Motive Power Committee continued its long deliberations on the subject of cost-effective haulage, the Branchline Committee was spurred on to renewed effort in weeding out and disposing of the uneconomic services. It was a process that generated little enthusiasm at the Railway Executive, where the staff were understandably loath to see their network handed to the opposition. But there was an answer to their dilemma — and it was already operational on the Western Region.

As we have seen, the Great Western Railway had begun to introduce diesel railcars from the mid-1930s. It was not a unique idea, for many railways abroad had produced similar designs, notably the County Donegal Railways (Joint Committee) in Ireland, which was about to bestow honorary retirement on its first lightweight diesel railcar, or "railbus", introduced in 1931.

The County Donegal was a world pioneer in the railbus field. Unlike other Irish lines, its management had decided against transferring traffic onto the roads, but had attempted to take the road bus to the rails instead. As early as 1926, the County Donegal's Traffic Superintendent had outlined ideas that were to prove revolutionary:

My idea would be to get an engine of the Ford lorry type, easily driven, and have it built into a chassis at Stranorlar by our own men, with a very light body, preferably aluminium, and fitted with comfortably upholstered seats, as in a bus, attractively painted in artistic colours inside and outside, one class only.

One man only to be employed: the driver would also issue tickets at halts and collect them from passengers alighting, and would also be required to assist in handling mails, papers and parcels at stations.

I have figured it out that we could almost pay for the car (the cost alone not to exceed £300) in one year by the savings effected by fuel alone, apart altogether from the reduction in wages...

Once a couple of secondhand petrol rail vehicles had been obtained, and adapted for the purpose, the County Donegal proceeded to implement its railbus policy. Where steam haulage had cost as much as $11^3/_4$d (nearly 5p) per mile, it was found that the railbus could operate for just $3^3/_4$d (about $1^1/_2$p). It was sufficient to produce a reasonable, if unspectacular, return from previously uneconomic services.

The diminutive railbuses were soon running 2,400 miles a month but, on November 19, 1926, disaster struck as perhaps it could only strike in Ireland:

As the 12.10pm bus from Stranorlar was running from Ballinamore to Fintown, and on a level part of the road, about a quarter-mile from the former station, while travelling at a moderate speed, the driver heard a loud crack, applied his brakes and, immediately after, the right-hand leading wheel flew off and ran down the slight embankment at the place into the bog below...

A month later the other vehicle was similarly struck, when "both front wheels flew off". But repairs were soon made, and the policy of substituting railbuses for steam-hauled trains was developed further. In 1931 the company introduced one of the very first diesel railbuses, and three years later, after gaining considerable experience in the field, the County Donegal brought railbus technology to a peak of development. The new vehicles seated about 40 passengers in comfort; they were fast, reliable, and extremely economical to run. By 1941, the company was running half as many railcars as were to be found on the entire British railway system. There was really little excuse for the excruciatingly slow progress made in Britain where modern rail traction was concerned.

The little County Donegal had proved that railbuses were suitable for the least remunerative lines, and developments elsewhere were indicating that larger faster versions of the railbuses, known as diesel multiple units, were capable of handling heavier traffic, and even relatively fast services.

By 1950, diesel multiple units were being introduced all over the world. The machines were generally powered by one or more road bus engines mounted beneath the floor, and the individual cars could be coupled together to produce

51

The pioneering 3ft gauge railcars of County Donegal, pictured in 1958. Above, a Walker-engined diesel. Below, railcar No. 19, travelling from Killibegs, passes No. 14 at Inver. No. 19, together with No. 20, now belongs to the Isle of Man Railways, where both were in service until 1989. They are in the workshops at Douglas awaiting restoration, but continue to be used to transport permanent way gangs in winter. Owen Prosser.

"units" of two, three, six, or more vehicles. With a driving cab at either end, the multiple units were particularly well suited to the operation of branch lines, for they could arrive, disgorge passengers, and accelerate away in search of fresh revenue in just a few minutes. They were also faster, cleaner and considerably more economical than steam traction. But although several British manufacturers produced such vehicles, they were yet to make an appearance on the BTC network.

In June 1950, several three-car multiple units were introduced onto the Great Northern Railway in Ireland to operate the service between Belfast and Dublin. So successful was the experiment that, by October, multiple units and single railcars were operating a quarter of all the services in Northern Ireland. In Britain, the Railway Executive found itself in the unusual position of condemning steam traction while continuing to invest in it and, according to Sir Eustace Missenden, there was no future at all for the branch lines:

> In the next 30 years many unremunerative lines and the smaller intermediate stations will be closed; time interval services will be operated where possible; and a cleaner and more up-to-date service must be provided if the railways are to survive...

> The steam locomotive has served the world faithfully, but with the march of progress it has been dethroned from its pedestal of public esteem... except in the eyes of enthusiasts. Smoke, steam, dirt, and smells... once the symbol of power... are now hurled at us as evidence of a failure to modernise and of the approaching end of the railway era.

Meanwhile, the railway press was viewing the situation with a mounting concern, as summed up by *Railway Magazine* in March 1950:

> [Comparison of] the recovery of several continental railways from the effect of the war has often been made with that made in this country... It is a constant source of dissatisfaction that countries such as France and Greece, whose railways suffered terrible devastation, should have made such a success of their rehabilitation schemes, whereas the future of Britain's railways is obscure...

> The praiseworthy experiment now being carried out on the Hetton-Sunderland branch line of competing with the buses in fares and service, could surely be extended by the conversion of many such branches to light railway working...

Of course, the Transport Commission, as both a railway and a bus operator had mixed feelings about such experiments and was understandably lacking in enthusiasm. In the same month, the Western Region took delivery of one of the first of the new standard steam locomotives — an 0-6-0 tank engine to replace similar models constructed between 1875 and 1905. Unfortunately, it was **very** similar to the machines it was intended to replace — a delight to the enthusiasts, but far from the cutting edge of technological development, and presumably just the sort of dirty, smelly machine that the Railway Executive Chairman wished to see eradicated. By the end of 1951, the Executive had introduced six out of 12 standard steam locomotives, although minor services were actually suspended that year for a lack of suitable coal.

Fortunately, a handful of independent observers were aware of the gravity of the situation, and notable among them was a professor of Dutch extraction by the name of Hondelink. Born in Holland in 1890, the professor later adopted British citizenship and established a reputation in transport circles second to none. Before the second world war he worked in an advisory capacity for railways throughout the globe, gaining vital experience in China, Japan, New Zealand, Holland, Britain, and many other countries.

With the Allied invasion of 1944, Professor Hondelink was given the task of restoring railway services behind Allied lines — a difficult and exacting job that progressed remarkably smoothly, giving a corresponding boost to the war effort.

After the cessation of hostilities, Prof Hondelink became a senior transport and communications consultant to the United Nations and the World Bank — a position that he was to hold for many years. Despite returning to his pre-war globe-trotting existence, the professor kept a close eye on railway matters in his adopted country, noting with alarm the increasing bureaucracy of the BTC.

Hondelink was not particularly enthralled by the nationalisation process, not for political reasons, but on account of the overwhelmingly top-heavy administration it produced. He was also far from happy with the strange BTC/ Railway Executive relationship, which appeared to have produced no fewer than 13 tiers of management where (according to the professor) five would have been more than adequate. On the 1947 Transport Act, he was forthright in his opinions, claiming that the legislation "…was conceived and passed in the greatest hurry; no time at all was taken to study and digest lessons which other world systems could have taught us".

In short, bureaucracy was strangling the BTC. And the push towards centralisation and standardisation was achieving nothing and wasting a great deal. The BTC had inherited 400 odd classes of steam locomotives and dealt with the problem by producing another 12 standard classes. The result was (naturally enough) 412 classes of locomotive and, as the professor pointed out with extraordinary foresight, the whole lot would soon be scrapped and replaced by a multiplicity of diesels.

There was plenty of evidence to back Hondelink's views at the time, for the number of administrative staff employed by the BTC, although commendably low in the early days, had almost doubled by 1950, while headquarters expenses had risen to £14.5 million, and would reach £18.5 million the following year. As the professor attempted to explain, the administration of the railways was certainly in a hopeless tangle:

> **The Railway Executive can be abolished completely. An executive board of members who individually exercise executive functions yet must submit to collective responsibilities and permanent consultations, plus regional officers whose authority and responsibility are seriously reduced, plus dual responsibility of the regions' chief officers (to their regional chief and executive member); this is a system which, wherever tried, has always proved inefficient.**

Such pronouncements did nothing to endear Hondelink to the socialist administration, although by 1950 it was becoming clear that Churchill might well return to power and the professor cannily switched his attentions to the Conservatives.

In the summer of 1951, the Branchline Committee discovered the Isle of Wight. The real problem for the island's railways was not so much a lack of traffic, but a marked imbalance between the summer and winter trade. The Isle of Wight was a popular holiday destination, and many visitors came by train. In the summer of 1945 for example, no fewer than 982,000 tickets were issued on the island, but a remarkable 1,830,000 were collected, suggesting that a fair proportion of travellers had begun their journey on the mainland. All the same, the island railway network was losing money on a year-round basis, and the Branchline Committee came to the conclusion that the whole affair could be closed with relative ease. It soon emerged that it had made a serious tactical error.

It was discovered that the busy holiday line linking Ryde Pier with Sandown carried almost 4,000 passengers per hour on summer Saturdays. It was estimated that no fewer than 62 buses an hour would be required to carry travellers to their destinations, if the railway were to close. But according to a prophetic letter from a Mr R F Hathaway, published in *Railways* magazine, the closure scheme smacked of something far more sinister than mere rationalisation:

> **...the island closure schemes are but the thin end of the wedge for even bigger things; there are those who stand to gain financially in countries which have "passed out of the railway age".**

In the event, the Railway Executive backed down, and the Branchline Committee was sent elsewhere in search of closure candidates. Whether sinister forces really were at work is hard to tell. There was certainly nothing sinister about the behaviour of the Executive, which might have acted a little foolishly, but was merely attempting to implement the policies passed down from the Commission. The Transport Commission, in turn, was bound by the various, and sometimes contradictory, requirements of the 1947 Transport Act. And it was still trying to integrate the nation's transport services. The Labour Government was almost dead by this time, and more or less viewing matters from the sidelines.

The real problem was the overwhelming size and complexity of the state machine and the plethora of committees that it created, some duplicating each others' work, while others pulled in opposite directions. In October 1951, after considering the matter for more than three years, the Motive Power Committee finally produced a report: diesels were very suitable for shunting duties; express units should be tentatively explored; and multiple units were worth further study for the branches! After a quite unnecessary delay of three years, the report brought only one positive result where branch line services were concerned — the establishment of a Lightweight Trains Committee to consider things further.

After six years of Labour Government, the Holy Grail of road/rail integration remained as elusive as ever. The high hopes of the 1947 Act were never realised, in part because the individual Executives had tended to concern themselves with their own schemes and ideas, but largely as a result of the BTC's failure to take control of long-distance road-haulage concerns, the acquisition of which was not fully realised until 1951.

On October 26, 1951, an elderly Winston Churchill returned to power, vowing to free his country from the shackles of socialism. He was not exactly in a position to do much about it at first, however, for the Conservatives had won with an overall majority of only 17. As the last ballot papers were counted, and the Tories slipped into power, their leader is said to have pronounced: "We've won… I have the reins of the country in my hands again. But we're in a bloody mess."

It was a sentiment that might, or might not, have rung true for the country as a whole, but where the railways were concerned it was all too accurate.

3.
The closures begin
1951-1954

Almost from the beginning of the working of these nationalised industries we have heard profound dissatisfaction expressed at the way in which they render their accounts. We hear from commercial industries that if they rendered their accounts in the same manner as the nationalised industries, they would find themselves in gaol.

Sir Peter Macdonald, MP for the Isle of Wight

No-one could claim that the closing of one small branch line was a matter of public interest in the wider sense of the word, but the closure of a whole group of branch lines is at once a matter of public interest.

John Maclay, MP for Renfrewshire West — Hansard, February 1954

WITH the return of Winston Churchill and a Conservative administration, most integration plans were halted and steps were taken to amend the 1947 Transport Act. Considered opinion, however, held the view that the nationalisation process was largely irreversible, and the search began for a compromise that could be enshrined in a new Transport Act. The Conservatives were quite clear on three points: the concept of an integrated transport system was now out of the question; the BTC was unlikely to survive in its present form; and the road haulage concerns should be denationalised as soon as possible.

The immediate effect at the BTC was to put development schemes on hold, for Sir Cyril Hurcomb had been firmly committed to creating an integrated system. Wearily, he abandoned further development, and began to bide his time before retirement. Such was the inertia within the Commission, that little changed and it continued to be assumed that minor rail services would be closed and their traffic handed to the roads, although it was rapidly becoming clear that the road services might soon be operated by private enterprise in competition with the state transport concern. As if to add fuel to the conflict, the Railway Executive at last discovered the diesel multiple unit and began tentative experiments with the new vehicles in competition with BTC road buses.

As the Branchline Committee widened the closure net, and introduced a number of underhand methods to achieve its targets, it came into increasing conflict with a fledgling protest movement. Matters finally came to a head on the Isle of Wight, where the pro-rail movement successfully dismantled the railway authorities' financial figures. But despite winning a moral victory, the protesters failed to make any impact on the Central Transport Consultative Committee (CTCC), which continued to recommend closure in almost every case it considered.

In October 1953, the Conservatives introduced their long awaited transport legislation — only road-haulage was to be denationalised, while the other transport concerns would remain in public ownership. The Railway Executive was abolished, and steps were taken to delegate power downwards to the regions. But although certain management functions were eventually delegated, the BTC took effective control of the railway system in the absence of the Executive, growing into a vast and bureaucratic organisation in the process. The branch line closure policy was pushed forward with some determination, but the pro-rail movement began to fight back by utilising increasingly sophisticated techniques. The first successful diesel multiple unit experiments caused a slight drop in the rate of closures. Finally, in 1954, the Commission announced a large-scale modernisation programme that included a degree of investment for the branch lines.

* * *

The return of a Conservative Government in 1951 caused a counter-swing of the ideological pendulum that was to throw the railways from one political extreme to the other in the following decades. No doubt the nation's railways would have thrived under a planned socialist economy — perhaps they would go on to thrive (albeit in a different form) under the Conservatives. All they really needed was a period of stability one way or the other.

Labour had not had sufficient time to produce a properly integrated system, and (in an admittedly difficult economic climate) the party had been too concerned with ideology to modernise the system. It could even be argued that Labour had a vested interest against modernisation: an early end to steam traction would have meant a reduction in the demand for coal at a time when the nationalised coal industry was in financial difficulties. And modernisation would mean a reduction in manpower — hardly in the best interests of a party whose grass roots lay in the trade union movement.

The railways had become a political pawn: but many believed the House of Commons was a far from suitable place for dissecting the ins and outs of the industry, and this appeared to be the view of Alan Lennox-Boyd, the new Minister of Transport, who said: "I do not think anybody would think it was a good idea for the Minister to assume day-to-day responsibility for the running of the railways." Whether or not it was a good idea, there can be little doubt that too much of the railways' dirty linen had already been aired in public, to the advantage of the soon-to-be-privatised road haulage operators.

The system appeared to have experienced all the negative aspects of socialism without any of the benefits — a top-heavy bureaucracy, without market safeguards or a policy of integration. Perhaps now, under the Conservatives, things would be different.

To those who were seeking to prevent the closure of railway lines, it certainly didn't look as though much was going to change. As early as December 1950, Owen Prosser (whom we left exploring the Kent & East Sussex) had decided that a body should be formed to fight certain closure proposals. The only militant pro-rail body at that time was The Light Railway Transport League, and an approach to the League proved fruitful, for its journal, *The Modern Tramway*, assisted by publishing a manifesto in December 1950.

As a direct result of the publication of Mr Prosser's article, affirmations of support were received from various quarters, most notably from Robert Aickman, founder of the Inland Waterways Association, who offered his very able assistance. The following year the two men were ready to hold a public meeting, and this was duly arranged for November 16, 1951, at the Fred Tallant Hall in London.

Prosser and Aickman addressed the audience on the seriousness of the situation and, from those present, was born the Railway Development Association. The primary grievance of the new Association (later re-named the Railway Development Society) was with the British Transport Commission's policy of closing lines which might have proved viable with the application of diesel railbuses or multiple units, and other examples of modern technology. Even in 1951, the BTC was designing and building steam push-pull units that were slow, dirty and expensive to operate. And they were being delivered to the lightly loaded branch lines that were most in need of modernisation.

But the message was gradually getting through and, after publication of the Motive Power Committee's report in October 1951, the BTC began tentatively to investigate the new diesel units. Predictably, the bureaucratic Commission decided that the best answer might be to create yet another new committee, and so the Lightweight Trains Committee was formed, and sent off to investigate.

Its first stop was in the West Country. The former Great Western Railway had had by far the greatest experience with railcars in Britain, introducing 30 single-car units between 1933 and 1941, together with a handful of multiple units. There had, however, been no significant advance in Britain since nationalisation, and the committee decided to extend its investigations to the near Continent as well.

Experiments in Germany and France had proved quite conclusively that railcars were able to fight off road competition. By 1939, the Germans had

A German railbus at Niendorf in 1958 — the vehicle was typical of those investigated by the Lightweight Trains Committee. A R Spencer.

introduced no fewer than 850 diesel units and, with characteristic precision, they made a simple claim to the BTC representatives: "These units have enabled unremunerative services on branch lines to be operated at a profit."

The more exuberant French were determined to demonstrate their showpiece. The Annemasse to Geneva line had been converted to multiple unit operation in 1949, experiencing an overwhelming increase in passenger income. At Annemasse, the branch terminus, income had risen from a paltry 19,000F to 126,000F, in a single year.

The French (busily introducing railcars since 1933) had found the vehicles cheaper to operate than steam trains — somewhere between 30 and 75 per cent of steam costs on a seat-for-seat basis — and very popular with the public. By 1952 they had built 720 railcars, from tiny single-car units for rural branch lines, to powerful multiple units intended for long distance express services. All were considerably more economical than their steam equivalents.

Using a steam-hauled French express train as a yardstick, the results of the Lightweight Train Committee's inquiries were broadly as follows:

Relative cost per mile

French steam-hauled express train	100
French steam-hauled stopping train	76
GWR steam-hauled stopping train	66-87
GWR 420hp DMU (4-car)	42
GWR 420hp DMU (3-car)	41
French 600hp express DMU (2-car)	35
GWR 210hp DMU (2-car)	24-28
French 150hp railbus (1-car)	16

The statistical evidence was so overwhelming that the committee set to work with enthusiasm, producing a report of its own by March 1952. Here, at long last, was official confirmation that steam railcars and push-pull units were no longer on the agenda.

A variety of diesel units were considered. The majority were large, relatively powerful, and designed to operate in units of three, but the committee also decided to investigate a lighter vehicle. The result was the AEC PUP, a joint development between the AEC company and the Railway Executive. It was felt that this smaller, lighter version of a conventional diesel unit might prove useful for "marginal or uneconomic services", but for the moment it was no more than an experimental investigation. Ultra lightweight vehicles, along the lines of the French railbus, were not really considered, although the committee commented that "there may be scope for the use of lightweight rail cars, possibly of the four-wheel type".

The change of policy had come not a moment too soon, for some otherwise successful urban lines were losing traffic to road buses at a frightening rate. The Birmingham to Walsall line, for instance, had experienced a 78 per cent loss of traffic between 1939 and 1950, and there were many similar examples.

The priority was to choose suitable areas to test the new units, and the committee came up with three schemes. The first would be in Lincolnshire, around Grimsby, Skegness, Boston and Retford. It was considered that 13 two-car units would be required, at a cost of £325,000, but the annual savings would amount to around £121,000, for the units would displace no fewer than 11 steam locomotives and 38 coaches.

The second railcar trial would take place in urban Yorkshire, linking Halifax, Bradford and Leeds. Here the requirement would be for eight two-car units at a cost of £200,000, but the vehicles were expected to save £25,000 a year, and generate new traffic worth £31,000. The largest scheme, involving 13 two-car units, two three-car units and ten four-car units, was to be based in and around the Lake District. The cost was put at £915,000, but once again the savings were judged to be considerable — £99,000 a year, with additional income estimated at £34,000.

As diesels became available, it was felt that Bristol, West Hampshire and the Waverley line between Carlisle and Edinburgh might also benefit from the new technology. The projected savings were substantial: a 25 per cent traffic increase on the Waverley route and, in Hampshire, replacement of eight locomotives and more than 100 coaches with just 13 diesel units.

All was not to proceed quite so smoothly, however. After protracted negotiations with the trade unions, it was agreed in principle that the new vehicles would not be used for shunting purposes. If they were to perform even the simplest of shunting manoeuvres, the union view was that they would become locomotives, requiring automatic attendance on the "footplate" of a fireman. It was later to prove an intractable problem.

There were other, more serious, difficulties. So enthusiastic was the Lightweight Trains Committee, that it neglected to consider the fact that the rival road buses (most markedly in Lincolnshire) were owned by its parent organisation, the BTC.

According to the committee, whose sole aim was to improve railway revenues: "Road services in the area do not show any great advantages over the railway in either speed or frequency, and on some routes are decidedly inferior." Its masters at the BTC, who had still failed to absorb the implications brought about by the change of Government, took a different view. Inevitably, once the report reached the Commission, the Lincolnshire scheme was vetoed, for the experiment was bound to damage the profitability of the buses operated by the Lincolnshire Road Car Company under BTC control. Undeterred, the committee recommended an East Anglian trial instead. But it is only against such a background that the subsequent demoralised state of rural railways can be judged, for there was a positive disincentive in the 1950s to upgrade the railway services.

The Railway Executive was charged with the task of operating the railways, but it was forced to obey directives from the BTC, which still had substantial interests in road transport. As a result there was often friction between the Executive and the Commission, the Executive dragging its feet on the subject of railway closures, and the BTC remaining unwilling to invest in railcars to make branch lines profitable. There were probably more than a few conflicts within the Railway Executive itself, for the work of the Lightweight Trains Committee was often contradictory to that of the Branchline Committee, whose primary role was to seek out and close unremunerative services.

But the report on diesel trains could not be ignored for ever and, after a quite

The experimental ACV lightweight train set during trials in the Birmingham area. Pictured at Henley-in-Arden, by S H Keyse.

unnecessary eight-month delay, the Commission agreed to the amended trial schemes put forward by the Lightweight Trains Committee, announcing the start of diesel multiple unit construction from November 1952. In fact, by this time, an experimental lightweight unit, known as the ACV set, had already quietly entered revenue-earning service earlier in the year.

As the newly-formed Railway Development Association suspected, the BTC had put pressure on the Executive from the very beginning to prepare a "programme" of railway closures. What the Association was not to know, was that the cuts were to run far beyond the branch lines, for the Commission was pressing for closure of the less remunerative secondary lines once the branch lines had been dealt with.

The Railway Executive was in a difficult position. It knew that diesel railcars were likely to ease the unprofitability of its minor services, but it was obliged to obey directives from the Transport Commission. Wisely, it took the middle road, and proceeded with closures as slowly as possible. Thus, despite the activities of a full team of railway officials on the Branchline Committee, closures proceeded at too slow a rate for the Commission, which was fretting to get on with closing the more financially significant secondary lines.

In December 1951 the Commission had sent a stiffly worded letter to the Railway Executive, in an effort to speed up the closure process:

It is hoped that the remaining investigations will be pressed forward as quickly as possible... The Commission wish to receive a report setting out shortly the reasons in each case which have led the Executive to decide that certain branches, which have been considered for closing, should be kept open. The Commission will also be grateful if you will now furnish the report on the Scottish lines...

...it is felt that the total effect of the closings already achieved or in prospect... will not amount to the "streamlining" of the railway system which has been described as the main objective.

The Railway Executive was playing for time. The new Conservative Government had made it clear that there were to be some major upheavals in the organisation of transport, and the Executive was loath to transfer traffic to BTC road buses, when future legislation might privatise the bus companies. Incredibly, it was not until September 24 the following year that the Transport Commission received a reply:

...many schemes are now delayed owing to their having to go to the Area TUCCs... in some cases such delay is up to six months... The Commission will realise that there are likely to be great difficulties in closing down many of the more important secondary lines. Some of them (such as the Dingwall to Kyle of Lochalsh and Fort William to Mallaig lines) are the only railways in large geographical areas. Such secondary lines represent national, social and eco- nomic obligations which the Executive can see no means of escaping... There is a further important point to be borne in mind in considering the closing of these lines. Since 1948, decisions to close branch lines have had regard to the fact that the Commission own or have a financial interest in many of the road passenger and freight services of the country. This not only means that much of the traffic diverted from rail is automatically picked up by existing road services of the Commission, but that the comparative ease with which alternative facilities can be provided is a powerful factor in counteracting opposition... Much, if not all, of this co-operation with road services might disappear if the Transport Bill goes through... in its present form.

A J Pearson, of the Railway Executive

The Government had already published a White Paper outlining the propos- als that were soon to be enshrined in the 1953 Transport Act. The shock news, for members of the Railway Executive, was that it was almost certainly their body which was going to be eradicated, rather than the BTC. The resulting stagnation in management activity caused all manner of problems. Integration plans had already been suspended at the Transport Commission, and now the various rationalisation and modernisation schemes of the Railway Executive were similarly affected.

In the meantime, the Government had entered into a less than healthy alliance with private road-haulage lobby groups. According to *The Times*, a paper that could hardly be accused of harbouring left-wing sympathies, it was no less than an attempt "to secure political favour at the expense of all serious consideration of transport economics and organisation". The road lobby had suffered grievously under the socialist administration and it had fought hard to bring the Conservatives to power. It was now busily tightening its links with the new administration, demanding higher lorry speed limits, motorways, and denationalisation of road haulage. The Government (backed up by an increasingly road-biased Ministry of Transport) agreed to every demand. It was a development that should have set alarm bells ringing at the BTC, but the Commission remained stubbornly complacent. In any event, the various activities of the Railway Executive were, paradoxically, starting to show a healthy return. Profits (before interest and central charges) had risen rapidly from £26 million in 1950 to £40 million in 1952.

Masked by the figures, however, was the awful reality that the railway system was continuing to decay. In the Midlands, the situation had become so serious that, in June 1952, the Birmingham Junior Chamber of Commerce decided to set up an inquiry of its own. Its report, published in February 1953, resulted in the West Midlands Railway Passenger Transport Scheme — an ambitious project to reopen railways and stations throughout the Birmingham area. No fewer than 56 new or reopened stations were envisaged, together with an intensive local service based around diesel multiple unit operation:

> Experience in other areas shows that track electrification where introduced has resulted in a considerable increase in traffic and there is every reason to suppose that the introduction of diesel traction within a network of comprehensive local services would have similar beneficial results... The mind of the public is so firmly made up in favour of road transport for local travel, that mere palliatives would not result in any substantial change-over to railway travel... a complete change of outlook by the railway authorities can produce the desired results...

The Chamber of Commerce had certainly done its research, for the report noted that the Railway Executive's ACV railcar was already undergoing trials between Marylebone and Princes Risborough. It was exactly the sort of technology the Chamber wanted to see introduced in Birmingham, but the Railway Executive, although generally interested in the report, was unable to assist. Hamstrung by its relationship with the BTC, its own impending doom, and severe restraint on capital expenditure, the Executive had no authority, and no desire, to get involved.

Far from taking the initiative where railway development schemes were concerned, the hapless Executive was about to be vilified in the press for implementing the closure policy passed down from the BTC. Early in 1953, a year that saw introduction of the Elizabethan, a crack express that achieved a post-war record speed between London and Edinburgh (but still failed to outpace the pre-war Coronation Scot), the branch line closure policy finally came to a head.

The Branchline Committee had reinvestigated the Isle of Wight and come to the same conclusion — that the entire island system was unremunerative and should be disposed of. Closure would not be easy though, for it was widely known by this time that diesel multiple units were about to enter service, and the railways on the Isle of Wight had an enthusiastic and vociferous following.

Publicly, the suggestion would be closure of just half the railway mileage on the island, leaving the more remunerative lines to be picked off at a later stage. The minor branch from Merstone Junction to Ventnor West had slipped quietly away the previous year but, in May 1953, the Executive outlined plans to close another 24 miles out of a total of just over 50.

The public announcement of the proposals in May 1953 generated an uproar, not just because the holiday island had an immaculate and delightful railway system, but because the Railway Executive had alleged that the railways on the Isle of Wight were losing no less than £271,000 a year. The Brading to Bembridge branch, and the lines from Newport to Sandown and Freshwater, would be closed — a move that would reportedly reduce the deficit by around £90,000. It was an outrageous figure — even allowing for the fact that the island trains were poorly patronised during the winter months. A deficit of such magnitude could only have accrued had the trains run empty for most of the year.

The Railway Development Association soon became involved. It was convinced that the Railway Executive had long been providing false figures to Transport Users' Consultative Committee inquiries so as to smooth the flow of closures, and the Association was determined to force a public debate on the issue. The result was a headlong confrontation between the Executive and the protesters which culminated in the most celebrated closure inquiry of the 1950s: The Great Isle of Wight Train Robbery*.

Edward Kenworthy FCA, Treasurer of the Association's Midland Area, set to work in consultation with F W Bright, of the Newport Chamber of Commerce, to analyse the claimed losses.

Meanwhile, the Isle of Wight County Council had engaged a distinguished barrister, Melford Stevenson, QC, to fight its corner. (Mr Stevenson was later to become known for defending Ruth Ellis, the last woman to hang in Great Britain.)

It was an unlikely alliance — a pro-rail group from the Midlands, a top barrister, and a county council — but it worked.

---

* So-called after the title of a book by R E Burroughes.

At the Transport Users' Consultative Committee hearing, Melford Stevenson argued that the objectors would be unable to present a proper case without access to all the facts. How could they debate the issue if they did not have before them an analysis of the losses as claimed by the Executive? Remarkably, the South Eastern Area TUCC agreed, and the inquiry was adjourned until June 1953 to give the authorities time to produce the relevant figures.

No-one was more surprised than the protesters at this turn of events. But when the inquiry reconvened in London, on June 20, the revelations were to put in question the honesty and integrity of the whole BTC organisation. Back on the island, the Council engaged an expert witness in the form of Stanley Hill, an accountant who had arbitrated in the nationalisation of the railways. His investigations were to produce some astonishing results, for it appeared that the Executive's figures were, quite simply, false or, according to Melford Stevenson:

> The issue is now clearer than it has ever been since the inquiry began. You have been presented by the Railway Executive with a set of figures that are false, possibly by carelessness or inadvertence. It is no part of my function to assign motives, but the figures have now been demonstrated beyond any doubt as quite wrong. If the same form of accountancy as has been applied to the Island were used for the whole of British Railways, their 1951 profit of £34 million would be turned into a loss of £40 million.

If the figures were really false, how exactly had the Executive falsified them? Firstly, it had quietly omitted the effects of contributory revenue generated by the threatened lines — in other words, the value of traffic that had been passing to and from the rest of the railway system. The effect of adding this figure was to increase the claimed income from £37,400 to £45,900. By this single step, the protesters proved that the branch lines were actually covering their direct movement costs, comprising wages, train working and maintenance.

It could be argued that the Executive was quite within its rights to omit contributory revenue from the accounts, but by doing so it had given a very false view of the savings that would result after closure, for much of the contributory revenue would be bound to disappear — the Executive wanted both to have its cake and to eat it. The suggestion that the Executive was unsure of the value of contributory revenue must be excluded, for the Branchline Committee had always made a point of providing a detailed analysis of the figures.

The second dispute arose over operating expenses, for the Executive had claimed some extraordinary estimates for maintenance of stock, particularly on the little Bembridge branch:

> In the case of the Bembridge line there was one engine in steam, three push-pull coaches (one used in the winter, two in summer, and three on Saturdays), and half a dozen coal wagons a week. For the maintenance of these, the Executive included a figure of £4,245. This was £80 a week for one engine, three coaches,

and six wagons...

The Bembridge contingent, though it represented 3.5 per cent of the total, was claimed to cost 7.5 per cent of the total maintenance bill. This [Mr Bright] had found generally to be the case with the figures in the maintenance and renewal section. The engines, for example, were shown to be replaced at a rate which could only mean brand new stock, yet the youngest locomotive in the island was dated 1896.

Isle of Wight County Press

In fact, far from being replaced new, the island rolling-stock had traditionally been replaced with equipment that was surplus to requirements on the mainland. Thus the Executive's figures — which gave the impression that the island was due to be re-equipped twice over with brand-new rolling stock — were quite fictitious. The same was true where the track was concerned. The Executive had put in a figure of £500 per mile for track maintenance. This was almost equal to the average national cost, but the island railways were single track, subject to speed restrictions, and largely maintained with secondhand materials.

The only figures that the County Council was able to verify from its own records were those for season ticket holders. The Executive had claimed a revenue of just £5 a year between Newport and Freshwater but, according to the *Isle of Wight County Press*, Mr Bright knew of revenue from three sources which totalled £98, including £53 from the County Council in respect of school children.

A table compiled by the county treasurer, analysing the total payments by the County Council to the Railway Executive in respect of scholars... shows the total as £1,721 and, on the Freshwater line, £53 12s 4d. None of this is included in income. Mr Bright added that season ticket income on the Brading-Bembridge line was given by the railways as £42, whereas the County Council alone paid £72. There must be other season ticket holders.

The whole affair smacked of sharp practice, even more markedly so when C P Hopkins, the representative of the Executive, came to be examined, and agreed to answer questions but refused cross-examination. "What's the difference?" inquired the wily Melford Stevenson, who knew very well what the difference was.

If the Railway Executive was wrong, then what exactly **was** the financial state of the threatened branch lines? Mr Hill, the expert witness, wisely refused to be drawn on an exact figure, although Melford Stevenson claimed that the annual loss was around £20,000, rather than £90,000, and the entire loss could be attributed to the Freshwater branch, as the other lines were more or less paying their way. Many years later, the BTC revealed the inaccuracy of its own figures, for the annual saving from all the railway mileage closed in 1953 (more

A Bembridge to Brading train at St Helen's, the only intermediate station on the three-mile branch which was closed in September 1953, a victim of the Great Isle of Wight Train Robbery. S H Keyse.

than 160 miles) was estimated to be no more than £146,000. On this basis, the savings on the Isle of Wight would have been about £22,000.

Perhaps of greater importance was the following admission by Mr Hopkins of the Railway Executive:

> ...the analysis of the position in the island was based on a system devised by the BTC in 1949 to permit the rapid examination of the position of any branch line. It had not been devised for any special line. Its basis was change... as between the position of the railways with the line open, and with it closed.

In other words, all the figures put forward by the BTC since 1949, and all those that might be put forward in the future, were suspect. It was a crucial turning point, marking the first public admission that the Branchline Committee might be using underhand methods to achieve closure targets. With Melford Stevenson sniffing at his heels, poor Hopkins was finally driven into a corner on the unlikely subject of railway sleepers:

> *STEVENSON:* You said, "In the Island we always use new sleepers". Can you

69

explain the most recent replacements then, where [secondhand] sleepers were used from North Kent and Faversham?

HOPKINS: You will recall that I wanted to close the Brading-Bembridge branch a few days ago. I thought it would help towards amity if we forewent economies.

STEVENSON: That statement is only useful as a general measure of how much reliability one can place on a railway statement.

The barrister concluded, with some justification, that "if a case with such a degree of prevarication and inaccurate figures had been presented in a court of law, it would have been thrown out with contempt".

The Isle of Wight inquiry was a small victory for free speech, but it did nothing to change the Transport Users' Consultative Committee inquiry procedure, or indeed to amend the policies of the Branchline Committee, the Railway Executive or the BTC. The protesters had proved that the Railway Executive's figures were largely false, and that the island railways (and presumably many others) were losing far less than had been claimed, even without the advantages of diesel operation. But besides making the Executive look more carefully at the figures in future inquiries, they achieved nothing of substance.

As a result of the inquiry, the Area TUCC recommended closure of the Newport-Freshwater line immediately, and gave the Sandown-Newport branch a two-year stay of execution. As for the little Bembridge line, with its single antiquarian locomotive and three carriages, the TUCC was divided and unable to make a recommendation.

The CTCC made a decision on its behalf, and the little branch line was put up for immediate closure. In its annual report, the central committee went on to make the extraordinary claim that it accepted the Executive's figures in full and repudiated any suggestion that the accountancy was questionable. Such pronouncements made a mockery of the consultation procedure and led many to believe that the central consultative body was merely an organ of the BTC, and not impartial as was claimed.

In October 1953, the Minister of Transport presided at a joint BTC/county council meeting on the Isle of Wight and succeeded in convincing the council that money would be available for road improvements. Thus, when the Sandown-Newport line came up for closure again early in 1956, there was little protest. And the Ministry had another trick up its sleeve, for the track was left in position. The logic of this move was soon to become apparent for, according to the Minister, the intention was to enable a private concern to purchase and operate the line if it wished:

...[the BTC] want it to be open to private enterprise to take over and run the line, if private enterprise believes that it will make a good thing of it when British Railways were unable to do so. Provided that we have adequate safeguards about the price paid to British Railways, I see no objection to that at all in principle. I can only mention that the rails have been left in the Isle of Wight right to the present time... that is for two years... waiting for some enterprising speculator to start running a service and, so far, no-one has been willing to do so...

During the Isle of Wight inquiry, Melford Stevenson had quoted from the minutes of a Southern Region/National Union of Railwaymen meeting where, according to the union, "the management admitted quite frankly that it was their intention at a later stage to close the railways altogether as far as the Isle of Wight was concerned".

A single small concession was ultimately obtained, for the Executive agreed to provide five years notice of closure in the case of the Ryde, Newport and Cowes line, and seven years for Shanklin to Ventnor. Otherwise the Isle of Wight inquiry achieved very little besides "exposing painfully undemocratic aspects of a country that calls itself democratic", in the words of John Arlott, the cricket commentator and rail enthusiast, writing in the *Hampshire Magazine.*

It was literally the end of the line for the island railways, but just the beginning for the eloquent Melford Stevenson who was destined to become a High Court Judge in 1957. He pursued the post with such vigour that by 1975, after disposing of the Kray Twins, the Angry Brigade, and a clutch of IRA terrorists, among others, he had gained a reputation as the toughest and most controversial judge in the land.

* * *

Late in 1953 the Government finally introduced the long awaited Transport Bill to abolish the Executives. Deep among the paragraphs of the new Bill, there was a subtle, but fundamentally important, clause. The 1947 Act had empowered the Commission to provide "adequate railway services" but, under the 1953 Act, the word "adequate" was dropped, leaving the BTC an option as to the sort of railway services it might provide — adequate, inadequate or non-existent.

Paradoxically, the BTC was reorganised along more complex lines to deal with the new initiatives, its membership growing from nine to 15. And another unfortunate side-effect of the new legislation was that, whereas the nine-member Railway Executive had included five railwaymen, the new-look Transport Commission included only two members with railway knowledge.

For some reason it had been concluded that denationalisation would be either politically or practically unacceptable. The intention, instead, was to transfer power to the individual railway regions, which would be controlled by Area Boards, rather in the manner of the former private railway companies. The aim was to give the BTC the right and authority to devolve management along local lines, with the intention of creating a new freedom that would allow for all sorts of novel schemes. It sounded exactly the kind of initiative that Professor Hondelink, the United Nations transport expert, had long argued for. Unfortunately, the Transport Commission and the remnants of the Railway Executive were left to work out the details of reorganisation themselves, giving the professor good reason to believe that the changes might be no more than superficial.

The new BTC Chairman, General Sir Brian Robertson, would encourage the railway regions to make commercial decisions of their own. It was felt, quite reasonably, that the former unwieldy management system had stifled the railways, whereas a return to regional loyalties would recreate a certain *esprit de corps*.

The 1953 Act was to have other effects, for it marked the end of the long and ultimately fruitless experiment in transport integration. Road services, which had proved so difficult to nationalise, would be sold off as rapidly as possible, and from the end of 1954 the 25-mile lorry limit would be repealed. The new freedom for road transport was, in theory, to be matched by a new freedom for the railways, for at long last the rates and charges legislation was to be adjusted.

The railways would be empowered in future to operate at a profit, and their freedom to set rates and charges was to be considerably enhanced. The outdated legislation requiring the railways to set standard charges to all traders wishing to consign a particular product was abandoned, the intention being to allow passenger fares and freight charges to mirror the costs involved in their carriage. The railway would no longer be obliged to publish charges — just the maximum figures — but these maxima would continue to be set by the Transport Tribunal which had the power to veto increases, as indeed did the Minister.

In the event, implementation of the scheme left much to be desired. So slow was the process of actually altering the charges, that it was not until four years later that a modified version of the new proposals was approved by the Transport Tribunal. Whereas road transport concerns had long been able to set their charges in a free market, the railways remained shackled by the Government: yet they were expected to compete in the same marketplace for the same traffic.

Only in July 1957, after a delay of almost 40 years, were the railways given the freedom to adjust rates to suit market conditions — to reduce charges in order to attract traffic they could carry economically, and raise rates for traffic they wished to deter. It had, however, come much too late. For some years the railways had been charging 14 per cent less than competing road haulage interests for uneconomic short-haul traffic, and five per cent more for middle-distance business. The whole operation was fundamentally uneconomic, and the cost had already begun to drive the railway system into a vicious spiral of decline.

The 1953 Act resulted in the sale of 24,000 lorries to small road hauliers, who proceeded to operate without the slightest restriction, undermining the railway's position. The process of disposing of the Commission's road interests was not brought to a halt until 1956, by which time the integrated system had been almost completely dismantled.

Professor Hondelink was profoundly disappointed with the 1953 reorganisation, for the Commission decided to oversee railway operations itself, taking up residence at the former Railway Executive headquarters at 222, Marylebone Road, and employing many of the old staff. The operation grew to such a size that it was soon necessary to build additional offices next door as well.

Although the new Area Boards were supposed to function rather as the board of directors of the former private railway companies had done, the result was nothing of the kind. The Area Boards took on extra staff, but very little extra responsibility, for the BTC had taken control of most of the Railway Executive's functions. The design and manufacture of locomotives, track, and signalling equipment remained under central control, as did negotiations over major wage claims and alterations to the charging structure.

It took more than a year to complete the reorganisation, and once the extraordinarily complex machine was up and running, the regions found themselves even more tightly restrained than they had been before. Wage claims and other costs were imposed from above, while the regions searched desperately for new business to pay for them. The result, according to Professor Hondelink, was an increase in complexity to a chain of command comprising no fewer than ten levels.

A policy that had been intended to strip away bureaucracy had actually increased it, for by 1958 the number of administrative personnel per mile of railway line had almost doubled from the days of the pre-nationalisation railway companies. And the ongoing railway closure programme served merely to make the situation worse for, although the number of rank-and-file railwaymen was gradually reduced, the number of clerks, secretaries, superintendents, committee members and managers increased.

By this time, income was slowly but steadily rising, but costs were beginning to run out of control, and 1953 saw the railway operating profit fall to £34.6 million, a figure that was more than swallowed up by central charges paid to the Transport Commission.

According to the professor, the rapidly worsening financial situation stemmed solely from poor management and the branch line closure policy was no more than a red herring to cover up for the inadequacies of headquarters administration. He calculated that a reduction in the number of BTC clerical staff, cessation of the standardisation programme, and a few other sensible economies, would improve railway finances to the tune of some £10 million a year —

"...an increase to no fewer than ten levels of command..."

considerably more than the closure programme was realising:

> I do maintain with all my vigour that such economies would far outstrip in value any that may be made by closure of stations and branch lines...

> If a complete railway administration, in the shape of a combined Commission and Executive, remains superimposed on the systems, with another level of boards and delegated executives interposed, then all the faults of the existing cumbersome, inanimate, rigid and slow-working machine will be made even worse than they are now.

Nothing was to change. Indeed, the number of administrative personnel continued to rise. Professor Hondelink was a world authority on transport affairs, but he had now drawn the fire of politicians of all shades of opinion in his own country. Trusted by no-one, his continuing exhortations to save the industry fell on deaf ears, for his views were quietly and comprehensively suppressed.

The innovative decentralisation policy, described by Professor Hondelink as "make-believe", proved quite worthless. It was, after all, a false situation. The Tories had assumed that the railways would simply shake off the yoke of socialism and return overnight to doing battle with each other. But, of course, they had now to contend with other, more efficiently managed forms of transport as well. And the Conservatives had made matters worse by introducing an administrative yoke of their own that weighed far heavier on the system than anything the socialists had created.

Conservative policies did little good and a great deal of harm, for just as the former railway companies had got used to the idea of working together as a national entity, they were instructed to make decisions of their own from regional centres. With old rivalries still lurking just beneath the surface, this was something they were only too willing to do. The result was little cross-fertilisation of ideas between the regions and few economies of scale.

Even quite innocuous ideas such as allowing the regions their own colour-schemes fell flat, for long-distance passenger trains began to take on a distressingly piebald appearance. It was a fine idea, but it had come at the wrong time, and regional identity began to appear as something of a retrograde step.

Yet, in some ways, this was a glorious Indian summer for the railways. Economies had as yet failed to bite, and for a few years there was something of a return to pre-war conditions. In the former Great Western territories in particular, where the drab uniformity of nationalisation had had little effect, the early 1950s were wonderful years. Once again, resplendent Kings and Castles hauled rakes of coffee and cream carriages to the Cornish Riviera, and the old guard of the GWR held their heads high once again. No-one really cared that the French and the Germans were pressing ahead with modernisation, for the heyday of the British railway system had been in the 1930s... it was a last chance to relive the golden years.

But according to Owen Prosser of the Railway Development Association, the lack of judgment shown by the BTC in those years amounted to an almost criminal irresponsibility:

> **The original BTC executive member for engineering went right ahead and designed steam engines, and had the authority to build them. They built dozens and dozens and dozens of small lightweight 2-6-2 tanks for branch line services in the 1950s, after I'd made the plea for more rail-buses...**

But the Commission was about to take a few decisive steps. In 1953 it decided to look into the economics of individual lines and services. The result of its enquiries made it clear that **something** had to be done to the branch lines, and it had to be done quickly. Among passenger services, express trains were returning a healthy surplus over movement costs of £33 million, while suburban services were generating a less satisfactory surplus of £7 million, but stopping and branch line trains were losing £14 million a year. On the basis of a survey conducted in October 1952, it appeared that almost **all** the branch lines were losing money.

Late in 1953 the Commission appointed a Modernisation Committee to investigate suitable areas for investment and, when the first draft of the Committee's report surfaced early in 1954, it included a recommendation for the cessation of at least half the stopping trains, involving closure of 30 per cent of the railway network. Clearly, if diesel multiple units were to save the branch lines, they would need to be introduced very rapidly.

Indecisive management, lack of communication, and a number of inexplicable delays, had created a deficit time-bomb, and a few arbitrary rail closures were doing nothing to ease the situation. No less than five years after formation of the Motive Power Committee, the railway workshops were continuing to churn out steam locomotives, and the stopping passenger services remained almost exclusively steam-hauled. The 1953 locomotive renewal programme had made allowance for more than 300 steam engines and only 68 diesels, all of which were destined for shunting duties. The following year, construction of another 330 steam locomotives was authorised, together with 125 diesel shunters, but the Western Region (presumably taking advantage of its new regional freedom) actually ordered 20 **steam** shunting locomotives.

There was mounting frustration among pro-rail MPs, and others, that branch lines were being closed that had never seen a modern diesel railcar — lines that might have proved economical with a little modern technology. But introduction of the new vehicles had been painfully slow, as witnessed by Rupert Spier MP in October 1953:

> I believe that if nationalised transport had really made an effort to convert some of these branch lines to light railways, and to employ... railcars, they could have effected considerable economies... All I have found out so far is that British Railways, after a great deal of effort, have instigated one diesel car service between Bangor and some place which is unpronounceable to me but which is spelled A M L W Y C H.

This was the very same ACV railcar spotted by the Birmingham Junior Chamber at Princes Risborough, and it was still the only post-war railcar on British Railways.

By June 1954, however, the first diesel multiple units went into service between Bradford and Leeds. And in October the same year, the Lightweight Trains Committee completed trials of the new vehicles in the Lake District, in the build-up to the far larger Cumbrian scheme:

Arrangement/No. of vehicles	Weight	Power	Fuel consumption
Power-car plus trailer (2-car)	$47^{1}/_{2}$ tons	300hp	4.7mpg
Two power-cars back to back (2-car)	54 tons	600hp	3.2mpg
Power-car, trailer and coach (3-car)	$83^{1}/_{2}$ tons	300hp	4.2mpg

The trials were generally satisfactory, for most combinations managed about 60mph, and both performance and fuel consumption were considered perfectly adequate. The only exception was the three-car combination, which (with just 300hp to draw on) had been reduced to a first gear crawl on the slightest gradient, and was considered too lethargic for general traffic.

While the diesel units plodded around the Cumberland hills, branch lines continued to close, and in October 1954 the attention of the Branchline Committee became focussed on North Wales. Faced with the complete destruction of rail services, Denbigh County Council held a joint meeting of all interested parties, including representatives of the Railway Development Association.

The Transport Commission had already closed the line from Ruthin to Corwen, and the remaining line from Ruthin, via Denbigh, to Rhyl was now under threat. One councillor asked how far the closure process would go:

> Now they are starting to drive the wedge home. Will it be the Denbigh-Mold line next and then the Mold to Chester line? Are we not to have any train service at all?

In this respect he was quite correct, for within a few years all these lines would be closed to passengers. Feelings were running high that night in Denbigh, and a Churchillian fighting spirit began to pervade the council chamber:

> Marshal your forces in the fight against a dictatorship of an impersonal kind which is becoming too rampant in this country... Let us realise that the battle will not be an easy one, for it is impossible to apportion blame when we condemn a national undertaking. There is not a soul to be damned nor a body to be kicked.

It was a good point. The citizens of Denbigh had found Hitler an unsavoury opponent, but nothing by comparison to the forces of the Transport Commission, something not lost on the County Council Clerk, W E Bufton:

> It is exactly the policy that Hitler adopted. After each nibble he said that no more territorial claims would be made. I wrote to the traffic superintendent after the proposals had been received and asked him whether he could give an undertaking that in the next ten to 15 years the Chester-Mold-Denbigh line would not be closed. He could not give that undertaking!

The mood of the meeting was further inflamed when it was revealed that the local Traffic Superintendent, a Mr Fisher, had made the following extraordinary remark in regard to the future of the line:

> The reason why railway fares could not be brought down was that it would deflect railway passengers from the roads!

Momentarily off his guard, the hapless official had revealed the true situation. There was the usual bandying about of figures, with the usual claims and counter-claims as to the true worth of the line, but it all came to nothing. The BTC was closing the line to passenger trains — not because it made large losses (for goods traffic was to continue in any case) — but because it intended to transfer traffic to its own road buses. The wishes of the local people, the anger

77

of their councillors, and the RDA's glowing description of railbuses, did nothing to alter the situation. The line, like many others, was doomed before the inquiry had even commenced.

* * *

After the usual prolonged gestation period, the final months of 1954 saw completion of the Modernisation Committee's report. Generally optimistic, the report recommended a programme of wide scale capital investment, but ended on a cautious note:

> **Railways are a national necessity. The need to modernise them is urgent and immediate. With the implementation of this plan, a long period of stability, good leadership and goodwill within the industry, British Railways can be made financially self-supporting. During the years of fructification of the plan, however, it will be extremely difficult, if not impossible, to meet the additional interest burden.**

In other words, unless some major capital restructuring was on the cards, the modernisation plan was almost bound to drive the industry into debt. Such gloomy forecasts were ignored at the BTC and, in January 1955, the substance of the report was published, under the title *British Railways Plan for Modernisation and Re-equipment* — a 15-year investment programme aimed at restoring the network to health. Publication of the plan provided little comfort for the County Councillors of Denbigh, however, for, according to the report, there was to be "a marked reduction in the stopping and branch line services which are little used by the public and which... should be largely handed over to road transport".

Neither was there to be a huge investment bonanza for the trunk lines, for half of the £1,240 million cost of modernisation would be swallowed up covering arrears of maintenance. The greater proportion of the remainder would be spent on pensioning off the recently introduced steam engines and replacing them with diesel and electric locomotives. After falling far behind the rest of the industrialised world in such matters, the BTC had made the dramatic decision to scrap thousands of steam engines and introduce new technology. Steam would eventually disappear entirely, although it was to be a slow process, for the report estimated that of 12,800 locomotives available for service in 1970, more than half would be steam.

All freight wagons were to be equipped with continuous brakes, and a plethora of antiquated marshalling yards would be swept away and replaced by a handful of modern facilities. Electrification on the Southern Region was to continue where it had left off before the war, making electric traction universal east of Portsmouth and Reading. Similarly, the East Coast Main Line, from King's Cross to Doncaster, Leeds and York would be electrified, as would the

West Coast line from Euston to Manchester and Liverpool. The Liverpool Street suburban scheme would be extended to Ipswich, Felixstowe, Harwich and Clacton.

The electrification plans were long overdue, and freight was crying out for investment. The inefficiency of operating loose-coupled wagons had become all too apparent by the 1950s, for research suggested that freight locomotives were spending half their working lives shunting. It was estimated that the eradication of loose-coupled wagons, and investment in new vehicles equipped with automatic brakes, would reduce the need for locomotives by about 2,000.

One of the first results of the plan was a rush to diesel traction by the regions. Each produced its own designs, some of which proved successful, while others failed miserably. But after such a late and over-enthusiastic start it was not surprising that the scheme ran into problems.

The extraordinary speed of the dieselisation programme proved to be a major economic blunder, for expensive diesels were being put into service before prototypes had even completed proper trials. The result was costly — not just in terms of hard cash, but in public confidence too, for the early diesels were chronically unreliable.

By the time the modernisation plan had been approved, the BTC deficit had reached a record £70 million. The railways achieved a £16.4 million working profit in 1955, but after paying central charges to the Commission, the profit had become a £21.6 million loss. Freight traffic was in a steady decline and passenger traffic, although apparently holding its own, was really losing out in a fast-growing transport market. To make matters worse, the rather vague financial assumptions of the modernisation plan were out of date before they had even been approved. During 1954-55, prices had risen by ten per cent, leaving the modernisation costings way behind, and threatening to engulf the modest 6.9 per cent return predicted by the committee.

As the railway modernisation schemes were hastily implemented, road traffic continued to increase. The Government already had a pretty shrewd idea that the future lay with the roads and, in the corridors of power, plans began to take shape. In February 1955, two weeks after publication of the railway modernisation plan, the Ministry of Transport announced a four-year scheme to modernise the road system: £212 million would be spent on motorways — not enough according to the British Road Federation, which claimed the scheme fell short of meeting the nation's urgent needs.

In April, with an election on the horizon, an aging Winston Churchill handed the reigns of power to Anthony Eden, who went on to tighten his grip the following month by winning the election with an increased majority of 58. The Conservatives now had 344 seats in the House of Commons and a clear mandate.

Portland Station on the branch from Weymouth on the day it closed, in March 1953 — before the search had begun in earnest for "unremunerative railways". Owen Prosser.

Meanwhile, the Branchline Committee was sweeping the country in its search for unremunerative railways, closely followed by the Railway Development Association, which was fighting every proposal that did not appear to be in the public interest. It was vital for the Association to concentrate its resources on the examples that appeared reasonably viable for, as the Association was all too well aware, a forthright condemnation of every closure proposal would have got it nowhere. John Betjeman (later Sir John and Poet Laureate), who had become Vice-president of the RDA by this time, reluctantly concluded that a selective policy was the only option:

> **I love the branch lines because they are little quiet worlds of peace and seclusion. But in order to try and preserve them, we have got to be what is called practical!**

One of the great milestones in the story of the railway closures came with the South Western TUCC inquiry into the Princetown branch in Devon. It was, by all accounts, an interesting branch line: 10$\frac{1}{2}$ miles long, winding steadily uphill from Yelverton on the edge of Dartmoor, to Princetown, a small community adjacent to Dartmoor Prison, high on the moors. Difficult and expensive to operate, with little indigenous traffic, the Princetown branch seemed an ideal candidate for closure, but there were special circumstances to confuse the issue. There was traffic to and from the prison, the atrocious Dartmoor weather (snow frequently closing the local roads for weeks at a time) and, finally, the spectre of tourism.

The Commission had done nothing to attract tourists to the line, but there was every indication that the Princetown branch, winding through some of the most rugged and beautiful scenery in Britain, would have proved an outstanding attraction. There were practical environmental reasons for retaining the branch too, for the roads of Dartmoor were quite unsuitable for heavy tourist traffic.

The Branchline Committee calculated a loss of £11,000, much of which, as it transpired at the inquiry, was being wasted on over-manning. The little branch supported no fewer than 19 staff, including four signalmen and seven permanent way men. As usual the objectors had no access to vital statistics, but they could count among their number some formidable names. Besides, Major G B Harvey, the Governor of the Prison, there appeared among the protesters a retired Lord Justice of Appeal, Sir Henry Slesser, one-time Solicitor General in Ramsay MacDonald's Labour Government of 1924, and a Dartmoor resident. According to Owen Prosser, of the Railway Development Association, he had retired there, "possibly with a sentimental interest to be breathing the same air as some of his old clients". Whatever the reason, he had also developed a more than sentimental interest in preserving his local branch line.

The South West TUCC, under the chairmanship of a ship-owner, Colonel Mark Whitwill, initially refused to allow the press access to the inquiry, but the story aroused so much interest that the national press followed every word of the debate. The TUCC, perhaps unnerved by the calibre of the opposition, was clearly split over whether to allow the closure or not. So heated did the debate become, that one member, in a moment of rare pique for such an appointee, announced to a railway official: "If you pursue your policy of self-extermination to its logical conclusion, you will be out of a job as soon as you have closed all the lines that don't pay." Wisely, the Committee decided that more time might be needed before it could arrive at a suitable verdict, and the unsavoury moment was put off for two months. When the decision was eventually passed down in September, it decided in favour of the protesters. The line should stay open, partly due to the "special circumstance" of the prison.

Much to the chagrin of those who had fought so long to save the line, the Central Transport Consultative Committee once again summarily dismissed the local verdict and advocated closure. It was an astounding decision, echoing a verdict some months previously, when protesters at the Horncastle branch line inquiry had found to their surprise that the East Midlands TUCC agreed with them, only to hear subsequently that the central body had over-ruled the area committee.

The Princetown closure procedure ran its fateful course. The last train departed in March 1956, and all appeared to be lost. But the BTC had reckoned without the tenacity of Sir Henry Slesser. The former Solicitor General was appalled at the CTCC decision and wrote in forthright terms to the late Viscount Garnock, President of the RDA:

> My principal grievance is that I was not offered an opportunity to put our case before the Central Transport Consultative Committee; I should have thought that at any rate if they were inclined to reverse [the decision of] the local body, who knew the conditions as they did not, they would at least have had the courtesy to offer us a chance of advocacy. As an old member of the Court of Appeal, I am rather horrified by this denial of natural justice, and had I been able to come would have spoken on this very serious matter.

The RDA hoped to use yet another eloquent condemnation of the Consultative Committee system as a lever to force change on the authorities, but it was not to be. It is rather more likely that opposition to railway closures from witnesses of the calibre of Sir Henry Slesser was instrumental in the Government's subsequent decision further to reduce the power of the TUCCs by means of the 1962 Transport Act.

Even so, it was not quite the end of the story, for the Dartmoor weather was to wreak wicked revenge on the authorities. In the winter of 1963, Princetown was completely cut off for three days, receiving food drops by helicopter. By 1971, road congestion was so appalling that the Dartmoor National Park Committee was considering banning cars from parts of the moor altogether. The next year two coaches met on a narrow lane and enforced a temporary ban of their own — traffic ground to a halt for three hours. It was estimated at the time that Dartmoor would have to deal with no fewer than 95,000 visitors per day by 1981, many of whom would gladly have used the Princetown branch had it survived.

The Branchline Committee had achieved 130 outright closures since 1947, although more than 200 branch lines, with a route mileage of 1,546, had been wholly or partially closed. The BTC tried hard to reassure its staff that closures were in everyone's best interests or, in the words of the Western Region railway staff magazine:

> The closing of branch lines and stations *does not mean* that the railways are dying on their feet. It means that they are moving with the times... and "streamlining" their services... remember that pruning is done to promote vigorous growth!

There was still a ring of truth to this statement in 1954, for the trunk routes and the secondary lines were still intact. Quite a few of the branches that had closed would have failed to survive even had the BTC introduced diesel operation and provided the TUCCs with accurate figures. And as the magazine was swift to point out, branch line closures were nothing new. Many infamous

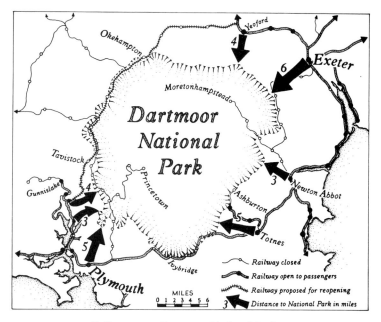

Rail access to Dartmoor National Park

There were once nearly 30 railway stations in, or within a mile or two of, Dartmoor National Park. Now there are none. Within three miles of the park there is only Buckfastleigh on the privately owned Dart Valley line — which currently has no connections with British Rail services at Totnes.

Access could be greatly improved with the reopening of Ivybridge station, between Totnes and Plymouth and — ideally — the relaying of the derelict stretch between Meldon quarry, near Okehampton, and Bere Alston, on the Gunnislake branch.

examples had failed to survive even until the Second World War. Among the worst offenders was the Fort Augustus branch in Scotland that had cost £322,000 to build in 1903 yet produced an income of just £907 in the normally euphoric first six months of operation. The line had been extravagently engineered with an optimistic view to its one day providing an onward Great Glen route to Inverness. This never materialised and, in 1933, the final year before the branch was laid mercifully to rest, it carried only 1,911 passengers who paid a total of just £179 for their tickets.

In all, the big four railway companies had disposed of some 240 miles of branch line between 1923 and 1947, with about 1,000 miles closing to passengers, but open for other purposes. However, a far higher mileage had closed in the first six years of nationalisation than in the previous 24 years of private ownership. The argument of the protesters was that lines were being closed without a thorough investigation of alternative operating methods, and that closure techniques were being "run in" on the minor branches in preparation for a much larger round of closures.

Not surprisingly, considering the wasteful operating methods employed, many of the early railway closures really did produce savings. According to the Central Transport Consultative Committee (hardly, of course, an unbiased source), the total annual saving from the branch line closure programme had topped almost £1.5 million, and most closures were realising even greater savings than had been predicted. The greatest damage had been confined to the very fringes of the network, where the continued existence of a handful of unremunerative lines investigated by the Branchline Committee would have been hard to justify by any criteria.

There were plenty of contenders for the title of "least remunerative branch line". Perhaps typical was the railway between Monmouth and Pontypool Road which, according to the Branchline Committee, earned just over £1,000 a year from passenger traffic prior to closure. Even less lucrative was the Headcorn to Tenterden section of the Kent & East Sussex, the last vestige of Colonel Stephens' light railway empire, which had been put up for closure after earning just £405 in passenger income.

Many communities had prospered with the arrival of the railways, but some had rather conspicuously failed to do so. A good example was the remote village of Llangynog in the Welsh borders, that had grown in less than meteoric fashion, reaching a population of 292 potential travellers by the early 1950s. Considering the sparsity of the population, the annual income of £252 from the Llangynog branch line was quite respectable, but it was not enough to sway the Branchline Committee, which recommended closure forthwith. Many other remote branch lines had survived as long, but the figures from Llangynog were probably a record of sorts.

In order to justify the closure programme, the Central Transport Consultative Committee report for 1954 contained an element of defeatism with regard to road competition:

> Both we and the area committees are satisfied that the Commission are reluctant to withdraw their transport services unless there is no reasonable prospect of maintaining them on a more or less economic basis. Later in this report we refer to our suggestions for making rail services more attractive, though we realise that these could not always be successfully applied, owing to the substantial advantages provided by the modern road facilities.

Despite such official pessimism, the diesel multiple unit experiments had proved an overwhelming success with the public. In the first three and a half months of the Yorkshire experiment, takings were up by £10,500, yet the CTCC prognosis remained a gloomy one: "Despite this substantial improvement in financial results, the point has not yet been reached at which the receipts cover the full cost of providing the service."

The vehicles might not have been covering full costs, but they were certainly running close. The first results from the West Cumberland experiment told a similar story, for the lines were now on the verge of profitability. The annual operating expenses of the former steam services had been no less than £150,000, against earnings of £45,000; the new diesels were costing £80,000 and producing revenue of £70,000. In other words, an operating deficit of £105,000 had been slashed to £10,000.

A comprehensive series of experiments on the Western Region in June 1955 proved the worth of diesel multiple units once and for all, when a four-car set operated a stopping train over the 193 miles between Paddington and Newton Abbot for an all-in fuel cost of just £2 2s. Fuel consumption was better than five miles per gallon.

Further proof of the efficiency of the new units came with the internal publication, by the Eastern Region, of a traffic census for March and September 1955. The new traffic costing service, introduced by the Chairman of the Eastern Regional Board, Sir Reginald Wilson, was exactly the sort of innovation that the railways needed. Unfortunately, other regions were slow to adopt the technique, and it was not until the arrival of Dr Beeching some years later, that accurate traffic surveys were produced on a national basis.

The census, covering 40 per cent of Eastern Region stopping trains, was conducted among the branches and secondary routes of rural Lincolnshire and East Anglia, where the BTC had opposed diesel experiments and, consequently, there were few of the new units in evidence.

Generally, the situation was pretty bleak for, apart from the services to the coastal resorts of Hunstanton, Mablethorpe and Skegness (which were very well patronised), the picture had been one of mounting losses. Overall annual receipts for the services were £880,000 against movement costs of more than £2 million. Some steam trains were costing five to nine times as much as they were earning, carrying an average of just 37 passengers per train — a 20 per cent load factor. Half the trains were earning less than 4s (20p) per mile, and quite a few were carrying fewer than ten passengers at a time.

In contrast, the modern diesel-operated services, apparently introduced on a few routes at random, had earned a total of £2,100, against movement costs of £1,600. Only one service was failing to cover costs, and quite a few were very profitable indeed. The report summed up by tentatively suggesting that, had all services been diesel operated:

...the direct cost of operations would have been covered by revenue, but there would have been no significant contribution to the costs of terminals, or of track, signalling and general administration.

It was a start. The BTC was beginning to realise that the railways needed to make a quantum leap of modernisation in the 1950s. This was the effect of the motor age. Proof came with the spectacular passenger usage figures of the first diesel experiments — the public was more than willing to return to the railways as long as the service was as good (or better) than road transport. Where it was not, people deserted the railways in droves.

In general terms, the British railway system of the 1950s was a drab and demoralised version of the same system in the 1930s. The motor car, on the other hand, had improved immeasurably in 20 years, and it was about to change out of all recognition with the release of compact, economical and efficient vehicles, such as the Austin Mini and 1100. In a consumer society, success or failure of a particular product might be said to depend on such qualities as value, comfort and reliability. The monolithic BTC organisation had failed to grasp that the same was true for transport undertakings.

As more than one commentator was astute enough to observe, the railways had become victims of their own heritage. If the flanged steel wheel had been invented in the mid-20th century, the railways might have been greeted as the saviours of the age — as it was, the Victorian infrastructure was regarded as anachronistic and outmoded.

Post-war fuel and raw material rationing had provided a breathing space by holding road transport in check but, after 1955, railway operating costs overtook income for the first time, and the system entered a spiral of decline. Hasty implementation of the modernisation plan did nothing to ease the situation; in fact, the waste associated with the new regime served merely to accelerate the impending financial collapse. In cost/benefit terms to the nation as a whole, the closure plans were terribly wasteful. Costly assets were liquidated for little more than scrap value, and the railway formation itself — the cuttings, tunnels and viaducts, built at such cost a century before — was being left to return to nature. It certainly didn't **look** like progress.

4.
You've never had it so good
1955-1959

Last Saturday night, for example, I was on Gloucester Station, and I asked the
guard of a train, what was the object standing at the platform and where was
it going. He told me: "That train has been running to Cinderford since 1907."

Whether he meant the timing of the train or the actual engine and coach set I
do not know, but it might well have been the latter since it appeared to be
contemporaneous with George Hudson if not George Stephenson... It appeared
to be carrying something less than an ordinary busload.

A J Champion, MP for Derbyshire South East, House of Commons, April 1956

*IN 1955 the Society of Motor Manufacturers & Traders set up a Roads
Campaign Council to co-ordinate the various road lobby pressure groups and
fight a "roads crusade" for motorway construction. With no effective opposition
from the Transport Commission and the pro-rail groups, the road faction won
almost all of its demands, and continued to tighten its stranglehold on the
Government and the Ministry of Transport. By 1957 the Roads Campaign
Council had spawned an all-party Roads Study Group within Parliament,
further strengthening the road lobby's tangled patronage and funding relationship with the Government, and weakening the waning influence of the BTC.*

*By the end of 1955 the railways were in a worrying financial plight.
Modernisation had caused considerable turmoil, but much of the problem lay
in the remote corners of the system — the rural branches and secondary lines
that were still largely steam operated and grossly overstaffed. Nationwide, the
passenger figures remained more or less static, but money was being lost
somewhere, and as far as the BTC was concerned, the scapegoat had to be the
rural branch lines.*

*It was, however, a confusing period for the Transport Commission. Con-
certed parliamentary action on the part of the railway pressure groups,
combined with favourable results from the diesel multiple unit experiments,
caused management resolve to waver. Suddenly the mood changed, and the
closure programme was eased. At the 11th hour, the Commission decided to save
the branch lines by applying a large and expensive dose of new technology in
the form of diesel multiple units for the major services and economical diesel
railbuses for the thoroughly unremunerative lines.*

Meanwhile, the financial state of the Commission continued to deteriorate, until a mild economic recession in the late 1950s precipitated a total collapse. To both the Ministry of Transport and the road lobby, which had felt considerable anxiety over the prospect of successful railway modernisation, this turn of events could hardly have been more satisfactory.

* * *

Mounting disquiet in the rural shires as to the very future of rail transport drew the attention of MPs in 1955 and prompted the Rural Transport Improvement Bill, introduced by Archer Baldwin, MP for Leominster, in consultation with Robert Aickman of the Railway Development Association. The RDA had by now grown from a small body of enthusiasts into an influential pressure group and the introduction of the Bill to Parliament was the culmination of a sustained and successful campaign by the Association. Superficially, the Bill was drafted to improve rural transport, but the real intention was to save railway branch lines by a combination of measures.

The main bone of contention was the unsatisfactory performance of the various Transport Users' Consultative Committees. The area TUCCs, overseen by a central body, had been created as part of the nationalisation process in 1948, to liaise between the Transport Commission and transport users; one of their major roles was to judge the merits of closure proposals put forward by the Commission. There was, however, mounting concern that the committees were not always acting in the best interests of the public. It appeared that of 118 closure proposals submitted between 1948 and 1955, the committees had supported the BTC proposals in all but two. There was now a widespread and quite justified belief that the Central Transport Consultative Committee, funded and staffed by the Commission, was not in the slightest degree independent.

The matter was repeatedly raised in Parliament to little effect and, as closure followed closure, and the local consultative committees continued to agree to the BTC proposals, MPs became increasingly frustrated:

> **I am beginning to wonder whether, in the light of experience, the role of these TUCCs should not be changed from one of acting as an advisory body to the Minister and the Commission, to one of acting as watchdog on behalf of the users… there seems to be a widespread feeling that these area committees are somewhat ineffectual and very remote.**

Julian Snow, MP for Lichfield and Tamworth, December 1957

But, according to the Government, the consultative procedure was perfectly adequate. Some years later, reeling from a barrage of criticism, the Parliamentary Secretary to the Minister of Transport gave a reply:

> **I want to make it clear that these committees are not "stooges" of the BTC, as some people are inclined sometimes to think or say… all I can say here is that**

the form in which the data are given to the committees is now generally agreed by the area committees and the Central Transport Consultative Committee and by the Commission itself.

Outside the Commission and the Government front benches, however, it was generally agreed that the Central Transport Consultative Committee was a most unsatisfactory body. Few observers felt that the area committees were so biased, but they were composed of lay people with little knowledge of railway operations, and they were too easily intimidated by the central body. The problem for the area committees was in reconciling local interests with those of the country at large — particularly after the railways began to lose money in 1955. Without any real understanding of the make-up of the frightening losses thrust in front of them at inquiries, they were unable to suggest economies, with the result that they usually advocated closure in the national interest.

The Rural Transport Improvement Bill set out to rectify the situation:

CLAUSE 1 would require the BTC to announce closure proposals in advance through advertisements in the local press and to furnish the relevant local authorities and the TUCC with all the statistics.

CLAUSE 2 would require the BTC to give reasons for closure proposals, should any interested party wish to know. This would expose the dubious practice of forcibly transferring traffic away from a particular line.

CLAUSE 3 was a retrospective version of Clause 2 that would have widespread implications if it become law, for it aimed to force the Commission to explain the reasoning behind every closure that had taken place in the previous five years.

CLAUSE 4 specified that if there were objections to a closure proposal, the whole matter should be handed to the Transport Tribunal which would be empowered to hold a local inquiry.

CLAUSE 5 dealt with updating the Light Railway Act of 1896.

CLAUSE 6 sought to exclude the TUCCs from the entire closure procedure.

The Transport Tribunal had been created under the 1947 Transport Act and was mainly concerned with rates and charges. But it was a neutral body and would be well suited to adopt the role of adjudicator at railway closure inquiries.

The most interesting section of the Bill was to be found deep in Clause 4, subsection 2: should the Transport Tribunal reach the conclusion that a railway was hopelessly uneconomic, it would give directions to the BTC to offer the line to another body for operation as a Light Railway; and the BTC would be empowered to sell the line to the highest bidder. This might be a locally constituted group of individuals, a local authority, or even a workers' co-operative.

The general aim of Archer Baldwin and the Railway Development Association was to force the BTC to downgrade the branch lines, both in terms of manpower and operating expenses, until they could pay their way. If a line was subsequently put up for closure, the Commission would be forced to give evidence in public detailing the economy measures that had been attempted. And the entire consultation procedure would be held before the Transport Tribunal, a truly independent body, rather than the TUCCs.

The Bill put forward some imaginative solutions to the rural transport problem, and to the delight of all concerned, it set out on the long and difficult road towards the statute book in 1955. The prospective legislation had arrived not a moment too soon, for some of the branch lines were carrying as many staff, wagons, coaches and locomotives as they had in Victorian times. But by the 1950s, manpower was accounting for no less than 62 per cent of total railway expenditure.

It was not so much that traffic had declined particularly in the intervening century (although road transport had made a great impact), as that economic circumstances had changed, leaving traditional labour-intensive railway operations quite unviable. A partial answer would, of course, be the introduction of diesel railbuses or multiple units but the most lightly loaded branch lines needed a more radical solution. The sensible answer was to run them by cheaper methods, perhaps under the provisions of a Light Railway Order.

There had always been a certain amount of confusion as to what actually constituted a light railway or tramway. Under the provisions of the original Act of 1868, and further legislation of 1896, a "light" railway could forego certain signalling, communications and maintenance requirements in exchange for limitations as to the speed and operating methods employed. Certain railway companies had experimented with Light Railway operation prior to nationalisation, but such practices had never achieved widespread popularity in Britain.

It was generally the most insignificant lines with little indigenous traffic that had operated under a Light Railway Order in the past, and most of them had closed. But the pro-rail movement was now advocating that the techniques be applied to more important lines, on the principle that a light railway was immeasurably better than no railway at all.

Substantial savings could be realised by simplifying signalling and communications, destaffing stations, and a few other strategic economies. And smaller, lighter versions of the Commission's new diesel railcars (smaller even than the ACV experimental vehicle) would reduce costs further still. Such a vehicle would be economic in terms of both fuel and manpower and very gentle on the track, which would lead to savings in maintenance. The standard British steam locomotive weighed about 70 tons; the coaches 25 to 30 tons each — a total of perhaps 150 tons for a three-coach stopping train. It was a lot of hardware to transport ten to 15 passengers, as was all too often the case.

By contrast, the three-unit ACV railcar weighed in at just 42 tons overall, and there was plenty of experience both at home and abroad to show that single units weighing as little as 15 tons could operate even more economically. Unfortunately, there had been little operating experience with railbuses in Britain. The branch lines were all in the hands of the Transport Commission, and they were mostly over-engineered and overstaffed to such an extent as to be quite unviable. By Edwardian standards the railways were superb, but by the cost-accounting techniques of the mid 20th century, they were uneconomic.

There may not have been much British experience in railbus operation, but British manufacturers had actually been producing such diesel vehicles for years, the majority of them for export. The Hertfordshire firm of Wickham built its first railbus in 1937. By the end of the war, the British company was exporting machines to Jamaica, Peru, Kenya and Uganda, and had built up a considerable expertise.

Most Wickham railcars were rated at no more than 200hp, and weighed as little as 13 tons, yet as early as 1945 they were proving more than a match for the torturous gradients and switchback curves of the Third World. These diminutive vehicles were considerably lighter than the BTC's railcar, yet they could carry about 50 seated passengers with unsurpassed economy.

In theoretical terms, assuming all other factors to be equal, a railbus was bound to have an advantage over its road equivalent by way of reduced rolling resistance. A steel tyre running on a steel rail was (and remains) fundamentally more efficient than a rubber tyre running on a Tarmacadam surface. And reduced friction meant a reduction in maintenance requirements, and improved fuel consumption. There was even evidence of a kind to substantiate the theory, for in the 1920s the West Sussex and other light railways had joined two former road buses back-to-back to create a rudimentary multiple unit, and found they ran quite successfully with only one of the two bus engines in operation!

New technology could assist in other ways too. British practice favoured staffed level-crossings. Even the lowliest of road crossings were equipped with a signal-box and staff at disproportionate expense. But on the minor branch lines the crossing-keepers might only be required to open their gates on half a dozen occasions during the working day. Once again, Continental European railway companies had made economies years in advance of their British counterparts by installing fully automatic crossings. But the BTC was not to attempt such an innovation until February 1961 when the first British example was installed at Uttoxeter. Progress had been remarkably slow, for the first lifting barriers had been tested at York as early as 1953, and legislation to allow fully automatic crossings had been available since 1957.

On December 9, 1955, the Rural Transport Improvement Bill attained its crucial Second Reading, and Archer Baldwin set to work to persuade his colleagues as to the desirability of economies in the field of railway operation.

The County Donegal Railways were cited: the system had almost closed, but after the introduction of modern diesel railbuses the passenger service looked relatively secure. The USA provided another example: a group of citizens had purchased an $18^1/_2$-mile branch line and operated it themselves — even reaping a four per cent return on their investment. The crux of Mr Baldwin's argument was that many uneconomic rural branch lines could be operated profitably by light railway methods, with simplified signalling, unstaffed stations and small diesel railbuses. He claimed that a ten-mile branch line could be maintained for around £60 per mile per year if operated by light railway methods, and a single diesel railbus would cost about £9,000, or less than £6,000 if mass-produced.

There was general agreement with the provisions of the Bill, especially from

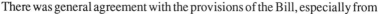

RAILBUS MISCELLANY: *Five different types of railbus would be ordered by British Railways in the late 1950s (see p101). They included, **right**, the Wickham model, built at Ware and featuring a Meadows six-cylinder 105hp engine and such modern fittings as pneumatic doors. The railbus pictured is bound for Craigendoran on the West Highland line. British Railways picture. **Above** — A Park Royal railbus arrives at Bedford from Northampton in 1958, four years before the former Midland line was closed. (Owen Prosser). **Facing page** — A manufacturer's picture of the Bristol Commercial Vehicles railbus, featuring a body built by Eastern Coachworks, Lowestoft.*

MPs with rural seats who knew only too well the damage that railway closures were causing — both to their constituencies and, consequently, to their own likely majorities. Typical of the support was that from J E B Hill, MP for Norfolk South:

If the Bill can produce one such diesel railcar service and if one branch line can find a new life on a lesser scale, then in my opinion the Bill will have amply justified its existence.

Inevitably the subject of the infamous Isle of Wight inquiry was raised. There were mutterings that the BTC, with a monopoly of road, rail and ferry undertakings on the island, intended to push traffic onto the roads until the remaining railways proved uneconomic and could be withdrawn.

Eventually, Hugh Molson, Parliamentary Secretary to the Minister of Transport, wound up the debate in remarkable terms: he described the branch lines as worthless speculative ventures that would never pay their way, and countered every argument put forward by the Bill's supporters. The ACV experimental railcar (operational now since 1953) was, he claimed, a failure. Apparently the vehicle had cost almost as much as a diesel multiple unit at £22,000, and had suffered reliability problems. But it is worth noting that the small run of railbuses produced two years later cost only £12,500 each. Mr Molson went on to claim that the BTC was actually underestimating the losses on rural branch lines by excluding the cost of track maintenance. His version of events was, quite simply, untrue.

Finally, when pressed on his Ministry's failure to initiate the promised road improvements on the Isle of Wight, the Minister responded with the extraordinary (but accurate) claim that "the roads in the Isle of Wight are of only very limited value to through traffic".

The Rural Transport Improvement Bill failed to attract enough support. From a near empty House of Commons, 31 members voted for the proposals and 27 against, but according to the rules of the House, the majority was too small for the Bill to survive. In the words of Owen Prosser, of the RDA:

The Bill failed, not through Labour opposition, although there was Labour opposition. In fact the big names of the day were there, including the immediate ex-Prime Minister, Clement Attlee, and that stormy petrel from the Welsh valleys, Aneurin Bevan. The Bill failed its second reading... through Tory apathy, because Mr Baldwin did not have sufficient Tories to support him in the Division Lobby.

Yet, with hindsight, it seems highly improbable today that apathy alone could have been to blame. Why did such high ranking politicians put their weight behind defeating a minor Parliamentary Bill? There was a Tory Government in power at the time, and a rural transport Bill which ran contrary to Government policy — as well as seeking to improve the amenities for those in remote areas — might have been expected to appeal to Labour politicians.

But Labour could hardly advocate the reopening of railways in private hands when it had gone to a great deal of trouble to nationalise the industry. Under the rules of integration, traffic was to have been directed to the transport undertaking that was best suited to carry it. And following the rules (if not the spirit) of capitalism, the socialists had allowed uneconomic nationalised railways to close, cheerfully transferring traffic to nationalised bus companies. To be fair, Labour was also faced with intransigent union problems where privately owned railways were concerned. Even had the party wished to approve a locally financed and locally managed railway, it would have faced insufferable union objections. Volunteer staff would be beyond the jurisdiction of the NUR, and they would be taking bread from the mouths of the bus drivers, some of whom were themselves NUR members.

For the Conservatives, the forces of capital naturally carried more weight. In a free market, the travelling public and the travelling freight consignment were free to choose their own transport, and if a railway failed to pay, it would have to make way for something else. Individual Conservative MPs were bound by loyalty to the Government and (as many were beginning to suspect) it was a Government whose victory was financed substantially from the pockets of companies with a vested interest in road transport.

Another possible explanation also had sinister overtones. It was simply that the Bill came dangerously close to transferring power from central government to the regions. And Westminster politicians from both the Right and Left found such an idea unpalatable. Both parties were opposed to moves that might reduce central government power, and that is what the apparently innocuous Rural Transport Improvement Bill sought to do.

Labour had made no secret of its desire for a planned centralised economy, but the Conservatives were less honest. They talked of freedom, but maintained a tighter financial and legislative hold on the railways than even Labour had done.

* * *

During 1956, the BTC's financial situation continued to deteriorate. In February 1956 the Commission applied for a ten per cent increase in freight charges, together with increases in passenger fares to cover rising costs. In the event, the Minister of Transport granted a five per cent increase for freight, but refused to allow any increase in passenger fares for six months. The hapless Transport Commission had become an instrument of Government economic policy.

Against a background of steadily rising prices, the result was catastrophic. Even the Ministry of Transport was later to accept that the loss to the railways was about £8.4 million; the BTC judged the figure to be nearer £17 million. Whatever the truth, the result was a crippling blow at a time when expenditure was running at high levels and profits were rapidly receding, for any loss of income meant the need to borrow, leading to interest charges being incurred and, in turn, further losses. It was a vicious circle.

However dubious the financial situation, the BTC was nonetheless beginning to reap the rewards of modernisation and, paradoxically, the greatest success story was on the branch lines, where the first handful of diesel multiple unit experiments had proved more popular with the public than anyone had dared to imagine. First indications were that the experiments had brought large increases in traffic: Birmingham to Lichfield had seen an increase of 210 per cent; Leeds to Bradford and Harrogate, 144 per cent; even the little Silloth branch in Cumbria had achieved a 66 per cent rise. The new vehicles were popular with the public, and they were very cheap to run: the BTC now had firm evidence that a multiple unit could operate for around 3s 4d (16.7p) per mile against 10/- (50p) for steam-hauled trains.

Gradually, the Commission began to move in favour of diesel operation. Orders were placed for 2,400 multiple units, to enter service by the end of 1958, with a prediction of 4,600 being required by 1961. Such was the demand from the regions, however, that by early 1957 the order had been increased to 2,741, then to more than 3,000, with a prediction of no fewer than 5,144 cars in service within 18 months. And the BTC was, at last, beginning to take the idea of a small diesel railbus seriously, announcing that a new unit would undergo trials during 1957. Intriguingly, there was even talk of a battery-electric vehicle to take advantage of cheap hydro-electric power. It would be tested on the Ballater branch line in eastern Scotland.

The overwhelming disadvantage of battery-powered transport has always been the prohibitive weight penalty of the traction batteries and, according to the Minister of Transport — who was very dismissive of multiple units, railcars, and battery-powered experimental vehicles in particular — the 25-ton railbus would require no less than ten tons of batteries.

As the decade progressed it became clear that the BTC, although somewhat slow off the mark, was becoming increasingly enthusiastic about the prospects for some of the rural branch lines. While there remained little doubt that a proportion, perhaps a substantial number, would close (early in 1956 the Transport Commission had actually warned the CTCC that large-scale closures were in the pipeline), the picture was looking decidedly rosier. As the favourable results of the diesel experiments began to percolate through the industry, the Commission's resolve to see lines closed began to weaken.

It was a confusing period. Some officials spoke in favour of railbuses, and even light rail methods, while others held the view that the rural branch lines should be closed *en masse*. Sir Reginald Wilson, Chairman of the Eastern Area Board, had long spoken in favour of closure, recommending that as many as 4,000-5,000 small stations should be eradicated. Others were not so sure — perhaps a little of the modernisation windfall should be invested to safeguard the branch lines? Eventually, even Sir Reginald seemed undecided. The Government, on the other hand, made its views perfectly plain and did everything in its power to resist cost-saving schemes for the rural lines. As a result, the policy objectives of the BTC began to slide further and further away from those of the Conservative administration.

Officials at the Ministry of Transport had laid their hands on confidential BTC documents relating to branch line economics which appeared to provide an overwhelming case for wholesale closure. The result was a flurry of memos on the timing and scale of an accelerated closure programme:

If we want [the TUCCs] to perform this task more quickly and more ruthlessly, then I think we and the Commission must give them more positive help. There seems to me to be a necessity for some really startling and comprehensive statement of Commission policy which could... be timed to coincide [with] or follow the announcement of the 1955 deficit.

Alison Munro, Assistant Secretary at the Ministry of Transport, in an internal memo, February 1956

By April 1956, the Ministry had gone so far as to draw up a broad plan, although the details were to remain shrouded in secrecy, for obvious reasons:

It should be possible to impress on the public the size of the amputation contemplated without listing actual services. Secondly, any such list will lead to the organisation of opposition — possibly on a national scale — which might otherwise have remained dormant.

Alison Munro, April 1956

In a vain attempt to limit the potential damage, Sir Reginald Wilson (who was by now beginning to favour branch line retention) wrote in these terms to Hugh Molson, the Joint Parliamentary Secretary:

...quite often these services were ancillary to other services and should not be charged, even theoretically, with a full share of the costs... The charges were, therefore, too heavy; on the other hand, credits were probably too light because they failed to take into account the contributory value of the traffic which these ancillary services brought to the main services.

Unfortunately, the figures have, in fact, become known outside the narrow circle for which they were intended, but I am glad that they have not gone further than the Ministry. But if the confusion they have caused in your office is any indication of the upset which would ensue if the calculations reached a wider public, then I feel amply confirmed in my view that the sooner the figures

themselves are forgotten the better it will be...

Of course, the financial figures were not forgotten — incomplete and inaccurate though they may have been — and, with the benefit of hindsight, they would have been safer almost anywhere but on the files of the Ministry of Transport.

Meanwhile, the light rail parliamentary lobby had suffered a setback, but reached the conclusion the issue was not quite dead. April 1956 brought a fresh opportunity to air its views when Parliament once again debated rural transport. Archer Baldwin received another brief from the RDA, and brought up the subject of Irish railbuses:

> **I have had sent to me by the Railway Development Association particulars of a railbus which is operating on the Sligo Railway, in Ireland. It is operating on a steel-rubber wheel. In fact it is a bus which is being converted at the cost of £100... If they can do that in Ireland, I should hope that something similar might be done in this country.**

Mr Baldwin rose to speak at 4.52pm. What he could not have known was that the mood at the Ministry of Transport had hardened against rail transport, and that the Minister would be waiting in ambush. The Minister of Transport, Harold Watkinson, had made inquiries in Ireland that very morning in anticipation of such a speech.

Exactly who the Minister's representative conversed with, and exactly what was said, will sadly never be known. The telephone might have been answered by some lowly minion in the railway yard who knew little or nothing about the railbus. Then again, it is quite possible that the affair was a Ministerial bluff. Or perhaps (as the RDA later assumed) the Minister's representative actually rang the avidly anti-rail Ulster Transport Authority. But the result was to silence further Parliamentary debate on the matter. At 6.34pm the Minister rose and settled the affair once and for all:

> **I asked one of my officers to telephone to Ireland this morning to find out about its present state of health. I learned that it was very bad indeed, and that steam trains are having to replace it for many operations. So I am afraid that the attempt to put a bus on the railway... has not worked.**

Whatever the truth of the matter, the official from the Ministry of Transport had certainly not spoken to the General Manager of the railway concerned, who later confirmed to the RDA that the railbus had achieved a considerable mileage and was in a good state of health.

The Minister went on to claim that the BTC had disputed Mr Baldwin's figures for the operation of a hypothetical ten-mile branch line, stating that the true cost per mile would be nearer £300 than £60, and that the line would require a full-time maintenance gang of four. The Government weighed in with some alarming traffic figures for stopping train services — allegedly, of 80 million

The Sligo, Leitrim and Northern Counties Railway railbus which achieved Parliamentary notoriety, pictured here at Manorhamilton. Owen Prosser.

train-miles operated the previous year, only five million had been moderately loaded (carrying more than 125 passengers); 45 million had been poorly loaded, and 30 million very poorly loaded, carrying fewer than 20 passengers.

Meticulously briefed by Ministry officials, Mr Watkinson continued to spew forth statistics. Holland had closed 691 stations out of 1,000, and a third of British passenger trains were covering no more than a third of their costs. Of course, the latter figure could just as easily have been used by the pro-rail lobby to justify light railway techniques, but Archer Baldwin and his Parliamentary conspirators were by now thoroughly demoralised. Despite the overwhelming evidence of the Isle of Wight inquiry, and the sensible arguments of the light railway faction, Parliamentary discussion about railbuses and light railway operating methods was effectively at an end.

Another reason for the failure of the rail lobby was that Britain's railways appeared to be turning the corner. Modernisation was well under way, and traffic (if not spectacular) was certainly holding its own. In 1956 the railways carried more passengers than in any year since nationalisation and, by the end of the year, nearly 400 multiple units were in operation, drawing in new business the length and breadth of the system. Fares and charges, however, continued to lag far behind inflation. In the summer of 1956, the Chancellor, Harold Macmillan, instructed the nationalised industries to freeze their prices to fight a rising tide of inflation. The Trade Union Congress refused to take part, and wages continued to rise. The effect was further to weaken the financial position

99

of the railways, and shorten the fuse on the deficit time-bomb.

Overall losses for 1956 hit £57.5 million and, for the first time since 1921, the railways experienced a working deficit, sliding £16.5 million into the red. The BTC explained it all away as a side-effect of modernisation, and it was partially correct, for the hasty implementation of the various schemes had been shockingly wasteful. The much vaunted main line diesel programme produced orders for no fewer than 230 locomotives, of which only 43 were to be constructed in the railway's own workshops. No fewer than 14 designs were involved, from seven different manufacturers. Privately, the Commission had estimated that at least ten per cent of the new diesel locomotives were likely to prove expensive failures. In the event, even that gloomy prognosis proved rather optimistic.

It had been predicted that the diesels would produce substantial operating economies through their availability for traffic. With no fire to clean and no boiler to wash, it was assumed that diesels would be available for almost 24 hours a day, the official estimate being an availability factor of 85 per cent. But so unreliable were the new machines that many failed to exceed 60 per cent, and a few managed no more than 50 per cent availability, or rather less than the labour-intensive steam engines they were to replace. One particular rogue averaged no more than 8,000 miles between breakdowns. By contrast, the diesel multiple units appear to have been comparatively reliable, although operating economies were not what they might have been, for the regions had all produced their own designs, resulting in a total of no fewer than 53 different vehicles.

Electrification plans were continuing apace, too. In March 1956, amid a fanfare of publicity, the BTC Chairman, Sir Brian Robertson, announced (rather prematurely as it transpired) that Britain's railways were about to witness "the end of steam". The first new overhead electrification scheme would be from Euston to Liverpool and Manchester and it would be completed by 1959. The line was to become a test-bed for one of the most prestigious and exciting modernisation schemes in Europe and, whatever else happened, the BTC was determined to make a success of it.

Generally, the Commission was confident about the progress of its modernisation plans and optimistic about the future. All the same, costs were beginning to run somewhat above the predictions and, in October 1956, a re-appraisal brought the BTC to the conclusion that more external finance would be required, partly as a result of mounting deficits. After receiving particulars, the Government grudgingly agreed that the plans still made commercial sense and authorised legislation to advance money to cover deficits and defray the cost of modernisation.

The BTC was very well aware that the Government had control of the purse-strings, but it needed more time, more cash, and less interference to complete the modernisation programme. From the safety of its ninth Annual Report, it launched an ill-timed broadside at the Government, demanding amongst other things:

> ...reasonable freedom and a period of stability to press on with reconstruction, and that the whole fabric of public transport will no longer be subject to periodic seismic upheaval on political account.

The change of attitude by the BTC was largely a result of the changed political circumstances. It had entered the 1950s as a vast Commission with a near monopoly on inland transport but, by 1956, it was mostly concerned with railway interests. The sale of British Road Services alone had resulted in the BTC handing over almost half its fleet of lorries to the private sector, but the numbers paled into insignificance against the size of the road transport sector in general: the easing of licensing restrictions in 1953 had allowed the lorry fleet to grow to more than a million by 1957. The effect was to change the BTC's attitude towards the Government, the road-haulage industry, and anyone else who chose to interfere. The Commission was now fighting the railway corner.

Meanwhile, pressure from the Railway Development Association was beginning to have an effect: not upon the Government, but upon the Central Transport Consultative Committee, which finally agreed that lightweight railbuses should be given a chance. Its favourable report on the matter led the BTC to authorise acquisition of a fleet of 22 vehicles during 1957 and '58.

The railbuses were purchased from four British manufacturers: two from Bristol/Eastern Coach Works, five each from Wickhams, Park Royal Vehicles and A C Cars and, in view of the European lead in the field, another five vehicles were ordered from the German company, Waggon und Maschinenbau, of Donauwörth.

It had taken the Commission eight years to introduce diesel multiple units, and another two to accept the principle of railbus techniques but, by late 1956, the Commission was firmly in favour of exploring new technology, advocating closure only as a last resort:

> Any plan for refashioning the railway system to suit modern transport conditions must first explore alternative methods of operation. Thereafter, those services which cannot possibly be made economic by modern rail methods but can be better catered for by road transport must be eliminated.

The railbuses were immediately put into service throughout the country, and it was perhaps fitting that one of the bravest and most innovative experiments was attempted on former Great Western territory, the GWR having pioneered railcar techniques almost 30 years earlier. The Western Region trial was wonderful news for the RDA, for the experiment was to embody almost every cost-saving measure it had advocated.

Kemble, on the main line between Swindon and Gloucester, was the junction for two rural branch lines, one running north to Cirencester, the other south to the little town of Tetbury. Both lines had operated at a substantial loss for a number of years, the longer branch to Tetbury reportedly carrying no more than 100 passengers a week in the last days of steam operation. They were, however, ideal candidates for railbus experiments. Tetbury, with a population of only 3,000, was typical of the smaller communities whose branch services were under threat, while the market town of Cirencester, home to almost 13,000, was representative of many larger centres. A great deal depended on the success or failure of the experiment, for the Western Region intended to provide similar services throughout the West Country should traffic levels prove satisfactory.

On February 2, 1959, the steam locomotives were retired and three A C Cars railbuses were set to work. Several new halts had been constructed, and the diminutive four-wheeled railbuses made up for their lack of seating capacity by operating an intensive service over the branches: eight trains a day to Tetbury and 14 to Cirencester.

Within a few weeks the results of the experiment became known. The Tetbury railcar (although generating a 250 per cent increase in traffic) continued to lose money, but the Cirencester line proved very successful, reportedly carrying 2,500 passengers a week, or an average of almost 30 per train. As the railcars seated only 46, the most popular Saturday services were often severely overcrowded, and on one notable occasion no fewer than 110 passengers squeezed aboard!

Above: The single diesel railcar whose introduction saw a 300 per cent increase in passenger numbers on the Buckingham to Banbury line (see over). It is pictured here at Banbury in August 1956. The period setting of the station, with its wooden stage-like platform, is spoilt by the removal of the roof. Pictured below, in 1951, is a Towcester to Banbury train at Towcester. The hopelessly uneconomic operation was withdrawn in 1951 and the successful railcar service covered part of the route. Both pictures, Owen Prosser.

*A brand new diesel multiple unit at Birmingham New Street in May 1955.
The units were used to shuttle passengers to the British Industries Fair at
Castle Bromwich. Owen Prosser.*

Even Sir Reginald Wilson appeared to have been swayed by the new
technology. According to David Blee, General Manager of the London Midland
Region, Sir Reginald was "more in favour of keeping such lines open, operated
with what he described as 'the lowest form of life', i.e. an ultra-cheap railbus".
It was becoming clear that a cheap and efficient railbus service would enable the
Commission to keep track on the ground, leaving open the possibility of
reinstating a full service at a later date, should the industrial, economic, or
population outlook warrant such a move. In a fast changing world, it was an
infinitely more sensible option than outright closure.

The London Midland Region had already introduced a conventional single
diesel railcar (as opposed to a lightweight railbus) between Buckingham and
Banbury. "All the indications," said the General Manager, early in 1958, "were
that it would continue to be a dead loss-maker; but I will be happy to try it." In
the event, the experiment generated a fourfold increase in traffic and a 28 per
cent reduction in costs, and had the London Midland Region utilised a railbus,
costs would have been reduced further still. The predictions of the Railway
Development Association had, at last, been proved correct: the railbuses were
economical and immensely popular with the public. It looked as though many
of the rural branch lines might be saved.

Elsewhere, the larger diesel multiple units were continuing to break records.
By February 1958, earnings between Birmingham and Lichfield had increased

almost threefold, while the Bradford-Leeds-Harrogate service (extended to Knaresborough in 1957), had earned £114,700, against £29,000 in the last days of steam. The following year, a new service between Leeds and Barnsley saw income increase by 416 per cent. Such figures produced an unsurpassed confidence within the industry, for the BTC was now convinced that it could make a success of the modernised railway services. Perhaps it was a little too confident for, in March 1957, the original modernisation plans were swept aside and replaced with new ideas that went a good deal further.

The Report on Diesel & Electric Traction, and the Passenger Services of the Future, was probably the most expansionist document ever considered by British Railways. Perhaps ominously, at a time when the Government was far from convinced that the railways had a bright future, it also represented the largest single investment programme on the railways since Victorian times.

The scale of the electrification proposals was quite staggering: 2,213 miles of overhead catenaries for the East Coast (including quite a few minor branches), 809 miles on the West Coast, 632 miles elsewhere in the London Midland region, 741 miles in Scotland and 346 miles on the DC third-rail system in the Southern region, together with 338 miles AC overhead to Weymouth and Exeter. The prediction was for construction work to reach a peak of 800 miles a year in the mid-1960s, the whole programme to be complete by about 1980.

It made the 1955 Modernisation Plan look half-hearted, with its modest provision for 1,200 miles of overhead electrification and 250 miles on the DC third-rail system, for the BTC was now intending to convert 2,800 miles to the overhead system within a few years, with an eventual aim of putting 5,100 miles under the catenaries. The cost was put at £250 million, against which branch line losses paled into insignificance. But there was to be money for the secondary lines as well. In addition to the railbus fleet, the BTC had placed firm orders for 5,144 multiple units, while construction of another 300 was under consideration. In the summer of 1956, the Commission even put pressure on a bemused Metro-Cammell, one of the companies producing multiple units, to speed the flow of deliveries.

The result, after years of tight financial control, was an orgy of spending. By the end of 1957 the overall cost of modernisation was re-appraised at £1,660 million. The Treasury was reportedly "somewhat surprised", for it was a very large sum of public money. Ministry of Transport and Treasury officials had previously allowed the Commission considerable freedom, but they gradually began to look a little more closely into railway affairs.

The problem, from the Treasury point of view, lay with the state of the economy. On September 19, 1957 the Government introduced a credit squeeze, cut public investment, and raised the bank rate from five to seven per cent to halt a run on the pound. Superficially, the financial situation was quite healthy (the bank rate fell back within a few months), but it was hardly a suitable time to announce massive increases in public spending. What the Treasury still didn't know was that the BTC's Modernisation Committee — the architects of modernisation — had warned that it might prove difficult (or impossible) to cover the interest payments on the modernisation schemes. In other words, financial collapse was imminent.

Perhaps the Transport Commission had been influenced by the mood of the times. In January 1958, Harold Macmillan was handed the premiership by an ailing Anthony Eden and, in July, the new Prime Minister uttered probably his most famous words:

Let's be frank about it. Most of our people have never had it so good.

* * *

For the railways, the good times were to prove very short-lived indeed. To an outside observer the picture must have appeared quite bright — large scale electrification would halt the decline on the main lines; diesel units had already matched road transport where stopping services were concerned; and railbus experiments had improved the prospects for the minor lines.

The railways should have faced a secure future but the reality was rather different. Money had been poured into a handful of prestigious schemes, leaving the greater part of the system starved of investment. And no-one had taken proper account of the long-term financial implications of piecemeal modernisation.

Few commentators understood the industry sufficiently well to realise what was happening. A marked exception was our friend Professor Hondelink, who returned from his work at the United Nations to find the situation at home sliding from bad to worse. In April 1958 he wrote to the Permanent Secretary at the Ministry of Transport, Sir Gilmor Jenkins, in a last rather desperate attempt to influence events:

A combination of modernisation and retrenchment can only have a disastrous effect, namely a few spectacular services here and there, but the railway system as a whole becoming a perpetual burden on the tax payer.

His advice was quietly ignored. In any event, road transport, and motorways in particular, were in the news. Work was well under way on the first eight miles of motorway, known initially as the Preston Bypass, but later to form part of the M6. Of much greater significance was the mileage already going through the planning stage — another 73 miles would be completed in 1959, 45 in 1960, and there would be a gradual increase in mileage thereafter.

Motorway construction was an enormously expensive process: it was estimated that the first stage of the M1 would cost more than £20 million, and such an outpouring of Government funds was bound to cost someone dear. In the event it was the Transport Commission that was destined to pay the bill. On December 5, 1958, Harold Macmillan opened the Preston By-pass, describing the motorway as "the symbol of the opening of a new era in motor travel in the UK". It was also to prove a problem to the railways, not so much through competition, but because the Government had long determined that the roads were the primary transport of the future.

Events began to move with lightning speed. In February 1959 the Government published a White Paper, *Proposals for Inland Waterways*. Like the railways, the canals had remained under the control of the Transport Commission in 1953. By the late 1950s their finances were in an even more parlous state than those of the railways, but the way the Government dealt with the problem was strikingly different, and it is worth looking at in some detail.

In June 1958, the Bowes Committee had reported to the Government with various proposals. It had recommended that the canals should be divided into three groups: class 'A' (such as the Severn, and the Aire & Calder) that were mostly profitable; class 'B', that carried a little commercial traffic but lost money; and class 'C' — of no commercial value, and mostly derelict or semi-derelict.

The Committee judged that class A canals should have profits ploughed back for investment and that class B should be reinstated to a prescribed standard and maintained thus for a period of 25 years to give future trade a chance. The financial burden would be met largely from the public purse. In the meantime, steps would be taken to find non-commercial uses for the waterways.

Generally, the A & B class canals would be treated in a similar manner to the trunk and secondary railways, but the C class canals, which corresponded more or less to the railway branch lines, were to be dealt with very differently. The future of each canal would be determined on its merits; some would be developed and others allowed to die. The real breakthrough was that any interested outside body, such as a preservation group or local authority, would be encouraged to share in the redevelopment of such canals — provided that it bore a proportion of the costs.

The Bowes Committee had produced an admirable report. It was honest and it provided plenty of answers and, by and large, the Government agreed with its findings. There would be a two-year experiment to test the proposals, and an Inland Waterways Redevelopment Advisory Committee to assist in the promotion of redevelopment schemes. One proposal that (perhaps inevitably) the Government was unable to commit itself to, was the provision that 900 miles of Class B waterway should be maintained at Ministry expense for 25 years. But it was very impressed with the idea of "privatising" the lesser waterways and it agreed with the Bowes Committee that abandonment was a "negative" option and redevelopment a "new and positive approach":

> The Government would be prepared to bridge a small gap by a special *ad hoc* grant towards the capital cost of the redevelopment... It is also important that voluntary organisations... which have shown so much interest in seeing canals preserved and restored, should take the opportunities for joint effort and contribution which the preparation of schemes should offer.

At the risk of jumping some years ahead of our story, it should be stated that the Government White Paper of 1959 led to the establishment of the British Waterways Board, whose enlightened attitude brought immediate results. Discussions were started with canal-users, local authorities and others, to formulate a policy for the restoration of the non-commercial waterways.

One successful restoration scheme was the lower section of the Stratford on Avon canal, proposed for closure by the BTC in 1955. This less than strategically placed backwater had lain abandoned for many years, but under the provisions of the White Paper, and the 1962 Transport Act which followed, the waterway was restored to health in a partnership between the British Waterways Board and the National Trust, using a mixture of state and volunteer capital.

If such schemes were suitable for the minor canals, then why not for the railways? After all, the conclusions of the Bowes Report were not so very different from the proposals in the Rural Transport Improvement Bill that the Government had gone to great lengths to destroy. If uneconomic canals were to be offered to private individuals or local authorities, then why not the uneconomic branch lines, for which abandonment was just as negative an option?

One reason was the high cost of abandoning the canals. It had been estimated that to close all the uneconomic canals would cost £600 million, but that only another £340 million would be required to keep them open to toll-paying pleasure craft. In the case of the Kennet & Avon, it had been judged that the cost of closure was more or less the same as that of restoration.

The canals had become essential for drainage, water supply and irrigation purposes, and it had generally proved necessary to leave a water channel in place to satisfy these requirements. Thus it could easily cost more to rebuild the canal as a water channel than to restore it to health as a thoroughfare.

There were hidden costs involved in closing the railways too which, by this time, must have become self-evident. The value of the realisable capital assets, such as station buildings, track and equipment, was largely offset by the cost of maintaining or demolishing worthless structures — the bridges, tunnels and viaducts. Fences, hedges, culverts and ditches all needed to be maintained in good repair by someone, and it was usually the Commission which picked up the bill. In addition, the replacement bus services were failing to fulfil their early promise and some routes were losing both customers and money at an alarming rate. Once again, it was the Commission which was generally liable, and the cost had proved prohibitive. But the Government had continued to treat the railways in a very different manner from the canals.

One possible explanation was that although the Government (and more particularly the Ministry of Transport) saw canals as useful from an amenity point of view, they were not seen as a threat to the supremacy of road transport. A privately operated, locally controlled railway was another matter entirely. Such a body might conceivably become a serious transport undertaking and, as such, it would be bound to create all sorts of problems — particularly with the road lobby.

Such a partisan position on the part of the Government may appear hard to believe but its behaviour is otherwise hard to explain. It had refused to heed the advice of experts such as Professor Hondelink, consistently thwarted attempts to run the branch lines economically and opposed the Rural Transport Improvement Bill that sought, as a last resort, to remove uneconomic lines from Government control.

So why was the Government acting in so biased a manner? Certainly, many of those in positions of authority saw the roads as the transport of the future, and the railways as the last vestige of a grimy, labour-intensive, heavy industry; and the Commission's extended reliance on steam traction had done nothing to alter such views. In government eyes, road buses would carry passengers more efficiently on the new motorways, and private haulage contractors could handle most of the freight. And it was these same haulage contractors that were to influence Government behaviour, for in the 1950s the Conservative Government owed a great deal to the road haulage industry.

According to *The Railwaymen*, the official history of the NUR:

> **The Transport Act in 1947 created something of a vacuum which was filled by the emergence of the Road Haulage Association, the principle agency for advancing the interests of the road-construction firms, the road-hauliers and motorists in Parliament.**

When the socialist administration had finally succeeded in bringing road haulage interests under state control in 1950-51, there was an upsurge of anger from the private hauliers. Consequently they went to great lengths to secure a Conservative Government — and to keep it in power.

Such patronage was expensive. The Conservative Government had handed back the trucks at knock-down prices, but the industry, sensing a political advantage, had demanded more. It wanted new roads, and the Government was glad to oblige, but the prize was to humble the railways once and for all and leave a road transport monopoly. It was a difficult objective, for the BTC was pushing ahead with modernisation schemes that might give the railways a real advantage. It was, however, bedevilled by mounting losses and this proved to be the key.

Exactly when the Government began to plan its assault on the railways is hard to judge. Under the influence of the road lobby, the attitude of the Ministry of Transport had been hardening for a number of years, and it was admitted in April 1963 that plans had been under active consideration for "more than three years", or from late in 1959. Probably it was from about the time of the October 1959 election. The patronage of the road haulage industry reached untold heights during the campaign, and according to *The Commercial Motor*, the journal of the Road Haulage Association:

> **The Conservative Party promise the answer to the haulier's prayers. Any financial contribution he makes towards this success may be partly selfish, but wholly natural.**

The financial contributions were most welcome and the Conservatives spent almost £0.5 million on advertising during the campaign. As there was no compulsion to reveal political donations in the 1950s, it is hard to judge exactly what proportion of this came from companies with road interests. By combining the available evidence with the picture revealed by the pattern of donations since disclosure became mandatory, it is reasonable to conclude that as much as a quarter of this budget came from these firms. In addition, the same companies provided finance for the various pressure groups that made up the road lobby. Harold Macmillan easily fought off the inexperienced Labour leader, Hugh Gaitskell, to return to power with an increased majority of 100 seats, and a clear mandate to push through the policies demanded by his supporters.

The hauliers were handsomely repaid, for the new administration was able to offer them a Minister of Transport who was not only road-biased, but a successful road engineering contractor into the bargain. His name was Ernest Marples.

And, as it transpired, the opportunity to humble the railways fell straight into Mr Marples's lap. In 1958, a substantial decline in the output of coal and steel had brought an eight per cent loss of traffic to the railways. Expenditure remained well under control, but a mild recession, allied to the after-effects of the rise in interest rates the previous year, caused income to fall, triggering the deficit time-bomb.

The financial house of cards collapsed: the railways returned a working deficit of £48.1 million, an overall loss of £90.1 million, and earnings well below the level anticipated in the 1956 modernisation proposals. The Commission had no reserves of capital, and was unable to cover the loss.

The Government demanded an urgent reappraisal of the financial implications of modernisation, and the Commission duly complied, publishing a report as a White Paper in July 1959, just before the election. The ambition of the modernisation plan had been to achieve a working surplus of £55-100 million on passenger services by 1963 and £5-35 million on freight. The Government felt these targets were drifting out of reach, and it hoped the White Paper would provide a few clues as to how matters had gone wrong. It particularly wanted to see a few examples of good housekeeping — perhaps a degree of retrenchment in view of the worsening financial crisis, or at least a plausible explanation as to the continuing losses.

But, despite the gravity of the situation, the BTC saw no particular need to cut back its plans. On the contrary, it proposed bringing forward expenditure into the period 1959-63 so as to bring forward the proposed financial benefits. There would also be a measured programme of rail closures amounting to about 1,800 miles in all, but excluding main lines which had previously been considered dubious, such as the Great Central and the Settle & Carlisle. The Commission also suggested that its financial structure should be reformed to remove the burden of high, fixed, rates of interest.

But it was already much too late for such changes. The problem was that most of the modernisation plans involved very long-term investment. Only a paltry 24 miles of overhead electrification had been completed, but there would be no sign of a return until the services were at least partially operational; 1,500 miles of concrete sleepers had been laid, and there was unlikely to be a return on that investment for several decades. To a lesser extent, the same was true of resignalling schemes, marshalling yards and locomotives — all were areas in which it would take several years for the financial benefits to become apparent.

If the Transport Commission had prepared accurate and reliable plans detailing expected financial returns, all might have been well, but officials at the Treasury and Ministry of Transport had discovered that many of the Commission's assumptions were flawed. A good example was the set-piece electrification from Euston to Liverpool and Manchester, that should have been the most easily justifiable of all the modernisation plans. The BTC had originally estimated that the electrification scheme would cost £75 million, convincing the Government that any borrowings would be repaid through increased returns. However, after a change of policy on the technical details of the scheme in 1956, an increase in scale during the "never had it so good" era, and a later, more realistic, appraisal of costs, the projected expenditure had doubled to £161 million.

A closer look at the proposed benefits indicated that income might increase by around £3 million a year, while operating costs would be cut by £5 million — a gross benefit of £8 million, or a net return of about five per cent on the investment. Unfortunately, interest rates were running at about five to six per cent at the time, which made it unlikely that the scheme would cover interest, let alone repay any capital.

The Commission replied that it had probably miscalculated and that the income would no doubt increase by more than £3 million following electrification. In other words, when its own figures indicated that its most prestigious modernisation scheme was unlikely to show a return, the Commission simply swept the figures aside. The affair was an unmitigated disaster for the BTC, for unfriendly civil servants proceeded to tear the modernisation schemes to shreds, and the unseemly wrangle gave the Government the ammunition it needed.

If the figures for Euston to Liverpool and Manchester failed to add up, then what were the returns likely to be on the less favourable routes? It emerged that the Commission had actually given the matter little thought, for it could give no clear indication as to which schemes were likely to produce a positive return at the end of the day, and which were not.

In reality, the Commission had actually underestimated the potential benefits of electrification, for had the costs been calculated on a different basis the results would have looked very different. For instance, the Ministry of Transport was already developing a technique for costing new motorway construction that took into account the value of motorists' time by attributing a value in its costings to the time drivers saved by switching to the new road. Had the Ministry allowed the Commission to cost electrification projects on a similar basis, most of the schemes would have proved overwhelmingly viable.

The Ministry might also have taken into account the fact that major railway investment projects were almost bound to save money in other areas — perhaps by tipping the balance against an expensive, but marginal, road improvement scheme. But it was too late to open a debate on the matter — most of the modernisation plans were already doomed.

Immediately after the October 1959 election, the Government asked the Parliamentary Select Committee on Nationalised Industries to examine the railways as a matter of urgency. The Select Committee responded with great speed, preparing and publishing a report by July 1960. Ominously, it had not had time to seek the views of outside experts, but the committee had sought the views of Ministry and Treasury representatives (who were now firmly opposed to the entire modernisation process) and officials of the BTC, who were determined to press ahead.

Generally, the Select Committee was satisfied with the way the Commission was handling its affairs. True, the losses were continuing to mount, but the 1959 figures had made it clear that increased efficiency was starting to have an impact on the financial situation. Track costs were down, movement costs were down, manpower was steadily being reduced, and the number of locomotives had been cut from 18,500 in 1955 to 14,000, with a reduction to 10,700 in the pipeline for 1961. The diesel multiple units — still accounting for only a small proportion of passenger trains — had, on average, increased revenue by more than one third on the lines to which they had been introduced, and the Commission was firmly committed to closing any lines that failed to show a decent return. Even the profusion of railway workshops was to be cut by half by 1964.

According to the BTC, the losses stemmed mainly from stopping and local train services, but the Select Committee disagreed. The financial crisis had been precipitated by a combination of factors. Firstly there was the awesome burden of British Transport Stock, issued to finance the nationalisation of the railways in 1947 and on which repayments were subsequently increased to keep the system afloat. By 1955 the interest repayments on British Transport Stock had reached £40 million a year and, as we have seen, the interest rate on Transport Stock was fixed, leaving the railways with an obligation to pay a handsome return to their former masters whatever the financial position.

The 1947 Act had empowered the BTC to establish a reserve fund to guard against contingencies, but for various reasons it had never done so. Such a fund would have helped to keep the railways from sliding into debt, and might have prevented the organisation from becoming enslaved to interest payments. It must also be borne in mind that Government advances to cover the cost of modernisation were just that — repayable advances. The money had been supplied from a special account that had accrued a deficit of more than £360 million by 1959. And there were substantial interest payments due on this account, irrespective of repayment of the actual capital.

This was how the financial situation had so rapidly reached crisis proportions. The BTC had been created as a transport monopoly with a statutory duty to break even, and its financial structure had been created according to those rules. After the disposal of road-haulage interests from 1953 onwards, the situation changed dramatically; the Commission had found itself with a rundown railway system, no capital, and trading in a competitive environment without the freedom to fix rates accordingly. By 1955, the railways were long overdue for investment — but with no reserve fund, and no opportunity for cross-subsidy from other BTC businesses, the Commission was obliged to borrow from the Government at commercial rates. Once the turmoil of modernisation had pushed the operating figures into the red from 1956 onwards, it was also obliged to pay interest on its short-term deficits.

According to the Parliamentary Select Committee, tight government control of railway fares and charges was largely to blame. Since 1938, prices had risen by 171 per cent, while railway passenger fares had increased by only 145 per cent and freight charges by 144 per cent.

Government interference had caused all manner of problems over the years — as in 1952 and 1956 when the Minister had intervened after the Transport Tribunal had agreed to grant fare increases. The financial implications of such outside interference were hard to quantify. The Commission had put the cost at about £50 million for the period 1949-55, and at least another £17 million in 1956. Some commentators put the cost of Government interference in that year alone at more than £50 million. More recently, in September 1957, the Government had announced without warning that capital expenditure in 1958 and 1959 would be restricted. The result — with schemes already well under way — was an expensive fiasco, as planning work was wasted and financial penalties paid to contractors.

Nor was the BTC itself totally blameless. It had failed to respond to private coach operators which were taking considerable traffic on some routes by adopting an aggressive pricing strategy. In November 1959, shortly after the opening of the M1 motorway, the coach operators had introduced a fare of £1 1s 3d (£1.06) between London and Birmingham, while the railways had continued to charge £2 2/- (£2.10). Even after Government controls were relaxed in 1957, the Commission had stuck to an inflexible charging system, based upon mileage, which took no account of local conditions. The same was true with freight charges, allowing the small private road haulage concerns to run rings around the unwieldy BTC organisation.

Branch line policy had also been mishandled. The Commission had deliberately run down the branches with the intention of closing them, then more or less cancelled the closure policy, pouring millions of pounds into multiple units in an attempt to turn losses into profits. But, as with the major electrification schemes, many of the branch line investments appeared unable to meet interest payments on the capital outlay, let alone produce a return. Had the Commission made it clear that certain lines were **unlikely** to produce a solid return but explained (both to the Government and to the public) why such services were worthy of investment, all might have been well. The real problem was that the Commission had failed to distinguish the commercially viable services from the socially desirable ones.

Tentative studies were already proving that it might be cheaper to subsidise certain lines than to close them down. An investigation in 1959 had looked in some detail at passenger services on nearly 1,400 miles of lightly used railway in central Wales, Devon, Cornwall and Scotland. The total income was £5.2 million, against expenses of £8.7 million, giving a paper loss of £3.5 million. However, the lines generated contributory revenue of more than £6 million, of which nearly £5 million would be lost after closure. The subsidy of £3.5 million could just as easily have been seen as an investment generating a healthy return.

Had such arguments been given proper publicity and consideration at the time, it would have become clear that such lines were not only worthy of retention, but of renewed investment.

Unfortunately, the Commission did nothing to support its own case — indeed, it appears to have had little idea as to where its own money was going.

Under Select Committee scrutiny, it emerged that the Commission was unsure of the financial performance of the individual railway regions. Nor did the Area Boards have much idea. It was also claimed that the Commission had failed to study the performance of individual lines and services even though, as we have seen, accurate records had been maintained (in a few areas at least) since the early 1950s.

Had the BTC kept a closer eye on the performance of the regions, losses might have been held in check more easily. As it was, the Commission only kept figures based on the **originating** receipts from each region, which tended to favour industrial areas, such as the North-East, and work against holiday destinations like the West Country.

All the same, the figures for 1959 make interesting reading. Ignoring central charges, three regions — North Eastern, Eastern and Southern — made a small profit. The Scottish region fared less well, but the majority of the £42 million operating loss that year could be attributed to the London Midland and Western regions. Perhaps rather more relevant was the fact that all the regions, with the exception of London Midland, had improved their financial position compared with the previous year.

The situation was not nearly as bleak as the Government was about to make out — passenger receipts were up by about £2 million against the previous year and operating costs had been substantially reduced. The real decline was in freight, particularly coal, where £13 million worth of traffic had been lost in 1959. Despite the decline in heavy freight, the figures remained quite buoyant. Passenger volume had hit a 20-year high, and parcels traffic had grown by 15 per cent since nationalisation. After carefully considering all the evidence, the Select Committee concluded: "There is no doubt that a large-scale British railway system can be profitable." It also tentatively concluded that a few services might be worthy of subsidy for "social" reasons. But it was not what Mr Marples wanted to hear. Railway finances were in a disastrous tangle and he had already decided to sort out the ailing industry once and for all. For the branch lines, many of which were busier than they had been for a number of years, the end was in sight.

5.
The Marples-Beeching axis
1960-1963

It is a difficulty which we all face, including the Commission, of trying to trace exactly where the money is being lost... the Commission itself admits that it cannot say with any precision where the money has been lost. All we know for a fact is that large sums of money are being lost...

...to talk as some do of the plan we have for the railways as being one for closures, and for closures alone, is claptrap and drivel. It has a positive and constructive side to it and that is what I want to emphasise.

John Hay, Joint Parliamentary Secretary to the Ministry of Transport

IMPOSING draconian cuts on a large nationalised industry can lead to the sort of nightmare of which politicians live in constant fear. As Minister of Transport, Ernest Marples's first move was to tighten control over the BTC management and rein in the modernisation programme. Early in 1960, the Ministry of Transport informed the Transport Commission that any investment project involving expenditure of more than £250,000 would have to be cleared with the Ministry, the ultimate decision resting with Mr Marples.

The effect of the new controls was virtually to wind up the modernisation process, for a scheme instigated at Area Board level now had to be cleared by the Commission's Works and Equipment Committee, the Commission itself, the Ministry and, finally, the Minister of Transport. The new system performed exactly as had been intended: it was quite unworkable. The Euston to Liverpool and Manchester electrification scheme was already well advanced, and it was allowed to continue, although financial control remained tight, and the completion date was set back several years. On the branches and secondary lines, investment ceased almost immediately, and the authorities began to prepare the ground for extensive closures.

Many voices would have to be silenced to bring about a bloodless road transport revolution: politicians, the rail lobby, the railway management, the unions... and the public at large. The Government replied with a systematic and well organised campaign.

* * *

In Government circles, the railways were considered to be far from essential; a next-to-worthless Victorian encumbrance in the age of road transport. What was the point of paying for railway modernisation when roads were already under construction to carry ex-railway traffic?

There was a genuine and rather naive belief that lorries would handle the nation's freight, the private car would look after personal transport, and road buses would more than suffice for those who could not afford (or chose not to own) a car. If the railways were to remain (and it was politically expedient that they should, in some form) the network would be cut to a size where profitability could be assured.

There had been an ongoing debate for many years as to whether certain railway maintenance and investment costs should be borne by the State. After all, the Government was pouring large sums into the construction of a motorway and trunk road network, why should it not pay to develop the railways as well? The railways were just as much a state network as were the roads: why should they be expected to operate profitably? The official reply was that the road system was effectively self-financing, receiving income from vehicle road fund licences and car and fuel taxes. But it was a contentious issue, for it was impossible even to prove whether the income covered the **true** cost of building and maintaining the road network, let alone other consequential costs.

According to the road lobby, the road "income" exceeded direct expenditure on construction and maintenance by a healthy margin. What it omitted to observe, however, was that income fell well short of covering the real cost, including pollution, accident damage, policing, hospitalisation and congestion. The National Council for Inland Transport, a generally pro-rail pressure group, later attempted to estimate the real cost of the road network and came to the conclusion that the annual roads income of £610 million covered no more than half the true expenditure of about £1,486 million. The shortfall of more than £800 million exceeded the railway deficit many times over, but such arguments were lost on a Government that openly favoured the road lobby.

Had the Government paused for a moment in 1960, weighed up the relative worth of various forms of transport, and reached the conclusion that individual roads should be placed under the same financial constraints as individual railways, the vast majority of minor roads would have been deemed uneconomic. The density of road traffic was spread just as unevenly as rail traffic, for half the vehicles were travelling on five per cent of the road network, leaving much of the system "uneconomic" in straight financial terms. The fact remained, though, that the railways were deemed a secondary, duplicate means of transport and, to Mr Marples, a Minister with a substantial interest in road construction, the answer was obvious.

Public opinion

The first, and probably the most difficult, task was to win the public relations battle, for an attempt to close a large proportion of the railway network was a policy that would cost the Government dear if it was handled badly. The message would be a simple one: that sacrifices would be needed by a few in the interests of the nation as a whole.

It might still have been an uphill struggle had the Government not brought out its big guns from the very beginning. It was decided that the Prime Minister himself would launch the campaign and on March 10, 1960, introducing a debate on the Guillebaud Committee report on railwaymen's wages, Harold Macmillan delivered a suitable speech:

> The carriage of minerals, including coal, an important traffic for the railways, has gone down. At the same time, there has been an increasing use of road transport in all its forms...
>
> First, the industry must be of a size and pattern suited to modern conditions and prospects. In particular, the railway system must be remodelled to meet current needs, and the modernisation plan must be adapted to this new shape...
>
> Secondly, the public must accept the need for changes in the size and pattern of the industry. This will involve certain sacrifices of convenience, for example, in the reduction of uneconomic services...
>
> The public has to accept that it cannot ask the industry to take on some of the old functions such as fell upon a common carrier, and some of the old restrictions which were quite reasonable when the railway was a monopoly, of which there are signs still, and it must also accept the inconvenience of certain lines being closed and other means of transport being made available.

The public had been told "to accept" it. There was an authority behind the voice of the Prime Minister that made the thing seem inevitable and, with the introduction of a few carefully worded slogans for the press, the campaign was well under way. One particular slogan gave the impression (without actually promising anything) that the Government was about to replace the outmoded railway network with a new improved version: "The railways are supposed to meet 20th century demands with 19th century equipment."

John Hay, Mr Marples's Parliamentary Secretary, generally put emphasis on the age and inadequacy of the railways, with remarks such as that "the existing system was laid down for horse-and-cart delivery and collection". Such remarks were deliberately intended to clear the way for a programme of railway closures.

Other claims were more defensive, such as Mr Marples's own Parliamentary reply that "traffic is going onto the roads because the people wish it to go onto the roads; I am not forcing it!".

The Parliamantary campaign which prepared public opinion for a campaign of closures laid great emphasis on the age of railway equipment. Yet, by this time, a substantial part of the network — including many of the branches that would close — had been enjoying modern diesel services for years. Pictured above is a 2-6-2 tank engine hauling a local service at Four Oaks, Birmingham, in 1956. The inset shows British Railways publicity for the new diesels about to replace it. Owen Prosser.

Another slogan that caught the attention of the press was an implication that closures would increase road congestion by no more than one per cent, equivalent to two months' normal traffic growth. This claim was quite false, being based upon a most dubious accounting procedure, but it was widely quoted.

The Government's big push centred on the outmoded nature of the railway network and the mounting losses. There were plenty of figures to play with, and the Government made good use of them: the Transport Commission was £353 million in the red by 1960; the Government had loaned £600 million; the overall railway deficit for 1961 would top £150 million, £160 million in 1962, and so on. Most spectacular of all were the near £2,000 million overall capital liabilities of the BTC. As £1,400 million of this was in the form of British Transport Stock, it was quite unreasonable to imply that such a figure represented a railway debt. To put the figures into perspective, the actual working deficit was running at around £60 million a year, against a gross national expenditure of around £7 billion, but these figures were given little emphasis.

119

The Government made clear its view that the losses were horrendous, and that they could only be reduced by eradicating the lines that did not pay. There was no direct reference to the extent of the proposed cuts, however, and the newspapers and the public produced answers of their own. Typical was the view of Professor Gilbert Walker, of Birmingham University, writing in *Westminster Bank Review*: "Railway route mileage to be closed cannot be less than 60 per cent. The proposition may be as high as 80 per cent." Even *The Times* fell victim to the misinformation campaign, agreeing that "half of total track mileage and a very much larger proportion in Scotland, Wales, South-West England and East Anglia" would close. When the authorities released the actual proposals a few years later in the Beeching report, their conclusions looked mild and well reasoned in comparison with these inflated expectations.

The Government naturally encouraged the view that railway closures were only of local importance and usually of a "rural" nature. This had been largely true during the 1950s, as the Transport Commission lopped off a few minor branch lines, but the plans of the Marples regime were on an altogether different scale. There was suddenly a very real threat to the entire railway infrastructure, although the official line continued to be that of minor rural hardship; of the necessity to "sacrifice" the convenience of a few unfortunate individuals who might in future need to take the bus.

Government policy undoubtedly paid off. The public, the media and even the specialist press began to accept the view that the Transport Commission was making overwhelming losses, and that the losses were largely caused by the rural railways. The only conceivable answer would be to cut the network.

The Road Haulage Association was only too glad to assist in the campaign and, in April 1960, its journal, *The World's Carriers*, went for the railway jugular:

> It is understood that the Government have already settled the principles of reorganisation, and it will be for the Board to work out their detailed application...
>
> We should build more roads, and we should have fewer railways. This would merely be following the lesson of history which shows a continued and continuing expansion of road transport and a corresponding contraction in the volume of business handled by the railways...
>
> A streamlined railway system could surely be had for half the money that is now being made available... We must exchange the "permanent way" of life for the "motorway" of life... road transport is the future, the railways are the past.

There was a lunatic fringe that took the whole thing even further. According to Colonel John Pye, Master of the Worshipful Company of Carmen:

> ...a look should be taken at the widths of pavements and, where possible, steps

be taken to cut them down to widen the road space... there should be more control of pedestrians.

Strangely, no-one objected, for in the early 1960s the motor car could do no wrong. Many of the claims of the Railway Conversion League — a dubious amalgam of thinly disguised road interests which campaigned for railways to be converted into roads — were equally ludicrous. The railways certainly had few friends at the time, while the road lobby was becoming ever more powerful. And that, really, was the problem. The railways had already lost the public relations battle.

General Sir Brian Robertson, the BTC Chairman, desperately mustered his troops in a last-ditch manoeuvre to turn the tide: "Our aim must be to counterattack and not merely defend!" But it was too late — the old soldier and his gallant staff were buried beneath a welter of invective from the heavy artillery of the road lobby, the Ministry of Transport, and the Government.

In a few short years, the road interests had become sufficiently powerful to influence political events, making it virtually impossible for the Government, or any future government, to hold out against them. From this viewpoint, the question of whether there was, or was not, a conspiracy to crush the railways... and who might, or might not, have been involved, becomes irrelevant. The road transport machine, once it had gathered momentum, was to destroy every obstacle in its path. Whether it began to move on its own accord — or was pushed — was no longer important.

Some people had once believed they could vote for Labour yet still keep Churchill as Prime Minister; many now believed that they could have motorways without losing the branch railway lines. The Government did nothing to dispel the illusion.

Parliament

Parliament posed a few problems for the Government. Opposition members had a nasty tendency to ask awkward questions and rake up unpleasant facts, and if the Government was to lose the support of its own back benches, the Marples plan would be doomed to failure. It was essential to push the negative aspects of the British Transport Commission for all they were worth — the losses, the mismanagement, and the accelerating cost of modernisation — while holding back on the positive aspects, such as the success of the diesel multiple unit programme. Unfortunately, the Select Committee on Nationalised Industries looked set to produce a fair and well-balanced report on the railways. Something stronger would be needed.

The Minister of Transport invited a select team of industrialists to investigate the "railway problem" and to find a solution. The trouble-shooting committee would be led by Sir Ivan Stedeford, Managing Director of Tube Investments, with Frank Kearton (later Lord Kearton), Joint Managing Director of Courtaulds, Henry Benson (later Lord Benson) of Cooper Brothers, a firm of Chartered Accountants... and Dr Richard Beeching (later Lord Beeching), Technical Director of ICI. Inevitably, the committee also included two top civil servants representing the Treasury and the Ministry of Transport.

But why did the Government actually appoint the Stedeford Committee? As early as 1956 the Transport Commission had made it clear that modernisation would take at least ten years to bear fruit. Meanwhile, decentralisation and more efficient working practices were beginning to show a return. Indeed, the Commission had already begun slimming its organisation down to size, predicting a rather alarming 1,000 station closures by 1963, together with a ten per cent cut in route mileage. In February 1959, the Commission had actually closed a trunk route — the old Midland & Great Northern Joint line that meandered for 170 miles across rural Lincolnshire and Norfolk and was reportedly losing £640,000 a year in the process. Perhaps it was a measure of the seriousness of the financial position that the line was closed in record time, with less than ten weeks passing between the announcement and the final implementation, which was unopposed by the Railway Development Association. If the Government was unhappy about the quality of management at the BTC it could have said so — and it had unlimited powers to do something about it.

The Stedeford Committee was set up for the sole purpose of facilitating railway closures. According to the Select Committee for the Nationalised Industries, which had already spent a great deal of time and effort investigating the railways, "a non-parliamentary planning board was later set up to cover much the same ground **for the Government's own purposes**" [*author's emphasis*].

There seems little doubt that the Stedeford Committee (originally a planning board, but later an advisory group) was set up to provide a smoke screen. The Government intended to cut the railways to size, but such a radical move would have been politically unacceptable without the backing and "evidence" of an expert committee.

Mr Marples would ensure that the committee reached suitable findings by effectively doctoring its terms of reference. The exact wording of the Stedeford Committee terms of reference were a subject of considerable Parliamentary interest. Mr Marples claimed they were both flexible and wide, although he went on to add that the Government had "laid down the broad plan", which implied that the committee would be concerned with no more than detail.

On April 6, 1960, in the face of repeated questions in the House of Commons, Mr Marples revealed what he claimed were the Stedeford Committee's terms of reference:

To examine the structure, finance and working of the organisations at present controlled by the Commission and to advise the Minister of Transport and the British Transport Commission, as a matter of urgency, how effect can best be given to the Government's intentions as indicated in the Prime Minister's statement.

As the Prime Minister had clearly indicated that many railway services would close, we must assume that the Stedeford Committee received a similar brief — to advise the Government on how best to close railway lines.

It was to be no ordinary Parliamentary Committee, however, for the Government needed a group that would produce an exclusive report for the Minister—which echoed the Minister's own views. Superficially, the Stedeford Committee would be an independent body reaching an independent conclusion, but in reality its task appears to have been simply to rubber stamp various conclusions that the Government had already reached. Perhaps understandably, the resulting report was not made public.

No member of the Stedeford Committee had railway experience, there was no BTC presence, no input from the unions, and no consultation as such, although the Committee hoped to take note of the views of various parties before producing its report — if it had time.

In the event, there was not sufficient time to take submissions from those opposed to railway closures — the rail lobby, the railway trade unions, user groups and other interested parties. But, strangely enough, the Stedeford

Committee **did** find the time to engage in consultations with the Central Transport Consultative Committee, the Road Haulage Association, and the Railway Conversion League.

The RHA saw a Darwinistic inevitability in the eclipse of the railways:

...no permanent subsidy should be granted to the railways before it is established exactly what services, passengers and freight are conducted at a loss... the railways' subsidisation would retard the natural evolutionary process in transport by which road services are replacing rail...

The railway system has a fairly long history of failure, and the decline in the importance of rail can no longer be concealed.

According to the available evidence, the Stedeford Committee had little or no contact with groups that might have helped to balance such views, besides accepting representations from the Locomotive and Allied Manufacturers' Association, and the Wagon Repairing Association — and **their** main concern was presumably with the number of jobs that would be lost on the manufacturing side if, or when, the cutbacks began.

Politically, the whole affair was skilfully orchestrated. Labour objections were silenced when the Minister revealed that the socialists had set a precedent for secret committees some years previously. Apparently, the Labour Minister for Aviation and Supply had received a secret report on efficiency in Royal Ordnance Factories. It was hardly comparable, for the ins and outs of the Royal Ordnance Factories were hardly suitable for widespread debate, whereas the future of public transport most certainly was. Labour MP Francis Noel-Baker was in no doubt as to the purpose of the Stedeford Committee:

The conclusion that many of us have reached about the Stedeford Group is that... the Civil Servants in the Minister's Department and the Treasury got cold feet.

When they saw the railway deficits mounting and they saw the Guillebaud Report [on railway wages], they lost their heads. Then they realised that things were in a mess and that if there was a row they might not get proper backing from the Minister of Transport, because he had always wanted to sell out on the railways anyway, and that therefore — to shift responsibility and to protect the Government and protect Ministers, who had not the courage of their own convictions — the Stedeford Group would provide an amenable and respectable-looking front and, incidentally, make it easier to ignore a good deal of the serious and factual reporting of the Select Committee.

But the truth was even more sinister, and many Labour MPs knew why. Back in May 1960, as the Government/Road Haulage public relations campaign reached its zenith, John Hay had spoken at the Road Haulage Association Annual Dinner. Relaxing in the company of friends, the Minister's Parliamentary Secretary made a speech which included the following tantalising items:

I know that our idea of getting advice on the detailed application of Government policy towards the railways from a group of businessmen... is a sensible approach which will commend itself to those present at this dinner.

We were very glad to know what you thought... and the views of your Association have been brought to the attention of Sir Ivan Stedeford's group.

...in the search for transport efficiency, the Government is prepared in a most practical way to do what it can to help. I refer of course to the road programme. It would be too optimistic to expect you to say that what we are doing is enough. No Ministry of Transport spokesman will ever expect that from his friends in the industry.

You and we worked together against the threat of nationalisation of road haulage. We won that battle. Now we must show that we were right to win it...

We in the Government will back you all we can... we shall try to make sure that the roads we have and the new roads we build give the best possible dividend... sometimes in this we shall be forced to require some sacrifices by individuals or by groups in the interests of the many. Road haulage will enjoy many of the benefits...

It was an extraordinary lapse. The Parliamentary Secretary had implied at least two significant things in his speech:

● It could be safely assumed that the (supposedly independent) Stedeford Committee would prepare a report in favour of the road lobby;

● That the road lobby, the Conservative Party (then in opposition), and perhaps even the Ministry of Transport, had "worked together" against nationalisation.

And what did Mr Hay mean when he said the assembled company would "require some sacrifices"? It might have been an echo of Harold Macmillan's March 10 statement, when the Prime Minister had first announced that sacrifices would be needed. But from the viewpoint of a private Road Haulage Association dinner, the phrase takes on a different and more specific meaning. Clearly, the railways, and railway travellers, were to be sacrificed in the interests of road transport.

That the Parliamentary representative of the Ministry of Transport should stand at a private function and openly toast the past and future patronage of a lobby group, leaves one wondering exactly where power lay at the time. Were Harold Macmillan and Ernest Marples really in control of events, or were they simply caught up in a private battle between the Ministry of Transport and the road haulage industry on the one hand, and the embattled British Transport Commission on the other?

Mr Macmillan had been a director of the Great Western Railway before the war and was known to have retained a degree of sympathy for the industry. Mr

Marples, on the other hand, had a personal stake in road transport that amounted to more than three quarters of the shares in his own road construction firm. Although the Minister claimed to have "divested" himself of the shares by this time, he had in reality put the shareholding in the hands of Mrs Marples. If there was a deliberate plan to inflict injury on the railways, it would be all too natural to assume that he was a willing accomplice.

Politicians are, of course, little more than front men where power is concerned. It was the anonymous civil service mandarins at the Ministry of Transport who wielded the real influence and they had a great deal to gain by supporting road interests to the detriment of the railways.

It was really just a matter of power, for the Ministry had been closely allied to the road lobby for so long as to become virtually a "Ministry of Roads". Road affairs necessitated a vast administrative machine, commanding a substantial budget, while the railways were virtually self-governing. By 1966 no fewer than 80 per cent of the Ministry staff were concerned with road matters while just one per cent handled the affairs of the railways. And the majority of this one per cent dealt solely with occasional accident inquiries. In the upper echelons of the service, 11 under-secretaries dealt with road matters and only one with the railways. Obviously, in order to gain promotion, it was essential to adopt a pro-road stance. If the railways had managed to leach back traffic from the roads to any marked degree, the Ministry of Transport would surely have been ravaged.

The Select Committee for the Nationalised Industries had cross-examined several key civil servants, including Sir James Dunnett, the Permanent Secretary at the Ministry of Transport, in an attempt to unravel Ministry policy, and it had received some masterful civil service replies:

> *Mr Albu (MP for Edmonton)*: **I want now to know whose business it is within this estimate of the country's general economy to make estimates of the return on capital invested in the railways... to put it crudely, whether the return on building more roads or modernising certain lines of the railway is likely to show the better return?**
>
> *Sir James Dunnett*: **That is a very difficult thing. The problem does not, in my experience, arise in quite that form.**
>
> *Mr Albu*: **You are saying that it is not the business of the Treasury or the Ministry to have a transport plan? I do not mean forcing everybody to travel a certain way, but a structure based on the consideration of giving the best economic returns?**
>
> *Sir James Dunnett*: **What kind of thing would you have in mind?...**

The Stedeford Committee's main source of information had been the Ministry of Transport, and the committee had been carefully briefed by Ministry officials on the inaccuracy of the Transport Commission's financial figures, and the general inadequacy of the railways as a means of transportation. Stedeford was already firmly opposed to the modernisation plans, and particularly to the electrification of the Euston to Crewe line (Crewe to Manchester being largely complete by this time). According to internal Ministry records on a top-level meeting between the Minister and Sir Ivan Stedeford on May 10, 1960:

> The Stedeford Advisory Group has sought, but completely failed to find any evidence, that the BTC's modernisation proposals had any adequate commercial basis. His view was that there was no prospect of railway finances moving from the "red" to the "black" during the first half of the 1960s, as claimed in the modernisation plans; it would be the late 1970s, if ever, before the railway system paid.

All the same, Stedeford needed to be sure that the Government had planned an adequate road network to replace the railways, because the Committee might otherwise be forced to recommend that certain traffic be encouraged back to rail transportation. Naturally, Mr Marples was only too willing to reassure him on the question of road construction:

> [The Minister] pointed out that [road] congestion occurred primarily in towns, and that in the future there would be still less congestion on the routes between towns. There were in any case objections to directing traffic to rail because of the economic burden this would place on industry...
>
> In the light of the future road schemes Sir Ivan agreed with the Minister's view and said that, in the circumstances, it was all the more important to prevent new railway modernisation projects being started.
>
> *Excerpts from Ministry of Transport notes relating to the meeting between Sir Ivan Stedeford and Ernest Marples, May 1960.*

By October 1960, after six months of intensive work (and three months after publication of the Select Committee Report), the Stedeford "Special Advisory Group" had completed its report. Mr Marples prevaricated over whether the report would be published, finally announcing that it would not, to cries of anger from the Labour benches:

> We have been told that we may not debate the report, to which, apparently, they attach real significance and on which they propose to base their legislation...
> [The railwaymen] take a very gloomy view of the present Minister of Transport. They see in him a Minister who is entirely disaffected, who has apparently no understanding of the railways, who hates them and the BTC and wants to write the whole system off, and whose whole attitude to the railways is one of utter frivolity and irresponsibility...
>
> If one looks at the relation between the Conservative Party and the road haulage interests, one cannot come to any other conclusion than that they have had a dominating influence on the policy of the Government and their attitude to the railways.

Excerpt from a speech by Francis Noel-Baker, Labour MP for Swindon

At least Marples had admitted there was a report. John Hay was later to deny that the committee had produced a report at all, merely that "advice has been tendered to my Right Honourable Friend and a number of recommendations have been made". It can now be revealed that this was more or less correct, for the Stedeford Committee's deliberations really **were** released as a series of recommendations — they were never actually compiled into a report.This was a most useful ruse which was used to good effect in later years when officials would declare, hand on heart, that the Stedeford Report did not exist. In a reply to a question from Robert Adley, the pro-rail Tory MP, in the late 1980s, Premier Margaret Thatcher was to state that the report could not be found, which was hardly surprising.

The findings of the Stedeford Committee remained such a well kept secret that even Barbara Castle was unable to see them on becoming Minister of Transport in 1966.

Mr Marples made only one, rather ominous, remark on the Stedeford Committee's deliberations. It had, he said, merely answered the questions that the Parliamentary Select Committee had asked.

According to Henry Benson, the only member of the Stedeford Committee to make any sort of public pronouncement on the report's contents, the committee had failed to reach unanimous agreement. Beeching and Benson had recommended the course of action that the Government favoured, and Stedeford and Kearton had taken a different, and unspecified, line. In the event, there was a damaging and divisive split, and Beeching was left to write the majority of the report.

Whatever the political situation within the Stedeford Committee, its final recommendations were pretty innocuous, according to the available records, and broadly in line with the conclusions of the Parliamentary Select Committee. Initially it had adopted a hard line with regard to modernisation, recommending in June 1960 that all schemes that had yet to pass "the point of no return", including the major part of the Euston to Liverpool and Manchester project, should be set aside for review. But, interestingly enough, the committee did not feel qualified to conduct the review itself, suggesting that another body be set up with very much broader terms of reference:

> ...to consider the size and pattern of the railway system required to meet current and foreseeable needs, in the light of developments and trends in other forms of transport, changing industrial needs and social habits, and other relevant considerations.

Presumably some members of the committee were unwilling simply to endorse the option of wide-scale closure being pressed upon them by the Ministry of Transport. All the other Stedeford Committee recommendations (released to Marples and the BTC in September 1960) were perfectly fair, and a number would even have pleased the rail lobby — had it only been aware of them. It suggested that the Commission's finances be restructured along more favourable lines; that the archaic fares and charges legislation be repealed; and that there should be closer scrutiny of railway capital expenditure, and a proper system of regional accountancy to clarify the financial picture.

The Commission had an excessive number of staff, said the Stedeford Committee, and fares and charges should be increased on marginal services:

Insofar as such services cannot be eliminated (and that will very often be the case) we think that higher fares can and should make a substantial contribution to eliminating the current loss.

But on the subject of railway closures, the committee had little to say, besides recommending that "a dated programme of further proposals be prepared".

As its deliberations came to a close, the committee even began to waver on the subject of the Euston to Liverpool and Manchester electrification. It agreed that the lines should be modernised and, although far from convinced that there would be an adequate return on capital, it noted that cancellation would waste £20 million that had already been spent, destroy railway morale, and damage Britain's standing abroad.

In the final analysis, Mr Marples's committee of industrial experts "could not give firm guidance" even on this issue, that had seemed so clear-cut to the Ministry of Transport. Its terms of reference had been doctored, and it knew it. Clearly some committee members had refused to play along.

The British Transport Commission

The effects of the Stedeford Committee's deliberations were felt almost immediately: Mr Marples further tightened his control over the railway system, subjecting the modernisation plans to close scrutiny and cutting investment. Many schemes were abandoned altogether, particularly those intended for the secondary and branch lines.

The committee had, of course, been unsure whether to endorse the Ministry's criticism of the beleagured London-Manchester and Liverpool electrification scheme, once the jewel in the crown of the BTC modernisation projects. But Mr Marples took the opportunity to halt further construction and cancel all future contracts. Although the scheme was eventually allowed to proceed, his actions demonstrated the real value of the Stedeford Committee, for the "Marples Gestapo" (as it became known among disaffected railwaymen) had succeeded in emasculating the Transport Commission overnight.

The next move in the Marples plan was to complete the process. In December 1960 it was announced that the BTC was to be abolished, and its constituent parts placed under the control of separate boards of management. General Sir Brian Robertson, Chairman of the Commission, had once warned the Government to stand aside and allow the modernisation schemes to run their course. Marples had neither forgotten nor forgiven Sir Brian for his outspoken remarks, and on March 15, 1961, he ousted the BTC chairman in favour of Dr Beeching, a member of the Stedeford Committee, who became Chairman on June 1, 1961. His task would be to simplify the organisation, oversee its final days, and implement the Stedeford Committee proposals.

Dr Beeching became Chairman of the BTC with a brief to implement the Stedeford recommendations. But his eyes would be closed to the country's broader transport needs. Railfotos.

Sir Brian was elevated to the House of Lords for his trouble, but he was greatly saddened by the collapse of the Commission. In May 1961 he undertook a farewell tour of the network and lingered awhile among the unfinished catenaries of the Euston-Liverpool/Manchester electrification scheme. To Sir Brian, who had defended the scheme to the bitter end, it must have been a sad and poignant moment. What really stung, leaving aside the political implications behind the move, was that Beeching was to receive a salary of £24,000 against the £10,000 paid to his predecessor.

Dr Beeching came to be vilified in the popular press as a cold and analytical accountant — an industrialist with a brief to destroy the railways. But, in reality, he was a scientist whose considerable intellect had aided his effortless rise through the ranks of ICI, Britain's most prestigious industrial concern.

Beeching was convinced that a detailed analysis of the railways' position would enable the losses of the Transport Commission to be turned into profits. Unfortunately, it would also be necessary to overturn the Commission's rather vague social obligations — which was exactly what the Government had in mind. To the Government, Beeching was the ideal appointee: an intellectual who could be relied upon to subject the railways to a rigorous statistical analysis, while ignoring the wider social aspects of the task.

The new Chairman rapidly appointed other private sector managers into the industry, including Philip Shirley, an Australian accountant from Unilever, and L H Williams, from Shell. The new regime set to work on a wide-ranging review of railway operations, producing a four-stage plan:

1) **A series of traffic studies to judge which services were viable.**

2) **Publication of the results.**

3) **Publication of Dr Beeching's own report.**

4) **The Government would be left to "reach its own conclusions".**

Cutbacks in investment, and a general feeling that the railways had little future, were already causing a knock-on effect throughout the industry. During a heavy fog on October 25, 1960, two loaded oil barges collided with the Severn Railway Bridge bringing the centre section down into the river — an event that could hardly be blamed on Marples. Such was the mood within the BTC at this critical time, however, that the bridge (due for upgrading as recently as 1959) was never repaired. It was destined to stand, useless and derelict until 1970, when the remains were demolished. Many other railway assets, some that had never been commissioned into service, were to share a similar fate.

An item of news that escaped widespread discussion in the general furore concerned the accident figures for 1961: 270,000 died or suffered serious injury on the roads while, on the railways, there was just a handful of casualties.

The objectors

There had been a number of obstacles in the path of earlier railway closures. One, although little more than a minor inconvenience, was occasionally embarrassing: the problem of protesters rooting up legislation from the Victorian era when, for one reason or another, the railway company of the day had been obliged to provide a railway service in perpetuity.

The other problem involved the TUCC inquiry procedure. True, only a handful of inquiries had actually found in favour of the protesters, but growing public resentment and increasingly sophisticated opposition might change the situation. If nothing else, concerted opposition might lead to future inquiries being drawn out for a considerable period, whereas the Government wanted the trains taken off, and the track removed, as quickly as possible. And if an inquiry found against closure, the Minister might even be put in the awkward position of having to overrule its findings. Legislation would be needed, and it arrived in the form of the 1962 Transport Act, which received the Royal Assent on August 1 that year.

The BTC was dissolved, and the railways were left in the hands of a British Railways Board, which was charged (amongst other things) with the task of eliminating the railway deficit. Generally speaking, the Board would function rather as the former Railway Executive had done, although the new legislation was framed with the intention of handing considerable extra powers to the Minister of Transport.

In keeping with the Government's intention to return the network to profitability, the railway rates and charges legislation was finally to be jettisoned completely in favour of a free-for-all, allowing the railways to tender for traffic on equal terms with the road hauliers.

The various capital liabilities of the BTC, standing by this time at about £2,000 million (£1,400 million as British Transport Stock), would be apportioned to the various boards that were to succeed the Commission, with the majority going to the railways. Of the debts apportioned to the Railways Board, around £400 million (representing half the modernisation capital) would be written off, another £400 million would continue as an interest-bearing loan, and the remaining £705 million (representing pre-modernisation debts) would enter a "suspense account". The Treasury hoped the money would remain "forgotten" only as long as the railways remained in debt, and that it might prove recoverable should the railway system show a profit in the future. It was a convenient skeleton for the Government to bring out of the cupboard and rattle at frequent intervals.

As an opening dowry for a reorganised and thoroughly demoralised Railways Board, the financial arrangements were hardly earth-shattering in their generosity, for the railways remained crippled by annual charges of almost £100 million.

The 1962 Act, like others before and since, covered a wide range of topics, but there were several disturbingly undemocratic aspects to the legislation. Various measures were taken to smooth the railway closure process and, predictably enough, all previous legislation that might conceivably hinder the process was repealed. But it was Section 56 of the Act that caused real consternation in railway circles, for this affected the Transport Users' Consultative Committees.

As we have seen, the Consultative Committees had never been very satisfactory bodies, but the 1962 Act sought to limit their powers still further. Since 1948, the area committees had held inquiries into the railway closure proposals put forward by the Transport Commission. Where a committee had come down in favour of a proposal, the judgment was usually confirmed by the Central Committee and the closure rapidly implemented. The area committees occasionally decided against closure, but they were usually overruled by the central body. In any event, the BTC was entitled to ignore all advice if it so wished, although this never occurred in practice. The system had worked (after a fashion) because the Transport Commission had put forward comparatively few closure proposals, and many of them had been quite justifiable, but the Government now intended to close a large proportion of the network. The new legislation promised a tightening of control over the entire procedure.

The committees were no longer to concern themselves with the wider social and strategic implications of closures (not that they ever had, of course), but with the simple question of "hardship" to individuals. The British Railways Board would put forward alternative road transport proposals and it was up to the objectors to prove that the new arrangements would be inadequate. The good news was that there was now a proper legal framework governing the advertising and implementation of the closure procedure, but the actual workings of the inquiries were considerably impaired.

There was to be no debate — something which was bound to be a little hard to enforce in a supposedly free country — and the committees had no power to make recommendations. They would report in future, not to the Central Transport Consultative Committee, but directly to the Minister of Transport. Where the previous arrangements had left something to be desired, the new consultation procedure was a sham and a travesty of democracy, for the TUCCs were empowered to submit a report, but they were instructed to ignore most of the available evidence.

The TUCCs were no longer to concern themselves with objections of a political or strategic nature, or those of holidaymakers (even though their patronage might constitute the major part of a line's traffic). Even the wider manifestations of hardship, such as the loss of property values to a town or community, would be unwelcome. The aim was simply to take submissions from those users of the line who lived or worked in its immediate vicinity.

The legal departments had worked long and hard to draft legislation to speed up the closure procedure, for the scale of the proposed closures was so vast that they could never have been implemented under the previous legislation. The intention was to keep discussion of financial figures well away from the TUCCs: in future, figures would only be supplied where committees requested them, and they would not be allowed to discuss them in public.

These provisions caused such disquiet that Mr Marples was forced to seek the backing of an outside expert. In August 1963, he invited Sir William Carrington, President of the Institute of Chartered Accountants, to comment on whether accounts should be provided to the Consultative Committees.

Sir William's general ruling was that the limited financial details were "appropriate for the purposes of the Consultative Committees", but he brought up many points of detail that are worth considering. It would not, he claimed, be wise to furnish TUCC inquiries with a detailed breakdown of income based upon the receipts of individual stations, because such figures might lead to inaccuracies. He recommended instead, that the estimate of income for a particular line should be based upon an extraordinarily complicated procedure.

During a census period of a week, the number of passengers joining and alighting from trains would be recorded at every station, converted into passenger-miles, and multiplied by the average fare. There was to be an additional safeguard for seasonal lines, where traffic would be measured at various times of year and "appropriately weighted in order to give the most reliable estimate". In the event, seasonal figures were never used to make adjustments of this kind, although they were sometimes provided separately to the TUCCs.

The great advantage to the Railways Board and the Government was that the figures effectively excluded any mention of contributory revenue (or the value of traffic passing from a branch line to the rest of the system) even though, as we have seen, it was of fundamental importance. It might be the case that almost all of the passengers boarding a branch line train would continue their journey on the main line but, with no mention of station receipts or contributory revenue, the TUCC would be unaware of this.

Sir William ruled that contributory revenue could only be a matter of "opinion or judgment". Whether he had been deliberately misled by the Minister, or had taken a unilateral decision to assist the Ministry of Transport in its plans, is not clear, for the contributory revenue of a given line was far from being just "a matter of opinion". Individual stations kept very accurate records of such things, and market research on a line-by-line basis would not have been difficult to arrange. In fact, the Railways Board knew in great detail the contributory revenue of particular lines. Before 1962, the Transport Commission had analysed traffic figures on threatened lines, identifying the "through traffic" component, and estimating how much of it would be lost after closure. Beeching himself was later to state that contributory revenue from through traffic varied between five per cent and 75 per cent of gross income.

The official view was that contributory revenue, although vital to any realistic judgment on the financial health and social importance of a given railway line, was outside the limited brief of the Consultative Committee inquiry procedure. It was not the committee's task to consider whether or not a line was financially viable, as this decision had already been taken. Why else would the Railways Board have chosen to withdraw the service? The task of the committees was simply to evaluate the hardship that might result from closure. Thus the TUCCs (and anyone else concerned with the inquiries) would have access only to the number of passengers carried in a typical week, and an "estimate" of the annual income based upon those figures. So complicated was the procedure that errors were bound to occur, and protesters were subsequently able to prove, on at least one occasion, that the number of passengers travelling between two stations had actually emerged as a negative figure!

Railway expenditure would be divided into three categories:

● **Movement expenses** — the cost of actually moving passengers from one point to another, including the cost of train crews, fuel, repairs and vehicle depreciation.

● **Terminal expenses** — the cost of providing stations, including wages and salaries of staff, repairs, heating, lighting etc.

● **Track and signalling** — not necessarily the total costs, but the cost of any additional signalling or track maintenance required solely for the service under review.

In addition to the "direct" costs described above, Sir William judged that the TUCCs should be made aware of any additional expenditure which might be required for renewals or maintenance during the five years following the inquiry, in the unlikely event of the line remaining open. This had been standard procedure for some time but, as an accountant, he must have realised that such figures were bound to give a false picture. Most heavy renewals on railway track or fixtures (such as stations, viaducts or tunnels) could be expected to have a working life of several decades. To provide these costs to the TUCCs within a "next five years" category, was to imply that such expenditure might be due every five years. Sir William Carrington's analysis of the figures was, in many ways, most unsatisfactory, but it provided the ammunition that Marples needed to silence his critics.

Fortunately, legislation could do nothing to silence public criticism, and Professor Hondelink, the United Nations railway expert, continued to battle away at a government that refused to heed his advice. The professor repeated his earlier message — that railway losses were mostly a result of top-heavy bureaucracy and poor management. Since nationalisation, the system had contracted, and the number of productive railwaymen had been reduced, yet headquarters staff had risen fourfold by 1962. The eradication of the BTC and cutbacks in the modernisation programme did nothing to stem the tide for, by 1965, there were nearly as many senior managers as there had been total headquarters staff three years before. It was all nonsense, of course: the sort of nonsense that pervaded the nationalised industries in the 1960s and '70s. Many of the clerks and managers, rather than looking for new traffic to improve the prospects for their industry, were involved solely with line closures. A number of them spent their working days massaging traffic figures in order to facilitate closure, and a more negative management post is hard to imagine.

According to Professor Hondelink, the losses on the branch lines were very small, and could be virtually eliminated with the application of a few economies. The Government, on the other hand, had put a great deal of effort into proving that railways would have to close, and proving that the remains of the system would be free to return to profitability when they did close.

There were no easy answers to the professor's arguments. Mr Marples, who was later to describe Professor Hondelink as a major thorn in his side, responded by instructing government and railway servants to avoid entering into discussion with him. Several attempts were made to discredit the Professor, not on academic or professional grounds where no fault could be found, but politically. Marples accused Hondelink of "going over to the Labour camp" through his association with the Labour Peer, Lord Stonham, and Labour MP Philip Noel-Baker, although the Professor had remained studiously neutral all along. Finally he was ignored altogether. Free speech could not be denied though, and in July 1962, Professor Hondelink rounded upon the Marples-Beeching plans in unequivocal style:

> Branch lines, wayside stations, even main lines and larger stations, have been deliberately starved of proper service to prepare them for closure and abandonment... the ever increasing rate of closures has now reached the stage where

partial and wholesale closures of certain main lines, including partial or total abandonment of some unremunerative passenger services, are planned...

No serious attempt is made to bring about the elimination of loss by improving operating methods, by meeting customers' needs, not necessarily with new equipment.

There was, he said, no evidence that closures had saved, or were likely to save, a penny. So complete was the legislation under the 1962 Act, and so incomplete the financial figures supplied under the Carrington formula, that even that most conservative of bodies, the Central Transport Consultative Committee, felt moved to sound a note of caution:

...there is an urgent need for the study of overall transport costs, including social costs (such as congestion, accidents and health services) for all forms of transport, and this should be published. The effect of subsidies, open and hidden, may be giving a completely false picture of the costs of various forms of transport...

...the negative policy of closing down uneconomic facilities, while contributing a small financial saving, is not the panacea it has sometimes been made out to be. Each closure diverts some business onto the roads.

That, of course, was the whole intention of the plan, but the change of heart from the CTCC had come too late, for its warning was not published until after the arrival of the Beeching Report.

Meanwhile, events began to move with bewildering speed. In the summer of 1962, Dr Beeching completed Stage Two of his plan and published maps indicating traffic density throughout the railway system. There were few surprises.

The unions

Many years later, the National Union of Railwaymen was to agree that its opposition to the Beeching proposals had been both ineffectual and lacking in direction.

That the main railway union mounted no serious opposition either before or after publication of the Beeching Report is difficult to understand, for between nationalisation and the Beeching cataclysm, more than 174,000 jobs had been lost. Branch line closures had proceeded without demur from the unions — perhaps they had accepted those BTC promises at face value: that "pruning" really would promote vigorous growth elsewhere. It was not until political events began to take a serious turn in 1959-60 that the NUR eventually established a Closure of Branch Lines Sub-Committee to deal with the matter, but even then the union took no effective action. Reports from local branch level continued to suggest that there was little point in opposing closures, for it was felt that the proposals were largely justified.

Whether by accident or design, the much more intensive Beeching plans came to affect the less affluent areas of the country first, with Scotland being particularly hard hit. When the railways had been reorganised in 1921, Scotland had not been given a statutory company of its own. The stated reason was that Scotland, weighed down by the sparsely populated Highlands region, was simply unable to support a railway company. As a result, the country was divided up between two comparatively wealthy English concerns, the LNER and the LMSR. Nationalisation was to change all that, creating a Scottish Region and, after the arrival of the Conservatives in 1953, the fundamentally unprofitable Scottish railways bore the brunt of the cutbacks while the wealthy South remained relatively secure.

One of Dr Beeching's first moves on becoming Chairman of the Commission was to examine the loss-making Scottish lines. A traffic survey was quickly conducted and, within a couple of months, the figures were released: of 2,750 daily trains in Scotland, no fewer than 2,000 were apparently running at a loss.

As a direct result, management drew up plans to withdraw 260 services and close seven branch lines outright on November 6, 1961. In the event, union pressure secured a stay of execution, but the Scottish railwaymen were well aware that they had won no more than a temporary reprieve, and delegates of both ASLEF and the NUR decided to lobby Parliament, spreading the word to their brothers in the South along the way. And so it was that about 100 railwaymen made the long journey to London, linking up with others from Lancashire, the North-East, and Wales as they went.

Astoundingly, on reaching their respective union headquarters in the capital, they were given a less than enthusiastic welcome. As the skirl of bagpipes could be heard outside NUR headquarters, only two members of the Executive Committee bothered to greet their members, and they were both docked an hour's pay for their trouble! The ASLEF delegation fared even worse: on arriving at their union headquarters, the members found the building locked against them.

Although the delegations were eventually given a warm welcome at Westminster by Hugh Gaitskell and other MPs, the affair was to do untold damage to the prospects of a united union campaign against railway closures. Whether Beeching had deliberately instigated cuts in the provinces first is not clear, but the effect was to split the unions.

In the South, where unemployment stood at less than two per cent and railway closures were expected to have little impact, the membership and officials of the unions showed little concern. In Scotland, Wales, and the less affluent areas of England, the impact was immediate and very serious, but the executive committees in London were unable to decide whether to take action or not. The inevitable result was no action at all and the unions dithered, wasting a rare opportunity to mount a concerted campaign.

By April 1962, details of some of the English railway closures became known and the unions, still prevaricating over how best to react, were caught largely unawares. It was not until June 1962 that the publicity machine swung slowly into action, dispatching circulars to branch offices, publishing leaflets, and organising meetings up and down the country. Even at this late stage, firm union action might have had the desired effect, but the campaign was lacklustre and ineffective, against a well-honed Railways Board publicity machine.

Meanwhile, the railway workshops, which had mostly done rather well out of modernisation, were feeling the pinch. As many as 11,000 redundancies had been envisaged as early as 1959, but three years later it became clear that Beeching intended to go a good deal further. A statement was issued by the management on September 19 detailing the revised plans. Many of the work-shops would be closed, others would lose departments, and the whole programme was to be carried through in just three years.

The railway unions now felt they were in receipt of the whole picture, but still they failed to organise any effective opposition. The NUR, with assets of more than £6.5 million, had spent just £7,547 campaigning against the closure plans. The only direct action proved to be a one-day national strike over the workshop closure proposals on October 3, 1962 — the first national stoppage since 1926. It was an ideal opportunity to rally the public to the railways' cause and fight the cuts, the implications of which were still not widely understood. But little was done. Only in South Wales did NUR men spend the day canvassing — the result understandably lacking the impact of a nationwide campaign.

In any event, Beeching swiftly defused the situation by making concessions on redundancy payments, and the half-hearted campaign against the closure policy rapidly degenerated into local discussions over the number of redundancies and their terms.

According to the NUR, the Railway Chairman "leaned over backwards" in his desire to reach a satisfactory compromise. And well he might, for had the unions taken concerted action and gained the sympathy of the general public, the future of the whole closure programme might have been put in doubt. As it was, the redundancy terms were unprecedented in their generosity and the union voice was effectively silenced.

So satisfied were the unions with the result of the negotiations, that in December 1962 the NUR Executive Committee voted unanimously to wind up the campaign:

> There can be no doubt whatever that the campaign has been one of the most successful the union has ever undertaken, but we feel that the time has arrived

for meetings at Executive Committee level to cease as from December 31, 1962.

It was a disastrous decision. Three months later the Beeching Report appeared and the union was, once again, caught quite unawares. All the NUR succeeded in doing was to reopen the debate over workshop closures, which proved a waste of effort for the newspapers were engrossed in the details of the Beeching Report. Had the unions spent the previous three years preparing a measured response to the Railway Board's proposals, and launched them on the media at the right psychological moment, they might have dealt the Beeching regime a devastating blow.

The most poignant side to the affair was that the South Wales NUR branch, which had worked alone to publicise the cutbacks during the strike, had made a unilateral decision to continue the fight. Convinced that a cataclysm was about to wreak havoc on the industry, the little branch ignored the platitudes from headquarters and fought on. In February 1963 (just before publication of the report) it canvassed other branches and lobbied MPs at Westminster with a measure of success. There was a sting in the tail, though, for when General Secretary Sidney Greene heard of their campaign, he reminded the South Wales men that the Executive Committee decision in December meant they would be unable to charge expenses to branch funds. It was a petty, officious and vindictive move that ultimately led to a debate at the union's AGM, and a vote in favour of continuing the campaign. But this was in July 1963, three months after publication of the report... there was little point.

In any event, the union response had already collapsed into farce. The NUR rejected the Beeching Report outright and called for strike action, a move that met with a positive response from ASLEF and the Confederation of Shipbuilding and Engineering Unions. At a meeting between Mr Marples, the TUC and the rail unions in April 1963, the Minister of Transport offered no concessions, leaving the ball in the NUR court. The Executive met later the same day and voted in favour of a three-day strike in May, but ASLEF was unable to agree, for the strike would have fallen during its Annual Assembly.

Once again, Beeching headed off the strike threat with concessions on redundancy terms. Down-graded staff would no longer be obliged to accept a cut in wages; men between the ages of 60 and 65 would have the option of retirement on almost full pay; and for those who were to be asked to relocate, there would be cheaper lodgings and free travel. The Railways Board had split the unions branch against branch, outmanoeuvred them, and finally bought their patronage for a handful of silver.

On May 9, 1963, the unions agreed to lay aside the strike weapon. The NUR continued a low key campaign, however, and a modest sum was put aside for the production of leaflets in 1963, but according to the official history of the union, the campaign lacked conviction:

In South Wales, the NUR men would be well aware of the often high cost of maintaining railways which crossed difficult terrain, and this may explain their more astute perception of the scale of the Beeching threat. These flashbacks to 1957 show Clydach, on the not untypical line from Merthyr which ran along the heads of the valleys to Abergavenny Junction. I L Wright.

The most popular [leaflet], *The Mis-shaping of British Railways… Retort* **[a pun on Beeching's** *The Reshaping of British Railways — Report*], **made clear the vast areas of Britain which would be denuded of railways if the report was implemented. But it was a slim leaflet and not a substantial, closely argued publication detailing a positive alternative… the kind of case likely to inform and educate influential opinion in the Labour Party.**

Beeching had achieved an overwhelming victory at the expense of just a single day's strike action. But the cost of the generous redundancy package and the relocation agreements was to be a high one in cash terms. As a result, many of the savings forecast under the Beeching plans were never realised, for when closures were implemented, staff were simply transferred elsewhere. The unions had won a few concessions, but Beeching had brought his plans through almost unscathed. The country was about to pay the price.

The management

The railway management had surprisingly little warning of the impending cuts. Morale during the late 1950s had reached an all-time high, and it was not until the virtual cancellation of the modernisation plans, and the arrival of Dr Beeching in 1961, that doubts began to creep in. The real shock was delayed until April 1962 when Beeching chaired the senior managers' conference in York for the first time, and outlined his plans for the industry. As public criticism began to mount, a defensive wall of silence descended around the Railways Board. It was not to be lifted for more than a decade. Few were willing to speak out, and when they did, it was generally in the most guarded of tones:

There are those who feel that these losses need not have been incurred after 1952, at any rate to the extent they have and, if this is right, to judge all the parts of the service now on the basis of the losses being incurred is open to question.

A J Pearson, Assistant General Manager, London Midland Region

Such criticism hardly amounted to a forthright condemnation of the Beeching regime but Pearson, like many others, was bound by loyalty to an industry to which he had devoted his working life. To speak out would only have meant dismissal, controversy, and untold damage to the railways.

According to the *Railway Gazette*, the Board was, by July 1962, experiencing a "grand resignation" of experienced managers. The result was an influx of outsiders: civil servants, army officers, industrialists and accountants. Pearson stayed to see it through, as did Gerard Fiennes, one of the best administrators in the industry during a period when the quality of management left much to be desired. It has been said that regional managers had kept their most able men in the provinces to avoid losing them to the BTC — whatever the reason, the higher echelons of the organisation were starved of experienced railwaymen, but they were desperately needed to balance the views of Beeching's army of outsiders.

Gerard Fiennes, who displayed a unique blend of common sense, business guile, and plain honesty, did more to salvage the position of the railways than almost anyone else in the Beeching era. Unfortunately, he was a little too honest with his views, having a perfectly natural tendency to condemn poor management and quixotic business practice. It was later to cost him his job.

British Railways managers, though not necessarily in full agreement with the Beeching philosophy, had enough work on their hands allocating a trickle of investment cash towards the inter-city services, without having to worry about the branches and the secondary lines.

According to Fiennes, General Manager of the Western Region at the time, the crucial challenge facing the railways was to improve the reliability and speed of main line services in order to compete with road traffic. He was probably right, for if the railways had lost the propaganda battle on the trunk lines as well as the branches, they might have failed to survive the 1960s at all. This view was supported by many within the industry: the branch lines would be sacrificed in order to satisfy the Ministry, but once the minor services had been eliminated, the railways would be free to concentrate on the trunk lines, where investment was desperately needed.

The branches were a social and political problem — a problem for the Government to solve. Some genuinely agreed with Beeching, but others saw the closure plans as a necessary evil to take pressure off the rest of the system, where competing road and air services were making a real impact.

That the railways had a task on their hands can be gleaned from the figures in Fiennes's own region: the fastest scheduled service from Paddington to Bristol before the war had been 105 minutes. It was not until 1954, nine years after the war, that the Castle Class locomotives were able to return even to that pre-war schedule but, with road traffic accelerating year by year, the Western region needed to cut minutes off the schedules, and it needed to do it very rapidly.

The early Warship Class diesel locomotives, introduced in 1959, cut the journey time to 100 minutes but, lacking power and reliability, were unable to maintain the pace. The following year the schedule was back to 105 minutes, and in 1961 it receded even further. It was not until 1971 that the fastest schedule was reduced to 100 minutes on a permanent basis.

Progress might have been slow, but the improved services began to pay dividends. The number of passengers carried in the region had fallen from 112 million in 1948 to a low of 104 million in 1960, but rose thereafter to 110 million in 1965.

As we have seen, the plunge into deficit in the late 1950s was largely due to a loss of freight traffic, but there were particular problems with the performance of the Western and London Midland regions. While other areas were gradually improving their traffic figures and reducing staff, the Western and London Midland were simply failing to do so, and performing badly as a result.

In the final analysis, this was the only justification the Government had had for cancelling the modernisation plans and initiating the chain of events that led to the Beeching Report. If Fiennes had pushed up the traffic figures with little more than hard work, a flair for publicity and rescheduled services, to what extent might traffic have increased had the BTC investment programme been allowed to run its course?

By the end of 1962 the writing was on the wall. The Transport Commission had gone, and the new Railways Board was preparing to push through the most savage round of cuts the industry had ever seen. Ironically, the Conservative Party was in difficulties too, for the economic boom of the late 1950s had proved short-lived, and the electorate was restless and ready for a change of Government. Within a matter of months, the Party was hit by the damaging Profumo affair that put paid to any lingering hopes of re-election. To some extent the fortunes of the Conservatives were set to mirror the decline they had so carefully engineered for the railways: it was a wicked irony.

In October 1962, Beeching addressed the Institute of Directors at the Albert Hall and outlined his plans. Even in Parliament, the war of words appeared to have been won for, during a debate in November 1962, there was considerable agreement with the Beeching philosophy. Perhaps the railways really were a relic of the horse-and-cart age; the stopping trains a ludicrous, outmoded form of transport.

The 1962 deficit had topped £160 million after interest, and Beeching was promising to sweep away the dead wood and balance the books. All would be revealed in the third stage of his plan, *The Reshaping of British Railways.*

6.
The Beeching Report
1963-64

Dr Beeching's report has proved to be the most staggering report ever presented to any government... He has closed the railways. If I stopped a train, I would be fined £5. Dr Beeching stops a third of the railway system and gets a cheque for £24,000... On the law of averages, as I should be fined £5, the Minister should be deported.

T W Jones, MP for Meirionnydd

ON March 27, 1963, Dr Beeching released the long-awaited report and traffic survey maps, entitled The Reshaping of British Railways. *The report set out to prove in the most straightforward terms exactly where the money was going, and went on to provide a few answers. According to the report, freight services would eventually produce a healthy return after substantial investment and reorganisation, but passenger services had little future. They were, Beeching concluded, bound to be squeezed almost to death between road transport (where short journeys were concerned) and the domestic airlines (for longer distance travel). Considerable emphasis was placed on the inadequacies of stopping and branch line services, and the figures were distorted so as to make individual lines appear quite uneconomic, and ripe for closure.*

The rail lobby could do little to dispute many of the figures in the report, for there was little alternative evidence. Fortunately, Dr Beeching made a serious tactical error by including an "example", demonstrating the income and expenditure for a hypothetical branch line.

It soon emerged that many of the genuine branch lines were costing considerably more to run than Doctor Beeching's hypothetical example, which suggested there there was plenty of scope for economies, and the pro-rail lobby proceeded to dismantle the report's assumptions — with a reasonable degree of success. All the same, the closure programme began to gather pace but, in the run-up to the 1964 general election, Harold Wilson, leader of the opposition Labour Party, promised to halt major closures. Within weeks he had been elected.

* * *

The introduction to the Reshaping Report made it quite clear that Dr Beeching did not intend (nor indeed did he have the power) to make final judgments. The Chairman of the Board had investigated and analysed every detail of railway operation, and it was now for the Government to decide whether to accept the doctor's medicine:

> Throughout these investigations and the preparations of this report the British Railways Board has had it in mind that its duty is to employ the assets vested in it, and develop or modify them, to the best advantage of the nation. Also, because the ultimate choice... must be made by the nation, it is a basic responsibility of the Board to provide, as objectively and comprehensively as possible, information which makes clear the range and nature of choice.

This paragraph, from the foreword of the Reshaping Report, appears to be in sharp contradiction to the following extract which appears on page two: "It is, of course, the responsibility of the British Railways Board so to shape and operate the railways as to make them pay..." Which route would Beeching follow? Would he objectively provide information to allow the nation to make a fair and equitable decision? Or was he bound by his terms of reference to produce a railway system that returned a profit above and beyond all other considerations — or even to cut the network to the point at which it would cease to pose a threat to road interests?

There was nothing wrong with the objective of returning the network to profitability, but it soon emerged that the report was really little more than a collection of figures, shamefully massaged to provide supposedly convincing evidence as to the overwhelming size and unprofitability of the network. It was, however, well written and concise in its arguments, and even Professor Hondelink was moved to concede that point:

> I have now digested the Beeching Report. My comment is as follows: Analysis clear, concise and capable; the accountant's work well done; the conclusions rough and unrealistic; the proposed implementation ruthless to the point of being suicidal...

The problem lay in Beeching's terms of reference, for he had not been asked to look into the social and economic value of railways, but simply to find a means of returning the industry to profit as quickly as possible. He might also have been instructed to err towards closure and retrenchment, for that was the thrust of the Reshaping Report's arguments. The report completely ignored various cost-saving measures that had been under consideration both at home and abroad for several decades; measures that might have turned marginal lines into profitable concerns. This was the ammunition with which the increasingly vociferous rail lobby was later to base its counterattack.

The Reshaping Report was constructed around a series of passenger and freight traffic surveys that were claimed as the first analysis of costs and income on a line-by-line basis. This was largely untrue, for the BTC had kept accurate records since the early 1950s; in fact, there was nothing new in any of Dr Beeching's schemes, for the handful of positive ideas in the report had all been included in the BTC modernisation plan of 1954. It was really only the clear and concise nature of the report that genuinely broke new ground.

Many proposals were perfectly reasonable, such as the necessity to move away from unprofitable wagonload and freight sundries traffic, and concentrate instead on train-loads, and container traffic... the so-called "liner train" concept, for which Dr Beeching had developed a particular enthusiasm.

Wagonload traffic had been fundamentally uneconomic for years. Wagons were picked up, shunted, carried to the next yard, shunted again, lost in sidings, rediscovered and finally delivered, after a long and expensive passage through the railway system. It had been estimated that freight locomotives spent half their working lives shunting and the other half hauling an average of just 20 wagons between marshalling yards. Someone had even proved that it was quicker to walk across London with a parcel than to send it by rail.

Where passenger services were concerned, several sectors were singled out for particular criticism — commuter services, seasonal traffic, stopping trains, and the branch lines. The prognosis for passenger revenue was a gloomy one for, according to the report, local traffic would continue to be lost to the roads, and long-distance traffic would be eroded by the airlines.

As expected, it was the minor passenger services that were to bear the brunt of the cuts. But closing branch lines was politically a far more sensitive issue than reorganising freight traffic, and the Reshaping Report went to considerable lengths to prove that the branch lines were fundamentally uneconomic... and to counter the arguments that diesel multiple units, railbuses and light railway operating methods might halt the decline. The analysis relating to the lines the Government had already chosen to axe left much to be desired.

Between 1960, when the first data had been collected, and 1963 when the report appeared, many lines had already closed, and it was clear that many others were a long way from profitability. The intention, however, was to provide an overwhelming case for the closure of a far greater mileage. Of a total route mileage of 17,800, the report concluded that around 5,000 miles should be closed to passengers, together with 2,363 stations, many on lines that would remain open to through traffic. And this was only the beginning, for Beeching promised a second report at a later date that would make further closures inevitable.

Almost a third of the national rail system and one third of the stations would disappear. With a few notable exceptions, almost every branch line was to close, leaving most of Devon, Lincolnshire, Cumbria, Wales, and the Highlands of Scotland, completely deprived of railway passenger services. A handful of trunk lines were to close as well — notably the Waverley route between Edinburgh and Carlisle, the Settle & Carlisle, the Great Central linking London and Sheffield, and the Somerset & Dorset between Bournemouth and Bath.

The report represented the most dramatic and far-reaching manipulation of the British transport system since the arrival of the railways more than 100 years before. How, then, would it be put into practice — against the will of the unions, the local authorities and (to a great extent) the public at large?

Passenger receipts quoted in the report were for individual stations, based on records kept throughout 1960. They appeared to represent a fairly accurate assessment of income. There was, however, a serious drawback to using such figures as a basis for determining the viability of a station, for income was based solely upon receipts for tickets **issued** at any particular place. The value of tickets issued at a holiday destination would, naturally enough, represent only a small proportion of the total value of the traffic flow to that point. The same was true for any station that tended to receive traffic rather than produce it. As Professor Hondelink pointed out, such a method would have rendered the summit station on the Snowdon Mountain Railway a substantial loss-maker, yet it was precisely this destination that made the line viable.

The result, when applied to the national rail network, was seriously to distort the passenger figures. But it was a distortion that should have shown up in the accompanying figures indicating the density of passenger traffic on a line-by-line basis. The fact that it did not, was due to another distortion built into the passenger density figures — they were collected over a single week in April 1961 — two weeks **after** the Easter holiday weekend. April was hardly mid-winter, but then neither was it of any great significance as a time for holiday or general leisure travel. Branch lines to holiday resorts, such as Skegness in Lincolnshire, carried a considerable volume of traffic throughout July and August — a volume of traffic so intense that closure of the line would be bound to create chaos, albeit for just a few months of the year. But the number of tickets **issued** at Skegness was comparatively small and, in April, the traffic volume was fairly low. The result was a major distortion of the facts.

Innocently or otherwise, the figures had been manipulated in such a way as to benefit the lines that the British Railways Board intended to retain, and against the lines it wished to close. Yet the Beeching Report was a document on which many historic (and quite irreversible) decisions were to be taken. It was no less than a scandal that these decisions would be reached on the sketchiest of information.

These in-house traffic figures were of the utmost importance, for there was little alternative evidence for the Transport Users' Consultative Committees to consider when a line came up for closure. Of course, bearing in mind that the Board had already decided to close a third of the system, any move that reduced the theoretical receipts of the least productive third could only strengthen the case for closure. In the event, that is exactly the way it worked. With a collection of statistics and graphs, the Board was able to demonstrate that one third of the stations contributed less than one per cent of the total passenger receipts and even half the stations contributed only two per cent. Similarly, one third of the route miles carried only one per cent of the passengers, and one third of the freight route miles carried one per cent of the freight.

These apparently damning figures provided a clear message for the press, and were much quoted at the time. It was very difficult for anyone to argue for the retention of 5,000 miles of track and 2,363 stations that contributed only one per cent to the railway's revenue. In reality, the situation was quite different — but there were no other figures available. Besides the distortions already mentioned, the report failed to look at the actual costs relating to individual stations: many of those on that unlucky third of the network were unstaffed halts that may have contributed little revenue, but they cost even less in upkeep. Many other lightly used stations could, equally, have been de-staffed to achieve significant savings. Today, such flimsy evidence would be torn to shreds at the inquiry stage, but in 1963 there was little organised opposition to rail closures.

Having "proved" that a third of the network was generating virtually nothing in the way of revenue, the Board needed to show exactly what the losses were on particular lines in hard cash terms. This was a little more difficult for, in glaring contrast to road transport, an allowance had to be made for all manner of expenses such as track maintenance, stations, and signalling costs. There was an additional complication where freight or through passenger traffic confused the picture, but for the purposes of comparing the viability of minor branch lines, these components were dismissed.

The report provided vital statistics from a few real lines, together with the infamous maps that showed where the losses were being made, but Beeching also decided to include a theoretical demonstration to prove that diesel multiple units and branch lines were simply unviable. He must have regretted it the day the report was published and in quiet contemplative moments for the rest of his life, for certain of his theoretical assumptions were later borrowed and used to some effect by the pro-rail lobby.

The report offered as an example a hypothetical single-track branch line, with stations at two-and-a-half mile intervals and a service of one train per hour in each direction between 7am and 10pm. There were rather a lot of stations and, as the hypothetical hourly service was assumed to run seven days a week, it already sounded pretty uneconomic, as few rural areas would have demanded such a generous schedule.

Nevertheless, the costs were broken down as follows: track maintenance and signalling costs would account for £58 per mile per week, and the stations (presumably staffed) would account for another £19, giving a total fixed weekly expenditure in the region of £77 per mile. It is worth recalling that less than a decade before, the Transport Commission had replied to the claims of the Rural Transport Improvement Bill's supporters by giving a figure of £300 per mile per year for maintenance, or just under £6 per week!

Then there were the train movement expenses to consider: steam-hauled trains (at the rate of 15s (75p) per mile) were calculated to cost in the region of £168 per track-mile per week, and a diesel multiple unit service (at 4s (20p) to 6s (30p) per mile) was reckoned to cost between £45 and £67. On these figures, the most economic rail service would cost £122 to £144 per mile per week, and with revenue at 2d (less than 1p) per passenger mile, would need to carry 15,000 to 17,000 passengers per week to break even. Naturally, the Board chose the higher figure when summing up, although it did make the concession that, with the addition of profitable freight traffic, this hypothetical line might break even at lower traffic levels.

For comparison, the Board considered the economics of a bus service that might operate economically for about £28 per mile per week... or less than a quarter of the rail cost. The evidence appeared to be overwhelmingly in favour of road transport, for the Beeching Report claimed that a bus service would make a profit carrying fewer than 3,500 passengers per week.

At this point, the Board betrayed a little too much of its enthusiasm for road transport and suggested that the bus service might run even **more** economically with a two-hourly schedule. Almost unbelievably, it failed to provide the figures for a two hourly train schedule by way of comparison. If it had, it would have become clear that the diesel multiple unit could cover **all** of the inflated costs carrying some 12,000 to 13,000 passengers. And with the inclusion of some strategic station and signalling economies, the railway might have broken even at as low a figure as 8,000 passengers per week; even less where freight traffic was available to share the costs.

Indeed, if full maintenance costs were covered by other traffic, the hypothetical rural passenger service would prove economic carrying just 2,700 passengers and, taking into account the benefits of contributory revenue, it becomes clear that the line might even provide a small return at these low levels of passenger use.

But what of the diesel railbus, a vehicle that had been in operational service for several years by this time? Beeching dismissed the railbus in a single paragraph, claiming that the vehicles cost 3/- (15p) per mile to operate, and provided no particular advantages over cheaper road vehicles. However, elsewhere in the report were the figures for the Gleneagles-Comrie line in Scotland, where a railbus had been operating for some time at a movement cost of 2s 4d (11.5p) per mile. According to the Beeching Report, expenses amounted to no less than ten times the earnings of the line: but a closer look at the figures revealed a different story.

Despite carrying an average of only five passengers per train, the contributory revenue generated by the line effectively boosted income to the point where the railbus covered all movement and terminal expenses. Mile for mile, the Comrie branch line railbus cost half as much as a diesel multiple unit and rather less than a road vehicle.

Dr Beeching had tried to prove that a railway needed to carry about 17,000 passengers a week to break even — but he proved nothing of the kind. The reality was nearer 8,000 passengers, and often much fewer.

Of course, such arguments would be academic when a bus service could operate at a profit with just a handful of passengers. But could it? Would all the ex-railway passengers actually transfer to the new bus service? What allowance had the Board made for road repair costs, environmental damage, accidents, and all the other hidden road transport costs?

In fact, no allowance at all had been made. And it was not an oversight, but a whitewash, for the Beeching Report was compiled in order to "prove" that minor railway lines were fundamentally uneconomic; any fair comparison with road transport would have damaged the case.

Some months after publication of the Beeching Report, a private study was conducted into one of its intended victims, the branch between Watford and St Albans, which bore many similarities to Dr Beeching's hypothetical branch line. Traffic was difficult to predict without access to figures, but "reliable sources" suggested a total of some 7,200 to 9,200 passengers a week.

On the Railway Board's own figures, total annual expenditure on the line amounted to £41,236. However, the study concluded that a few sensible economies would result in a saving of £14,950 a year, leaving an expenditure of £26,286. If revenue was then based on a more realistic $2^1/_2$d per mile (rather than 2d as suggested in the report), income would just top expenditure at £26,364. Clearly, the line **could** have been made self-supporting, even ignoring the contribution made by freight traffic. Whatever the true economic position, the challenge by the rail lobby was successful, and the Watford to St Albans branch was one of the lucky few to survive the Beeching era.

The veritable whirlwind of facts and figures was of crucial importance, for with the Railway Board's conclusion that even a single-track branch line might require as many as 17,000 passengers per week to stay afloat (combined with its avowed intention to return to profitability), more than half the system was potentially at risk. In the passenger census week, ending April 23, 1961, only the major trunk lines had carried more than 17,000 passengers. On the Board's figures, it appeared as though cutting a third of the system was quite a generous compromise.

The Beeching Report was instigated with the sole intention of eliminating the railway operating deficit. It was a cold, and ultimately futile, exercise in purely theoretical accountancy.

Had the Beeching Report been produced as part of a wider evaluation of future transport needs, the result would have been much kinder to the railways. For instance, there was no account taken of where traffic that was forced off the railways would actually go. What problems would rail closures create in terms of road congestion? What damage would be caused to the economic development of hard-hit regions? Most of north Devon, Lincolnshire, Wales, and large areas of the Scottish Highlands would be deprived of rail transport: what would be the economic and social cost to these regions? Clearly this was someone else's headache. Most critically of all, the report ignored the possibility that the closure of branch lines (and the consequent loss of contributory revenue) might damage the viability of the lines that remained.

There was little discussion of future transport needs. In what areas was road traffic likely to reach saturation point? Nowhere in the report was the future of the private car questioned: on the contrary, there was a clear assumption that the volume of road traffic would continue to rise — presumably indefinitely.

The report did grudgingly accept that commuter services were essential in and around London, Glasgow, Edinburgh, Newcastle, Manchester, Liverpool, Leeds, Birmingham and Cardiff. But accepting that commuter services were essential to Britain's nine most important cities was tantamount to accepting that these cities were already saturated with road traffic (as indeed they were). And if the Beeching Report really had reached such a conclusion, why was there no discussion on the future of public transport around other important centres, such as Bristol, Plymouth, Southampton or Sheffield?

In other areas, too, the report's arguments were sadly lacking. Holiday traffic, particularly during the peak periods of July and August, had long been seen as a lucrative sideline for the railways. It was a traffic for which they were ideally suited — large numbers of people, travelling over long distances, and generally moving in the same direction. But there had been a steady decline for a number of years, brought about by changing holiday patterns and the increasing popularity of the private car. The Beeching Report compared traffic for each of the four summer months of 1961 with the average winter figure:

Winter Average	100 per cent
June 1961	118 per cent
July 1961	147 per cent
August 1961	143 per cent
September 1961	121 per cent

Once again, the way the statistics had been presented was grossly unfair, for they related to traffic on the entire railway system. The seasonal traffic increase on branch lines to holiday destinations would have been far greater than the figures suggest. Taking figures from the **whole system** to calculate seasonal fluctuations, yet judging individual holiday lines on the basis of passenger receipts during one solitary week in April, would clearly make it easier to write off seaside branches.

Many lines received an influx of trade during July and August that exceeded their winter receipts many times over, but the Beeching Report had neatly sidestepped this inconvenience by presenting the figures in an underhand manner. Railway lines that were profitable for just two months of the year may have deserved to close — but they were never given a fair trial.

As far as the main lines were concerned, the report accepted and welcomed the fact that holiday traffic could help to fill service trains. But service trains, if properly scheduled and advertised, should already have been filled close to capacity, and from that viewpoint additional holiday traffic (where it required extra capacity) was seen as a liability.

There appeared to be some justification for this view, for in 1959 it was discovered that out of 30,000 coaches, only 18,500 vehicles were used for express services and just 5,500 of these were utilised on a daily basis. Of the remaining 13,000 coaches, 2,000 were found to have left the depot on no more than ten occasions in the entire year. It was an accountant's nightmare, and (on paper at least) it was easily cured.

The seasonal peak would be "controlled" by the imposition of compulsory reservation schemes and selective fare increases. Beeching reckoned that, by adopting such a policy, it would be possible to scrap 6,000 coaches, at a saving of £3.4 million a year, against a loss in revenue of £500,000. But, according to at least one authority, these figures were quite wrong. Not only was the cost of maintaining 6,000 coaches actually about £2.7 million, but this was only an **average** figure, and included average maintenance and depreciation charges. The true cost of maintaining 6,000 elderly carriages that left the depot only occasionally, and were already fully depreciated, was really minimal. It would have been more prudent to retain the carriages until they were life-expired, and then decide whether the seasonal traffic justified purchasing replacement vehicles.

In the event, despite scrapping 15,000 passenger coaches between 1961 and 1966, the railways' total maintenance and depreciation bill increased by £13.75 million in the same period. Disposal of 6,000 carriages had lost the Railways Board at least £500,000 in annual seasonal revenue and saved absolutely nothing. And what of the displaced passengers? Probably, although the report ignored this point, they went out and bought a car.

In 1963, the motor car seemed to herald a new age of personal mobility and, as far as the railway's passenger receipts were concerned, the motor car was clearly identified as the villain of the piece.

According to the authors of the Reshaping Report, the railways were caught in a pincer movement between road transport and the airlines. They observed that, in the United States, "the process is almost complete". The assumption was that Britain's domestic airlines would be left with a virtual monopoly over long-distance traffic, as had happened in America:

> On the Scottish routes, air makes quite serious inroads into the loading of day trains, and will continue to do so. Even though trains may be speeded up, they will not match city-to-city transit times by air over such a distance, and erosion of daytime rail traffics between London and Scotland will probably continue to the point where some trains will have to be withdrawn.

Certainly the railways had much to fear from the airlines at the time, but the report made no attempt to examine air terminal and flight path congestion — or the road congestion between airport and city centre — that would inevitably follow such a capitulation. In the event, British European Airways made a loss of about £1 million on domestic services in 1963-64, and by 1966 losses had risen to £1.6 million, pushed up by the belated electrification of the London to Manchester railway. Ironically, the railway modernisation scheme had snatched 30 per cent of the air traffic overnight. By the early 1970s the electric trains were running through to Glasgow and, a few years later, the 125mph High Speed Train was stealing back air traffic on the Edinburgh route. Although domestic flight passenger volumes rose by 14 per cent a year between 1956 and 1966,

The bus network was dense... but services were not forced to be frequent...

The High Speed Train was a crucial weapon for BR in its battle with both the airlines and in gaining a bigger advantage over road journey times. A diverted HST is pictured on the Leamside line, south of Newcastle, with Penshaw Monument in the background. This line's future was uncertain at the time of writing but part of it was among routes being evaluated for a Metro link to Sunderland. Neville Stead.

there followed years of stagnation — largely because the railways had introduced competitive technology. And, in 1963, Beeching knew perfectly well that such developments were in the pipeline. Not only did the airlines fail to attract the bulk of the long-distance business, but (in the Britain of the time, at least) it was a comparatively unprofitable traffic which perhaps had more to do with feeding the international routes out of Heathrow than providing a real alternative to rail.

For shorter journeys, and journeys of any kind in rural areas, the Beeching Report viewed the motor bus as an excellent form of transport:

> With the exception of northern Scotland and parts of central Wales, most areas of the country are already served by a network of bus services more dense than the network of rail services which will be withdrawn, and in the majority of cases these buses already carry the major proportion of local traffic.

The bus network was certainly dense — as outlined in the maps thoughtfully provided with the report, which indicated an impressive spider's web of bus routes embracing the country far more thoroughly than the railways had ever done. What the report failed to observe was that many of the bus routes it had so dutifully reproduced saw only a handful of buses a day. Some had only a solitary weekly bus, and there were a few on which services disappeared altogether in the winter months. Another point the report's authors could have made was that the future of the bus network was intimately related to the future of the motor car. Any rise in the level of road congestion would affect bus travellers just as it would effect those with private cars. But the report glossed over problems on the roads, remarking that "road congestion is being reduced in many places".

And, in a magnanimous gesture, Dr Beeching even made it clear that he would be handing the bus companies a little bonus:

> Taken as a whole they have enough spare capacity to absorb the traffic which will be displaced from the railways... and which will provide a very welcome addition to the revenue of the bus operators.

Finally, and most damning of all, the report overstretched its brief and advocated a degree of road construction:

> In parts of Scotland, in particular, and to a lesser degree in Wales and the West Country, road improvements or road construction may be necessary before adequate road services can be provided as full alternatives to the rail services which exist at present. Some of these road improvements are required, in any case, for development of the motor tourist trade, on which the future of these areas so greatly depends.

The motor bus network looked quite effective on paper, but in reality the bus services were irregular, unco-ordinated, slow and inefficient. One of the major assumptions of the Beeching Report was that rural rail passengers would happily switch to buses for short journeys, yet continue to use the train for long-distance travel. But the 1960s were witnessing a dramatic growth in private car ownership. Rather than switch to alternative means of public transport, passengers were taking the closure of their local line as an excuse to buy a car, and once they had become motorists they were deserting public transport altogether.

As a statement of transport policy, the Beeching Report was fatally and disastrously flawed. The idea that losses could be substantially reduced, let alone eradicated, by disposing of a third of the network was, as discussed, a highly dubious one. Yet, according to A J Pearson, Assistant General Manager of the London Midland Region, the sudden and dramatic implementation of the closure plan would harbour even greater dangers:

> To introduce at this time a dramatic [closure] programme such as the Railway Board's first report contained, has sunk deeply into the consciousness in this country, as it was undoubtedly designed to do, and it is bound to create and intensify a negative attitude to the lines and services that remain that will be very hard to remove.

As the branches and cross-country lines were lopped off, public confidence collapsed, and the secondary and trunk lines began to wither. Faced with an onslaught of road competition, the railways appeared simply to be capitulating.

* * *

Many commentators were to find fault with the conclusions of the Beeching Report, although no-one was to present a more devastatingly concise reply than Roger Calvert of the National Council on Inland Transport.

The NCIT had been created by a consortium of pro-rail groups in 1962. Under the Chairmanship of Lord Stonham, a Labour Peer, and with technical guidance from Professor Hondelink and Roger Calvert, it was to achieve a measure of success in fighting the Marples/Beeching proposals.

Mr Calvert was well qualified to oppose the Beeching philosophy, indeed rather more qualified than Dr Beeching was to impose it, having worked for many years for both the New Zealand state rail system and British Railways. His technical knowledge of railway operations was to prove invaluable to the rail lobby.

The National Council on Inland Transport was convinced that the losses claimed by the Railways Board were exaggerated, and that the whole Beeching plan was based on false assumptions and dubious figures. It was, however, very difficult to get any opposing arguments across. The only forum for open discussion on railway closures was provided by the TUCC inquiries, but since the passing of the 1962 Act, their role had become a most ineffective one. The NCIT was determined to find a legal loophole through which to alter the consultation procedure; and it nearly succeeded.

In October 1963, during the inquiry into the proposed closure of the Southport to Preston line, it put forward a challenge to the local TUCC. If British Railways refused to provide a breakdown of the claimed earnings on the line (in this case presented as £52,700), the TUCC would surely be unable to verify the accuracy of the figures. And if the TUCC failed to make every effort to verify the Board's financial statements, it might technically be breaking an obscure Act passed in 1958 to regulate the conduct of tribunals and inquiries.

In the event, the Chairman of the TUCC declined to ask the Railways Board for a breakdown of the figures, citing the wording of the 1962 Act: that the Committee was only concerned with questions of hardship. The NCIT then approached the Council on Tribunals, but the claim against the TUCC disappeared under a welter of legal minutiae, for it was ruled that the TUCCs were independent bodies and their inquiries were not held "by or on behalf of a Minister" and, therefore, they were not bound by the provisions of the 1958 Tribunals and Inquiries Act.

The NCIT decided it might be worth playing for higher legal stakes in order to clarify the position. In November 1963, Roger Calvert and T C Foley, the Council's Secretary, discussed the inquiry procedure with the Secretary of the Central Transport Consultative Committee and procured a CTCC policy statement, which they passed to the Hon Sam Silkin, QC.

Counsel's opinion was that the 1962 Transport Act contained several small, but significant, loopholes. Technically, the TUCCs were not allowed to consider financial matters at all; their task was simply to make a judgment upon the question of "hardship" to passengers which might result from the closure of a railway service. Not surprisingly, hardship had proved a little difficult to define in legal terms and, in practice, the committees simply balanced the evidence submitted by the Railways Board against the weight of the opposition.

But the question of hardship was not quite the be-all and end-all of the consultative procedure, for the TUCCs were allowed to view certain financial figures if they so wished. These figures were often requested by the committees, for they were understandably concerned that they might be led into suggesting an alternative bus service costing more to run than the railway.

It was a crucial point for, if the committees were to see the figures, then it was reasonable that the protesters should too. And if the TUCCs were to become involved in matters of finance, by comparing the cost of the existing rail service with that of alternatives, it followed that they should also consider possible economies to the existing service. The question was really in the hands of individual TUCC chairmen, who had the power to run inquiries more or less as they chose.

Naturally, even an outright victory at local committee level might be a hollow one, for the local body could be over-ruled by the Minister of Transport. All the same, it was felt that a test case might be worth fighting, for, if necessary, the affair could be dragged to the House of Lords — a procedure that might hold up the Beeching plans for many months.

An opportunity arose in May 1964, when the Railways Board put forward proposals to withdraw the Manchester to Buxton service. It was, in many respects, an excellent choice on which to test the protesters' case. The line carried a considerable volume of commuter traffic into Manchester, while Buxton (situated high in the Pennines) attracted plenty of tourists in the opposite direction. Even more useful was the fact that winter snows often made roads in the area impassable. In short, the Buxton line exhibited almost every characteristic that made branch railways worthwhile. Most of the two-day inquiry was spent dealing with an overwhelming caseload of hardship claims, but late on the morning of the second day, Sam Silkin was granted leave to speak on behalf of the NCIT. He began by outlining the assumed role of the TUCCs under the 1962 Transport Act:

The public is being asked to swallow, as it were, this particular Beeching pill,

and your committee has been appointed to hear the objections, all the objections; and yet, Sir, as I understand it, you have been told by some authority, I do not know what, that all you can do is to assume that the pill is going to be swallowed, and advise the powers that be what pain and sickness the patient is likely to suffer as a result, and how you suggest going about relieving that pain and sickness. But when it comes to analysing the pill or even examining the patient to see if he really needs any medicine at all, you are told this is not your job.

His next task was to persuade the Chairman of the Committee to accept a different interpretation of the 1962 Act and take account of the arguments put forward by the NCIT. This proved more difficult, for the Chairman was determined to scotch any such move from the start:

May I interrupt? It is not our intention to report on the economics of the railway proposal, and if there are any questions about that they are for the Minister and we shall not report on them. Any time devoted to that will be time wasted.

Nevertheless, the Committee allowed the barrister to continue, and eventually he came to the *pièce de résistance* of the protesters' case — an examination of the accuracy of the Railway Board's financial claims, which had been investigated by Roger Calvert.

British Rail had put forward the usual figures: movement costs of £142,600, terminal costs of £70,600 and maintenance of £51,000... a total of £264,000 a year. When projected expenditure in the dubious "next five years" category was included, the total costs for the line came out at £318,000 a year against income of £140,000. A loss of around £180,000 looked pretty clear-cut, but Roger Calvert countered by applying Beeching's own theoretical figures to dismantle the Railway Board's assumptions.

The terminal costs of £70,600 were for ten small stations, where Beeching had suggested that a cost of £2,500 per station would be a reasonable figure, giving a total of just £25,000. An analysis of the timetable revealed that British Railways was claiming a movement cost of around 6s 6d (32.5p) per mile where Beeching had suggested 4s to 6s. And on the basis of information supplied by British Rail, the line was carrying 24,000 passengers a week which equated to 24 million passenger miles a year. At the 2d a mile fare that Beeching considered to be a reasonable average, the income of the line should have been in the region of £200,000.

Thus, by using Beeching's own figures (which had been formulated to show the inadequacy of branch railways), Calvert reduced the loss from £180,000 to £42,000; and he was able to go a good deal further. Half the stations could be de-staffed at a saving of £11,500, and rationalisation of the timetable would save an additional £12,000 on signalling, and £15,000 on movement costs. The result, excluding income from goods and parcels traffic, would be an annual profit of nearly £6,000, assuming all his presumptions were accurate. He went on to point out the unreasonable basis of the "next five years" expenditure assumptions and suggested that the line might be partially reduced to single-track to effect further economies.

Summing up, Mr Silkin rounded triumphantly upon the secrecy of the Railways Board:

Silkin: I think one would want to say, Mr Calvert, that despite your own considerable experience you have been handicapped in making these computations and suggestions by having only the skeleton figures which the railways have supplied?

Calvert: That is so; it would be necessary to have many more figures in order to produce a detailed analysis.

Silkin: Have you done the best you can with these figures, and on that basis are you confident that the line, as modified, could easily run at a profit, whether or not the line as it is at the present time is running at a profit, taking everything into account?

Calvert: I am quite confident the line could be run at a profit.

There followed a break for lunch while the TUCC members ruminated on their invidious position. If they refused to take account of the protesters' evidence, there was every possibility that the NCIT might take the matter to a higher authority. If they agreed, and informed the Minister that the railway should remain open along the lines suggested by Roger Calvert, they would effectively have accused the Railways Board of either incompetence or false accounting.

When the inquiry reconvened, the Chairman thanked Mr Silkin for his submission but refused to allow cross-examination of the railway staff, who presumably needed time to prepare a response. Mr Silkin, with no other evidence to offer, then entered into a detailed exchange with the Chairman as to whether the committee was willing to accept, and act upon, Roger Calvert's evidence. The NCIT needed to know for, if the committee were to ignore the evidence, the matter would indeed be placed before the High Court.

He was never to receive an answer, nor (as it transpired) was he to need one. The Consultative Committee sent an interim report to the Minister who promptly reprieved the line. The Buxton inquiry resulted in an outright victory for the protesters, for the Government had backed down when faced with detailed evidence and simply withdrawn the closure proposals. But there were to be few repetitions. During later inquiries, committee chairmen (probably operating under new directives) simply refused to consider outside evidence.

Roger Calvert's figures were of paramount importance. He had proved that the Railway Board's estimates not only failed to take account of possible economies, but failed to add up when measured against the "typical" values published in the Beeching Report. And it was possible to apply the same techniques to any railway.

Beeching had suggested that a diesel multiple unit could be operated for around 5/- (25p) per mile. If the Railways Board was claiming that a line should close because the costs were higher, it followed that it was either presenting false figures or failing to make reasonable economies. The same was true of the "terminal expenses" — the cost of operating stations. Beeching had suggested £2,500 for each small country station, yet the Railways Board usually claimed considerably more. Very probably the stations **were** costing more, for the issue was not so much that the railway figures were downright false; rather that they had long since chosen (**or been instructed**) to prepare particular lines for closure, and facilitate this by maintaining costs at a high level.

This issue as to whether lines had been deliberately run down was a contentious one. Without a doubt, where management had several years' advance warning, it "rearranged" maintenance schedules to fit in some hefty renewals in the years following the proposed closure. Of course, this was not necessarily a malicious policy, for there really was little point in investing scarce resources on lines earmarked for closure. The deliberate rescheduling of traffic onto alternative routes, on the other hand, was intended merely to increase losses. After all, if a line was due for demolition, the most sensible option from an economic point of view would be to make good use of the assets before scrapping them... perhaps by transferring heavy and damaging freight traffic onto the line in its last days.

In fact, the lines destined for closure were deliberately and systematically starved of traffic in their final years, and the policy could be seen most clearly on the threatened trunk routes. Even before publication of the Beeching Report, traffic had been run down on the Great Central and the Somerset & Dorset, leaving passengers with no doubt as to the fate that awaited both lines.

By the end of 1962, both railways were operating without proper maintenance, and through express trains and freight services had been re-routed. New technology that might have eased the financial situation, such as diesel units or automatic crossings, was notable only by its absence. It was easier to kill a railway by starvation than by strangling an otherwise healthy concern, and Beeching had been preparing the ground long before publication of the Report. Whatever the truth of the matter, the cutback in investment was one of the reasons for the comparatively buoyant financial situation of the railways in 1962-63, for the Beeching regime was spending very little on maintaining the lines on the closure list.

Gerard Fiennes, manager of the Western Region, was later to claim that railways were never deliberately run down in order to pre-empt closure or, in his own words: "A railway manager likes managing railways. The more railways he manages, the higher his salary and the more impressive his status." Perhaps Mr Fiennes was innocent, but others certainly did inflict deliberate damage, sometimes by a subtle rescheduling of the timetable, and occasionally in a most blatant manner. Individual managers were not really to blame though, for the problem was a political one. Many of the lines condemned in the Beeching Report had been under sentence since the mid-50s, and with closure long considered a formality, operating economies would have been counter-productive.

Roger Calvert went on to apply his "basic railway" formula (based, of course, on Beeching's own theoretical figures) to other lines on the closure list, with astonishing results:

Movement & station costs		Income	Profit/loss (direct costs only)
Liskeard-Looe			
BRB	£12,900	£7,100	-£5,800
Calv	£6,350	£7,100	+£950
Isle of Wight			
BRB	£289,000	£147,000	-£142,000
Calv	£101,500	£250,000	+£148,500
Oswestry-Gobowen			
BRB	£17,966	£4,800	-£13,166
Calv	£3,900	£5,100	+£1,200
St Erth-St Ives			
BRB	£17,934	£9,100	-£8,834
Calv	£12,320	£12,100	-£220
Hull-Scarborough			
BRB	£397,000	£366,400	-£30,600
Calv	£135,250	£366,400	+£231,150

BRB = British Railways Board
Calv = Roger Calvert

These figures took no account of track and signalling costs (which might or might not be subsidised by freight or other traffic), neither did they include expenditure under the "next five years" category under which British Railways often claimed an extraordinary sum to justify closure. On the other hand, nor did they did take account of possible operating economies and, in many cases, there was considerable scope for such improvements.

What the figures did show was a very marked discrepancy between the Railway Board's estimates and those of Roger Calvert. In a rational, and reasonably democratic country, it might be assumed that such wide variations would give rise to an inquiry in order to set things straight. But no such thing happened: no-one had the right to challenge the official figures — not even experts of the standing of Roger Calvert and Professor Hondelink.

Mr Calvert investigated 95 lines in all. He first made an assumption that British Railways' income figures were correct, but that costs could be reduced to Beeching's "typical" figures. This revealed that 36 examples would be able to cover movement and terminal expenses and ten of these (where the track would remain in place for other passenger services) were effectively covering their full costs already. A further six would have been profitable as long as annual track costs could be kept below £1,000 a mile — a figure which many authorities (including Gerard Fiennes) believed to be a reasonable one for a lightly loaded branch line.

Calvert's next move was to reassess income on the branch lines at the rate of 2d per passenger-mile. Under these conditions no fewer than 53 per cent of the lines destined for closure appeared capable of covering all relevant expenses.

The balance was to tilt even further in favour of retaining the branch railways when he considered the benefits of contributory revenue to the rest of the railway system. As we have seen, British Railways knew the exact level of contributory revenue for any given line, although this information was not provided to the TUCC inquiries.

What could not be judged with any degree of accuracy was just how much of the contributory revenue would be lost after closure. Would potential travellers take a bus to the nearest rail-head? Would they buy a car and stop travelling by rail altogether? Or might they travel the whole journey by bus? There were a host of variables that made the question difficult to answer. The ever-optimistic Railways Board claimed that the majority of passengers would continue to use the railway system and that there would be little loss of contributory revenue after a branch line closure. It was to be another 20 years before this rose-tinted view was finally and unequivocally disproved.

From the viewpoint of the early 1960s, however, Calvert took advantage of all the available data and came to the conclusion that closure of 67 per cent of the lines under threat would leave the railways worse off financially. In other words, as many as two thirds of the Beeching closures would not only cause massive disruption to the travelling public but also lose money for British Railways into the bargain.

In the event, there were no new closure proposals between September 1962 and June 1963. Implementation of the wide-ranging 1962 Transport Act had taken a considerable time and, very probably, the Government wished to allow a decent interval for the furore over the Beeching proposals to die down before getting on with the task. Time was running short though, for a general election was fast approaching, and closing railway lines was not the sort of policy that was likely to prove popular with the electorate.

Paradoxically, while the closure process ground almost to a halt, the working deficit of the railways showed an encouraging improvement. A record deficit of £123 million was set to fall to £81 million by the end of 1963 and to £67 million the following year.

Besides the near cessation of investment on the threatened lines, there were several reasons for this strange state of affairs. In the main, the turn-around was due to the belated effects of the modernisation schemes instigated in the late 1950s. Chronically unreliable diesel locomotives were starting to earn a little revenue, and the diesel multiple unit programme was showing a healthy return. It should be noted, however, that the financial improvement had little to do with railway closures for few had been implemented by this time.

Meanwhile, the Labour Party was busy brushing its radical wing under the carpet and reassuring the electorate that a Labour victory at the forthcoming election would not mean a return to the heady days of the 1945 socialist experiment. During a triumphant party conference in October 1963, Harold Wilson put his finger on the national pulse and promised to forge a new Britain:

We are redefining our socialism in terms of the scientific revolution... The Britain that is going to be forged in the white heat of this scientific revolution will be no place for restrictive practices or outdated methods on either side of industry.

He had words of encouragement for those who objected to the loss of their local railway lines as well. Should Labour form the next administration, Wilson would call a halt to all "major" rail closures pending a wide-ranging and thorough review of the nation's transport requirements. Presumably railway lines would be reprieved where the technological heat was due to burn with a particular intensity. There were no specific commitments, but the message appealed strongly to the electorate, and went a long way towards swinging the national mood away from the Conservatives.

Railway closures were bound to affect almost every parliamentary constituency, and the Railways Board did nothing to assist the beleaguered Conservative Government by launching full tilt into the closure schemes, bringing the largest candidate into public view at a critical time.

So wide-ranging were the proposals affecting the former Great Central trunk line between Sheffield and London, that no fewer than five different Consultative Committees became involved, and the consultation procedure proved quite unable to cope with such a major inquiry. The line was so long, and the arguments for retention or closure so technical from a strategic point of view,

The Great Central was engineered to a very high standard, exemplifed by Besford viaduct, north of Nottingham, seen here in 1960 with a northbound coal train crossing. Colour-Rail.

that the local Transport Users' Consultative Committees were unable to make any realistic judgments.

The Great Central ran right down the spine of the country: from Sheffield via Nottingham, Leicester, Rugby and Aylesbury to its own London terminus at Marylebone. It had been the subject of a war of attrition for some years, even before Beeching arrived on the scene, for the line had been upgraded in the early 1950s, but a later change of heart had resulted in plans for partial or complete closure.

This unhappy line held the dubious distinction of being probably the least useful duplicate trunk route, passing through a mixed bag of Midlands towns and cities that were all served by at least one other main line. And further south, between Rugby and Aylesbury, the line ran for almost 60 miles through open country that looked unsuitable even for local traffic.

Closure would have made a lot of sense, were it not for a couple of minor points in the line's favour. The Great Central was the last, and one of the finest, of the trunk lines. Completed as late as 1899, it was built on the grandest of scales. Probably the most ludicrous extravagance imposed by its larger than life founder Sir Edward Watkin, was construction to the European loading gauge, somewhat wider than the British standard, and a source of considerable expense in the shape of larger tunnels, bridges and earthworks.

Watkin was no fool, however. He had an eye on (and a substantial shareholding in) the channel tunnel then under construction. If the scheme had come off, the future of the Great Central would have been assured, but British xenophobia and the vagaries of European politics put paid to the channel tunnel for almost a century. Until that is, the late 1960s, when British Rail again became involved in a tunnel scheme. Unfortunately, Dr Beeching had already exterminated a ready-made high speed link from London to the heart of the Midlands.

The other unique quality of the Great Central lay in its ability to carry through traffic from the North-East to the South and South-West. A short connecting link between Woodford Halse on the Great Central, and Banbury on the former Great Western Railway, provided a route of great strategic importance, enabling long-distance express and freight trains to travel cross-country, avoiding a circuitous and congested detour via Birmingham or London.

Much political capital had been made of the Great Central's failure to make a profit during a long and chequered career and, as a trunk line between Sheffield and London, it was certainly surplus to requirements by the 1960s. However, had services been modernised and rescheduled to make better use of the line (which was potentially faster than the rival Midland route), it might have had a bright future. The Railways Board did not agree.

Since January 1960, through express trains from London had been rerouted and replaced by a languid "semi-fast" service terminating at Nottingham. The north-east/south-west traffic was cut to a single daytime express between York and Bournemouth. It proved to be the first shot in a six-year war of attrition aimed at precipitating outright closure. Sure enough, the second move came in 1961 when British Railways proposed the withdrawal of all local passenger services between Sheffield and Aylesbury.

So great was the extent of the proposed closures that it proved necessary to arrange three separate TUCC inquiries at Nottingham, Leicester and Aylesbury. The local Consultative Committees, aware of British Railways' intention of closing the line outright, were hamstrung by their brief to look only at local problems of hardship. With genuine reluctance, they agreed to most of the closures, leaving the strange parting shot that they "would have preferred" to recommend a new diesel multiple unit local service between Nottingham and Aylesbury. All the same, they came reluctantly to the conclusion "that this would not be immediately possible under present circumstances".

Most of the closures were rapidly implemented, leaving the trunk line with little through traffic and a few token local services. In the spring of 1963, the Railways Board took the process a little further and withdrew all Sunday trains between Nottingham and London.

There was not a great deal of traffic left. The semi-fast services had been skillfully scheduled so as to avoid connecting with local trains traversing the short link between Banbury and Woodford Halse, leaving the connecting line under-utilised. In December 1963, the Board applied for closure, and the area TUCC, which had no understanding of the wider strategic implications behind the proposal, reluctantly consented to the local trains being withdrawn. Then, despite (or more likely because of) the admission that the Board intended to close the Great Central outright, nothing further occurred. The derisory service continued, the line lost money, and the closure debate moved, temporarily, elsewhere.

In January 1964, Lord Stonham of the NCIT wrote to the Prime Minister, Sir Alec Douglas Home, and outlined the state of the nation's railways. Home had succeeded to the Premiership in October 1963, being chosen as the least divisive of the available candidates. Sir Alec was far from being every Conservative's ideal choice for Prime Minister — not even his own, in fact — and most of the wise money had gone on "Rab" Butler, an able politician who might have better handled Harold Wilson. Wilson had promised a scientific revolution, but Home appears to have been confused by the whole process of modern government, having once reputedly remarked: "There are two problems in my life. The political ones are insoluble and the economic ones are incomprehensible..."

Sir Alec was, however, a kindly soul, and during his short stay in office, he found time to reply to Lord Stonham and express incredulity that anything underhand might have occurred on the railways:

It is difficult to resist the impression that you are seeking to imply that the Board are proposing closures of services and stations which can be made to pay.

This most certainly was the case and, as the election approached, the closure process began to accelerate. In March 1964, Marples announced the first major round of closures, approving no fewer than 21 candidates, including most of the railways in Lincolnshire — Peterborough-Boston-Grimsby, and the branches to Skegness and Mablethorpe.

Coming just before the summer season, the latter proposal generated even more public concern than the Great Central plans had done. The various lines through the Lincolnshire Wolds served a population of more than 180,000, and passed through no fewer than 14 local authority areas. The seaside resorts of Mablethorpe and Skegness received almost 500,000 railway visitors each year, an influx that (according to the local MP) would necessitate 27,000 bus journeys should the closures be implemented. This was not a very practical proposition in the early 1960s for, as it was, the police were regularly turning road visitors away from Skegness on summer Saturdays.

Amid general public uproar, the East Midlands TUCC voiced objections, and the Minister of Transport hurriedly instructed the Board to come up with some revised closure proposals. The result was almost identical: Peterborough to Boston; Firsby to Grimsby; Willoughby to Mablethorpe and Lincoln to

Firsby via Midville. In other words, there was to be a reprieve for Skegness, but the other lines would go.

While major closures made the headlines, the branches involved in the railbus experiments of the 1950s were quietly fading away. In April 1964, after a protracted battle, the branches to Tetbury and Cirencester in Wiltshire were finally closed.

One of the new halts constructed to serve the railbuses in 1959 had been sited within spitting distance of a remote public house and little else. Fittingly, it was from the aptly named Trouble House Halt that the now obligatory coffin loaded with empty whisky bottles was put aboard the last Tetbury train and sent up to Dr Beeching in London.

At least the line had been the subject of an experiment to reduce deficits. Many services had never even seen a diesel multiple unit, let alone a railbus. At the local TUCC inquiry into the Taunton to Barnstaple closure, the Railways Board stated that "dieselisation" had "been examined", and would not make the service remunerative, "even under the cheapest working methods". It was a common response to questions from knowledgeable passengers expounding the benefits of diesel railcars, and an identical reply was given during the nearby Taunton to Yeovil inquiry.

This was a classic example of the sort of rural branch that Beeching had in mind for closure; a 25-mile line linking two country towns, a scattering of villages, and connecting with trunk services at either end. One might have assumed that the Taunton to Yeovil railway was short of passenger traffic, yet this was not the case. Most trains carried 30-40 passengers, rising to 60 or more at peak times. On Saturdays, trains were exceptionally well patronised, each unloading 100-150 passengers at Taunton throughout the morning and carrying them all home again in the afternoon. It was not particularly heady stuff by inter-city standards, but this was one of the quieter branches on the Beeching closure programme, and the line had never seen the benefits of modern traction equipment.

Some lines could not even approach such traffic figures. The little branch between Tiverton Junction (on the main line between Taunton and Exeter) and Tiverton, just four miles away, was carrying only 100 passengers a day. Annual income was put at just £3,500 against movement costs amounting to no less than £21,600, or around 10 shillings (50p) per mile. Yet even Beeching had suggested that a three-car diesel multiple unit could operate for half that amount, and the handful of passengers travelling to Tiverton could have been carried in a railbus for even less.

Whereas the lines involved in the railbus experiments were generally insignificant, those involved in the early diesel multiple unit trials were mostly of greater importance. Among the exceptions was the Silloth branch line in

The introduction of diesel multiple units on the line from Carlisle to Silloth saw passenger figures rise by 66 per cent — not enough to stop it falling beneath the Beeching axe. Neville Stead.

Cumberland. The line had been one of the very first to experience the new technology in 1955 during the Cumberland trials, something that had caused great excitement in the local press. Railcars had brought a renewed confidence in the future of the line, and prompted an increase in traffic from the grateful residents of Silloth. Now the whole experiment was to be swept away and the line abandoned.

On the evening of September 6, 1964, the last train was preparing to leave Silloth for the main line. By popular request the usual railcar had been put aside in favour of steam traction and, as dusk gathered, the engine stood ready for departure bedecked with a wreath on the smokebox door.

The anger and frustration generated by the closure process in these far flung corners of the network was intense. Distant authorities had seen fit to modernise the local branch line, but nine years later the railway was to be eradicated altogether. To the ordinary citizens of a small town on the Solway Firth, the affair made little sense.

The authorities had expected trouble prior to a general election and, sure enough, an ominous crowd of 9,000 or more had gathered to mark the occasion, watched over by eight police officers and an Alsation dog. Detonators were placed on the line, missiles hurled at the police and, finally, members of the local

169

Labour Party sat in front of the locomotive, only to be driven away with blasts of hot steam. The objectors fought to place a placard on the engine: "If you don't catch this there'll be another one if you vote Labour at the next election..." In the battle for the smokebox door, a locomotive inspector finally triumphed, and the placard was unceremoniously removed.

It was not until 8.30pm that the 7.58pm from Silloth finally departed. And, as the tail-light of the last train dimmed and finally disappeared from view, the citizens of Silloth returned quietly to their homes through the cobbled streets of a smaller and sadder town.

The Labour Party was indeed to form the next administration, but there would be no more trains to Silloth.

.

7.
The axe falls
1964-1969

It was a mild wet night with a strong wind making the three gas lights that were alight on each platform flicker. No staff were on duty at the station and except for the gas light in the passengers' section of the booking office the station rooms were in darkness.

And the last passenger stood on the deserted platform and thought of all the many journeys that had started and ended there... and of the friends he had travelled with. And realising that a point had been reached where it was more pleasant to look back than forward, he left the still lighted station, and as he walked down the drive, the flickering lamp over the station entrance grew fainter...

Although the last train had gone, the last passenger left, the station lights were still on, flickering in the wind and the rain.

Stanley Keyse, of the RDA, on the closure of Sutton Park station, Birmingham

ON October 16, 1964, Harold Wilson led the Labour Party to a less than decisive parliamentary victory, winning an overall majority of just four seats. In the run-up to the election, the Labour leader had pledged to halt all major rail closures pending a national transport survey, but with the election safely won, the pledge was soon forgotten and the closure process (overseen by the new Minister of Transport, Tom Fraser) continued to accelerate.

It was not until the arrival of Barbara Castle in 1966 that an attempt was made to reverse the policy, although her initial attempts to stabilise the system —through the Network for Development plan—met with derision from the road lobby and protest from the pro-rail groups, which felt the proposals went nowhere near far enough. Mrs Castle went on to mastermind the innovative 1968 Transport Act that promised grant aid for unremunerative rail services and increased taxation and restrictions on heavy road vehicles.

The 1968 Act proved, however, something of a disappointment. The Government lost its nerve in the face of concerted opposition from the road lobby and eased the lorry taxation proposals. And the unremunerative railway grant system actually caused a fresh round of closures, for the level of grant stipulated proved too generous, leading the Government to refuse aid in many cases. By

1970 the Beeching plans were more or less complete, but overall financial viability remained as far out of reach as ever.

* * *

After 14 years of Tory rule, the arrival of a Labour Government was hailed as a generally positive and populist victory. The outcome of the election had been greatly influenced by transport policy, and the Labour Party gained many votes — perhaps enough to tip the balance — by claiming that major railway closures would be halted.

Mr Wilson had, for example, given a personal pledge that the Whitby-Scarborough line, one of the most scenic routes in the north of England (if not the most remunerative) would remain open. "I confirm," he said, "that an obviously major decision such as the proposed Whitby rail closure would be covered by that statement in the Labour Party manifesto." The citizens of Whitby saw no reason to doubt his word. After all, Harold Wilson had denounced the entire closure process in the most forthright terms during a debate on the Reshaping Report the year before:

> Over the last ten years, 3,600 miles of railway have been closed. That is 19 per cent of the mileage previously in operation.

> Presumably this 19 per cent must have been the least remunerative of the lot. Presumably that is why it was first selected for closure.

> Yet its closure saved only seven per cent of the working deficit of British Railways in 1960, and this takes no account of the additional cost to the nation of the closures, or of the loss of main line traffic caused by loss of feeder services...

> If the closure of one fifth of the railway mileage makes so little difference to the operating deficit of British Railways, what will the next one third do?

At the time of the election, the fate of no fewer than 38 railway lines was in abeyance, the outgoing Minister of Transport having consented to closure, but the services remaining in operation. Two were large-scale proposals and one (the line from Dumfries to Stranraer) had provoked considerable opposition from a strategic point of view, providing as it did, a direct link with the ferry service to Northern Ireland.

Immediately after the election, Wilson saw fit to argue that his pledge had been worthless, for it was claimed that under the 1962 Transport Act it was impossible for a Minister to overturn a previous judgment on closure. The new Prime Minister did, however, make vague promises to keep the track in place pending the all-important transport review, and the protesters were largely silenced.

A positive sign that the new administration had some faith in the railway

Above: A local train at Castle Douglas on the doomed strategic route to Stranraer, April 1960. P B Booth, N Stead collection.

Below: Harold Wilson's pledge to reprieve the Whitby to Scarborough line proved worthless after the election. This picture shows a Middlesbough to Scarborough train on the picturesque coast line at Staithes in 1955. In fact, this part of the line, north of Whitby, had succumbed as early as 1958. Neville Stead.

173

network came in January 1965, when Anthony Wedgewood Benn, the Postmaster General, formalised an agreement with Dr Beeching under which the railways would contract to carry the bulk of Royal Mail parcels traffic for the next ten years. A few weeks later, faced with a demand for a nine per cent pay rise from the unions, British Rail announced that large pay increases would threaten the success already achieved through the Reshaping Plans. But, as we have seen, the financial improvements in 1963-1964 had little, if anything, to do with the Beeching plans. The closure of 148 railway lines had, on the Railway Board's own figures, yielded a saving of only £6 million, against an overall deficit of £125 million in 1964, and there was a hidden cost behind the closure policy, for the Railways Board was paying a subsidy to the bus operators of almost £100,000 a year. By 1966 it was to reach £0.5 million.

Beeching had promised a second report on the railways and, on February 16, 1965, it arrived. In keeping with an agreement to inform the unions in advance on questions of policy, the Board allowed them a whole 24 hours advance notice, providing a union briefing on the 15th!

The report, *The Development of the Major Trunk Routes*, argued that, of the 7,500 miles of railway advocated for retention in the first report, only 3,000 miles should be actively developed. It was the result of an internal study to find the size of network that would suit conditions 20 years ahead, assuming that the commercial restraints of the 1962 Transport Act were to remain in force.

The Times generally backed the second report, noting that Beeching had carefully avoided the word "closure", as in the first, and advocated instead that certain routes should be "selected for retention", which was just another way of looking at the same thing. The *Times* leader summed up the report in hawkish mood:

> **Dr Beeching has provided, invaluably, a solid foundation on which to build a transport policy... There is no reason at all why, at a current cost of around £70 million a year, and a great deal of unproductive activity by a great many people, the railways should be excused the prudent housekeeping demanded in other branches of national life.**

Something *The Times* failed to point out was that the second Beeching Report had concluded that even a 3,000 mile system would not necessarily guarantee profitability. The Report had looked further: to explore options for an even smaller network, to the point where the railway would link just a few major cities such as London, Manchester and Glasgow. Newcastle, for example, would find itself at the end of a single-track freight branch from Leeds!

Few commentators took the conclusions of the second Beeching Report seriously, although it did at least provide evidence that theoretical accountancy would ultimately mean the end of the railway system altogether. It was the first official admission that retraction and closure could not guarantee profitability.

A fortnight later, the Trade Union Congress prepared a response. The Railways Board Report was not, it said, "sufficiently well argued to make constructive comment possible". The TUC also reached the inevitable conclusion that "non-selected" routes would, ultimately, be destined for closure, as there would be no real saving in switching traffic to the "selected" routes unless this was so. In any event, said the TUC, the report was fundamentally flawed, for the future of British Rail could not possibly be determined outside an analysis of transport policy as a whole.

Where the first report had been acclaimed in many quarters as a lucid and concise analysis of the railways' position, the second, produced while the painful closure procedure was well underway, failed totally to catch the public mood. The Beeching philosophy had run out of steam.

As if to pour cold water on the idea of further rail cuts, the provincial bus drivers flexed their negotiating muscles in the wake of Beeching's first round of closures, and chose March 1965 to demand a pay increase of no less than 16 per cent, together with a reduction of two hours in the working week. When the employers offered 11 per cent, the drivers threatened to strike. The management replied that strike action might threaten certain rural bus routes on a permanent basis. Many of them had only recently been introduced to replace defunct railways.

Public transport appeared to be falling apart at the seams, something that could not fail to catch the attention of the nation at large. One result was an unprecedented demand for driving tests: later in the month, the Ministry of Transport took on 150 new examiners to clear a backlog of 430,000 test appointments. There had been a record two million tests in 1964 — 250,000 more than the previous record.

As usual, there were plenty of suggestions from the road lobby as to what the Minister could do with his railways... A certain Brigadier T I Lloyd advocated the use of closed trunk lines as road coach super highways. The coaches would have 9ft diameter wheels, and stop at railway stations "razed to ground level" and "reconstituted as combined stopping places for coaches and access points for other traffic". How the recently launched Mini would cope with rapidly advancing 9ft diameter wheels on a single track motorway was a problem that the Brigadier had yet to address. The scheme was typical of many, more or less lunatic, proposals at the time, such as the suggestion to build "four or five" dual carriageways across Wales, an idea put forward by the Country Landowners' Association.

Meanwhile, the Railways Board continued to implement the closure plans and, amid mounting concern, the Labour administration did nothing to stop the process. It took some time to force a statement from Harold Wilson but, when it eventually came, at the end of March 1965, the pro-rail movement, and the citizens who had voted Labour to halt the railway closures, were far from satisfied. The Prime Minister had simply changed his mind.

In a statement laced with ambiguity, he claimed never to have had any intention of seeking powers to reverse closure decisions on lines that had "already ceased to exist" (*sic*). And true to post-war government form, he also claimed not to have been aware of the grave financial crisis his party had inherited. Of the 38 closure proposals inherited by the Labour administration, 25 had already been implemented. Two months later, only six of these lines remained open, and the Government had added another 13 to the list, with 144 in the pipeline.

On June 1, 1965, after a little under five years in the service, Dr Beeching retired as Chairman of the Railways Board when Harold Wilson decided against renewing his contract.

Perhaps Beeching had reached the conclusion that his policies would never achieve the elusive goal of profitability... or perhaps the Government had reached the same conclusion on his behalf. It was later claimed that Harold Wilson had wished to give Beeching more time to achieve some positive financial results, but that the Prime Minister had been over-ruled by a generally pro-road cabinet!

Paradoxically, Beeching had fought hard on behalf of the railways in certain areas, upsetting the road lobby in the process, particularly where the "liner train" freight project was concerned. In 1964 the railway chief had given evidence to the Geddes Committee that allowance for the passage of heavy freight vehicles was adding about 70 per cent to motorway construction costs — a view roundly condemned by the Ministry of Transport. Shortly afterwards, Beeching had agreed to chair an investigation into road/rail track costs. One of Harold Wilson's first moves had been to confirm the appointment but, under intense pressure from the road lobby and the road transport trade unions, the new Prime Minister had backed down. There would be no independent review of transport costs, and Dr Beeching accepted his life peerage and returned to ICI, having failed to secure a chairmanship for which he would probably have been well suited.

What no-one outside the railway industry could possibly have known, was that the national railway losses were set to increase substantially in 1965, after a gradual fall to £125 million in 1964. Dr Beeching's critics were already voicing doubts that the financial improvement had been caused by the closure process at all, and might well have been a hang-over from the BTC modernisation investments of the late 1950s. If this was indeed the case, Beeching might have realised by mid-1965 that it was high time he returned to ICI.

In four short years, Beeching had become known as "the axeman" and the "butcher" of the railways, but the furore generated by the closure programme had drawn attention away from other areas, such as overmanning and inefficiency, where considerable cost-savings could have been made.

Five years of cuts had yielded virtually nothing, while the waste associated with the programme, coming so soon after the BTC's substantial investments, had reached tragic proportions. In May 1965, the *Daily Mail* reported that a dozen new locomotive boilers were rusting away at Derby, their usefulness overtaken by the diesel programme. Around the country, thousands of coaches had been scrapped, while new replacement wheels lay rusting at Swindon... and in November, three steam locomotives were treated to a major overhaul, and scrapped immediately afterwards.

The vast freight marshalling yards, authorised under the 1955 modernisation plan, were proving largely redundant, for the railways were now concentrating on "train-load" goods traffic that needed little or no trans-shipment. A classic example was the Thornton New Yard, in Fife, constructed in 1955 at a cost of £1.35 million. Those planning the yard had thoughtfully provided coaling, watering and stabling facilities for steam engines, together with 15 miles of sidings, in a yard designed to accommodate loose-coupled wagons. And there were other monuments to the follies of the Transport Commission, including the vast Kingsmoor yard near Carlisle which was never fully utilised. Ten years later, as the steam locomotives were withdrawn, and the loose-coupled wagons were scrapped by the thousand, such yards had become expensive white elephants.

The anachronistic loose wagons were not being scrapped fast enough, however, and the appallingly unprofitable freight sundries traffic (that Beeching had rightly condemned) continued much as before. In 1961, the sundries business had lost £13.5 million on a turnover of £38 million but, six years later, losses had grown to £18 million on a turnover of only £22 million. Even uniforms were being wasted. Three redundant porters received smart new uniforms in Newmarket, as did 61-year-old William Botterill, redundant for three months from nearby Aldeburgh. He decided to send it back.

Beeching had gone, but his legacy remained, and Prime Minister Harold Wilson agreed to intensify the closure programme. Throughout the whole of 1964, the Conservative Transport Minister, Ernest Marples, had authorised the closure of 991 miles of railway; Tom Fraser, the new Labour Minister, was to authorise 1,071 miles before the end of 1965.

Not only would the prophesies of the Beeching Report be fulfilled, but the Railways Board had decided to look even beyond the Reshaping Report for likely candidates. Its next intended victim proved an unusual choice.

Beeching had spared the Oxford to Cambridge cross-country line, and with good reason, for it provided a purpose-made "London bypass" — a direct link between the South-West and the east coast, avoiding the capital. Suddenly the

line was faced with closure. It was an extraordinary move, under an administration that claimed to have put a certain amount of strategic planning into its
transport policy. Not only was the line useful for the purpose of keeping rail
passengers and road traffic out of congested London, but it also linked the
rapidly expanding new city of Milton Keynes with other areas of rapid growth,
such as Peterborough, Oxford and Cambridge.

In July 1965, the Minister consented to closure — a decision that was not
to be implemented immediately, for there were problems arranging alternative
bus services on a local basis. The greater part of the line closed to passengers
in November 1967, with just a small section between Bedford and Bletchley
being retained.

By the end of 1965, there were few realistic closure candidates left. Why,
then, did the Labour administration continue the process? According to Roger
Calvert, of the National Council for Inland Transport, the new and inexperienced
Labour Government had been bullied into submission by the powerful civil
servants at the Ministry of Transport. Others were to lay the blame with Tom
Fraser, a determinedly road-biased Minister of Transport. Whatever the views
of individual politicians, the real pressure for an acceleration of the closure
programme was coming from the road lobby. In 1965 it commissioned Professor
Victor Morgan of University College, Cardiff, to produce a road study. Inevitably, he came down in favour of a massive increase in spending on roads, and
the road lobby increased pressure on the Government, demanding another
1,700 miles of motorway and a £7 billion road programme.

The future looked grim for the railways. Government opposition to closures
had mysteriously evaporated, and the pro-rail groups were in disarray, for
proposals were being put forward with such speed that organising opposition
proved a hopeless task. Since 1964, lines had been closing at the rate of almost
ten a month.

In August 1965, however, a proposal was successfully challenged. The
Railways Board had suggested closure of the East Suffolk line from Lowestoft
to Ipswich and provided an alternative bus schedule that would pick up
passengers en route and connect with London bound trains at Ipswich. The
prospective Liberal candidate for Eye, Don Newby, rounded up a posse of press
hacks, local worthies, and a couple of Suffolk mayors, and put them aboard
three buses to challenge the timetable. After 50 miles of hard driving they
reached Ipswich 23 minutes behind schedule... long after the departure of the
London train. All the same, British Rail insisted that the line should close,
informing the TUCC hearing that losses were running at around £250,000 a
year. That might have been the end of the story, but as luck would have it, Gerard
Fiennes had recently been appointed manager of the Eastern Region and his
timely intervention turned the East Suffolk into a *cause célèbre* for the protest

movement.

Fiennes' case, initially sketched out on the back of the proverbial envelope, was very simple. A package of economy measures, together with a frequent diesel multiple unit service, would form the nucleus of a "basic railway"... a line operated as economically as the demands of safety and expediency would allow, while retaining as much of the former traffic as possible. The light railway concept had first been advocated at the turn of the century (and was later put into practice by Colonel Stephens and others) and similar "basic railway" proposals had been put forward by the Railway Development Association and other groups since the early 1950s. But Mr Fiennes was the first highly placed railway official to develop an enthusiasm for such economies. A quick calculation suggested that maintenance and renewal costs could be cut to as little as £30,000 a year for the 49-mile line, and the total expenses reduced from a claimed figure of several hundred thousand pounds to just £84,000. Even after allowance was made for a drop in income from £120,000 to £90,000, the basic railway formula had turned a £250,000 loss into a modest £6,000 surplus.

Such calculations made a nonsense of Beeching's entire closure policy, and generally vindicated the views of Professor Hondelink, Roger Calvert, and other members of the protest movement. Fiennes caused a storm at the Railways Board by daring to challenge the official line, and he rubbed salt into the wounds a year or two later by pouring scorn on the railway closure programme:

> **In 1962 the Marples/Beeching axis began to define their territorial ambitions about rural railways. They laid it down in general that rural railways did not pay, which was true; and could never pay, which was false. They did not, therefore, require more than the most elementary arithmetic on the losses either in general or in particular. They took no account of the new techniques; either coming into operation like diesel traction, or just round the corner like automatic level crossings, mechanised track maintenance, token-less block signalling, and "bus stop" operation which could cut the cost of rural railways by more than half.**

Gerard Fiennes was unceremoniously removed from his post, but the East Suffolk line survived. It was a rare victory during a period of utter despair.

The year 1965 had seen the loss of the Ryde-Newport-Cowes and Shanklin-Ventnor branches on the Isle of Wight — despite the fact that the Board had previously undertaken to give advance warning of closure. Some reports claimed the Ventnor line was carrying as many as 250,000 visitors a year and, according to Professor Hondelink, the entire island network could have returned to profitability had the Railways Board charged visitors a supplementary fare of 3d (1p) each for the journey along Ryde Pier. Such arguments fell on deaf ears at the Ministry, however, and the TUCC inquiry in 1964 was followed by ministerial consent to closure. So great was the income from the branch lines,

179

Ryde pier, 1966: after the closure of the service to Newport and Cowes and the Shanklin to Ventnor branch, only the Ryde-Shanklin line remained. Patrick Henshaw.

that a society was set up with the intention of operating a private service between Ryde, Newport and Cowes, in co-operation with the county council. As negotiations began, the Railways Board tore up the track and scuppered the scheme.

Tom Fraser did refuse to allow closure of the only remaining line on the island, leaving British Rail (which had long hoped to rid itself of the Isle of Wight lines altogether) with an obligation to maintain services on the busy holiday line between Ryde and Shanklin. BR subsequently announced that the line would close on a temporary basis while electrification was carried out, to reopen utilising ex-London Underground tube vehicles. Despite an estimated cost of around £680,000, it was envisaged that the scheme would prove no more than a temporary arrangement for, according to an internal memo, the Railways Board intended to put the line up for closure again in 1975.

In October 1965, a month that saw a number of major closures, including the once-busy line between Hull and York, the Railways Board at last announced its intention to discontinue passenger services on the Great Central, with the exception of a few Nottingham to Rugby local trains. The final Ministerial decision was to be long delayed though, for the country was once again approaching a general election.

Another large-scale closure proposal involved the former Somerset &

Dorset main line — no less than 72 miles of it, between Bournemouth West and Bath Green Park. Bournemouth West station had already succumbed to an electrification scheme on the nearby main line, but the line westwards towards Bath was to receive an extraordinary, if brief, reprieve.

On December 31, 1965, Wakes Bus Company withdrew its application to operate a Blandford-Glastonbury-Midsomer Norton service along the approximate route of the Somerset & Dorset. According to contemporary reports, a variety of reasons were put forward for the company's withdrawal, including staffing problems, logistical difficulties — even a quite justifiable fear that the route would prove unprofitable.

British Rail, running scared that the consequent reprieve for the railway might turn into something more permanent, scrapped the schedule of 20 trains a day, and introduced a derisory skeleton service of eight trains, supplemented by buses. For more than two months, while surplus track and fixtures were scrapped, the ghostly service continued, and it began to look as though the Somerset & Dorset, once counted among the most evocative of all British railways, would refuse to die. But it was heading for a lingering, untidy death.

Only two years before, as winter storms cut communications in the area, the Somerset & Dorset train crews had fought to maintain services over the Mendip Hills. Many men had offered a lifetime of service to the line, a line that was much-loved and well patronised. Those same men were now under obligation to act out the last rites.

It was something that Tom Fraser, far away in Whitehall, could hardly be expected to understand. Many of the rural lines had become ingrained into the communities they served; integral and indispensable threads binding the rich tapestry of rural life. The Somerset & Dorset served a scattering of rural towns, but the population along the line was a sizeable one, and it was set to grow very rapidly indeed in the following decades.

A forlorn Blandford Station after the closure of the Somerset & Dorset trunk line. Author's picture.

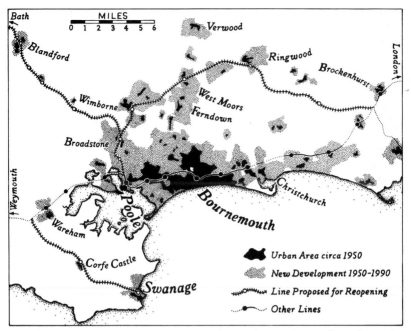

Few areas of Britain, or indeed Europe, have witnessed growth on the scale experienced around Bournemouth and Poole in Dorset. There were already signs of this impending growth when the line from Brockenhurst to Poole was closed in 1964. By the late 1980s, Wimborne, Ferndown, West Moors and Ringwood had merged into a single conurbation and new development had obliterated thousands of acres of heathland — and the former railway trackbed. Also illustrated are the ex-Somerset & Dorset line to Blandford and Bath and the Swanage branch, now partially reopened in private hands.

Towns such as Blandford, Wincanton, Shepton Mallet, Midsomer Norton and Radstock (with a combined population of well over 50,000) were to be left remote from the rail system. And remote from any system of transport, as there were no significant road schemes for the area. To a greater or lesser extent, such communities were to die a little with the loss of rail communication, and it was a blow from which many would never recover. But in comparison with some areas, the number of people affected by closure of the Somerset & Dorset was insignificant. When services in and around Mansfield in Nottinghamshire were eradicated, a population of almost 250,000 was left without adequate rail links.

The counter argument from the British Railways Board was that such lines cost a fortune to run; a sum out of all proportion to the social benefit of maintaining them. But as we have seen, the railway figures were at best dubious, and at worst, downright false. The Somerset & Dorset carried a considerable volume of traffic, but it had hardly seen a diesel multiple unit in the ten years since the vehicles had been introduced. It was not in the least surprising that the line lost money.

As early as December 1962, the clumsily named Branch Line Re-invigoration Society (later the Railway Invigoration Society) had put forward some interesting proposals aimed at restoring the line to health, convinced that the Somerset & Dorset could become a viable and profitable concern. The line had, like many others, been starved of investment since before the war, having seen precious few changes since Edwardian days. In 1913, the fastest through train completed its journey in a little under two hours; by 1962 the fastest time had slumped to two hours and 13 minutes, although the majority of trains travelled excruciatingly slowly, meandering at about 20mph between Bournemouth and Bath, with a journey time of almost four hours. The Society recommended that certain minor stations should be closed, others de-staffed, and a faster, more frequent service of two-car diesel multiple units employed in preference to the picturesque but expensive steam trains that still dominated the timetable. It was an imaginative plan and, together with a few signalling and operating economies, it might have saved the line. Inevitably, of course, the Society's report was ignored, and the Somerset & Dorset simply wasted away.

A handful of lines **had** benefited from new technology. As the Somerset & Dorset closure proposal was being implemented, the Ballater branch in Scotland had come up for closure. It was at Ballater that the BTC had introduced the revolutionary battery-electric railcar, a vehicle that had slashed movement costs on the branch. But the Scottish Region had done nothing further to reduce costs, leaving the rural branch line employing no less than four stationmasters, 37 station staff, 16 signalmen, four crossing-keepers and 24 men engaged in track maintenance. Although the passenger income produced a healthy profit against movement and station expenses, it went nowhere towards supporting the army of staff employed on the line.

Those "permanent" ways forged to Bath and Ballater a century before were to be obliterated — but there were no new roads to take their place. The roads of south-west England, and north-east Scotland were quite unsuitable for through traffic, and remain so to this day. A popular Ministry line in the 1960s was to imply that an area might be eligible for costly road improvements once loss-making rail services were safely out of the way. Many were taken in by this ploy, such as the tiny Bruton Labour Party, which implored the Minister to grant a stay of execution on the Somerset & Dorset line pending road improvements:

> British Railways have made a big mistake in hurrying this closure proposal and
> your consent to it was in error until the road programme for this area was

The battery-electric railcar introduced on the Ballater branch where the Scottish Region failed to make sensible additional economies. It is pictured here at Aberdeen in 1958. Owen Prosser.

complete... this programme cannot be completed for at least ten years. The retention of this line is the only way to relieve the chaotic congestion of the overcrowded roads in the area...

There is public outcry from end to end of this line.

There was no reprieve, and once a reasonable bus service had been arranged, British Railways withdrew the remaining trains and set about scrapping the remnants of the Somerset & Dorset. Cost had once again triumphed over all other considerations, for the reduced operating expenses of rural bus services provided a persuasive argument.

But had the railway really produced a loss? Evidence was coming to light that rail closures might be proving very expensive in wider terms. The question of cost versus social benefit had raged back and forth for some years, but late in 1965 the protesters tried a radical new approach, with considerable success.

Motorways had traditionally been costed by the Social Surplus cost/benefit analysis technique. The estimated "income" of a new motorway was assumed to be the saving of motorists' working time, vehicle time (in terms of fuel, depreciation etc), and sundry benefits to the rest of the road system, should the new road be constructed. When the number of "saved" passenger-hours had been calculated, they were multiplied by a prearranged figure (16 shillings (80p) per hour in the 1960s) to give a gross "income". As a rule of thumb, a motorway was considered viable if the social benefit exceeded the extra mileage costs incurred by travellers, the ongoing maintenance costs, and produce an annual return of about ten per cent on the initial expenditure. With the M1, for instance, construction costs had been put at about £23 million and annual maintenance at £200,000. At 1955 traffic levels it was estimated that the proposed motorway would show a rather limited return of around three to four per cent, although growth of traffic by 1960 was expected to push the return as high as ten-15 per cent, making the project firmly viable.

Many independent experts argued that similar techniques could be applied to railway closures: if the loss of a service produced longer journeys, the wasted passenger-hours could be calculated, and the resulting figure offset against losses.

When the lines from Oxted and Tunbridge Wells to Lewes came before a TUCC inquiry, the protesters applied the technique. Using the very same motorway costing formula, it was revealed that closure would result in 712,000 wasted travelling hours at a cost of around £570,000 per annum. British Railways, on the other hand, was claiming a loss of only £276,000...

So impressed was the local TUCC, that it came down firmly in favour of retaining the line:

> ...these hardships could not be alleviated other than by retaining the lines proposed to be closed... This arises not from lack of alternative bus services, existing or proposed, but from the inherent advantages of the railway to those using it...

The Tunbridge Wells inquiry was to prove a watershed for, by using the Ministry of Transport's own formula, the protesters had proved that the benefit greatly outweighed the cost of providing the service. A similar study on the Central Wales Line revealed that hidden benefits equalled about 60 per cent of the income from fares, producing a "true" income markedly higher than the sum claimed at closure inquiries.

Roger Calvert of the NCIT (who had already applied lateral thinking to the railway authority's figures) went a step further and applied the Ministry of Transport criteria to all the closures implemented between 1963 and 1966. The result was an effective annual loss of £36 million in passengers' time, against the £17 million that the Board claimed to have saved by axing the services.

Even Stanley Raymond, the new Chairman of the Railways Board, was thinking along similar lines. In January 1966 he proposed a "Transport Highway Authority" to determine priorities for investment and raise money to pay for the infrastructure costs of rail, road, air and water transport. The cost of maintaining the railway "highway" would have been £130 million after interest the previous year — more or less equal to the entire railway deficit.

He went on to ask awkward questions about cost. How were the railways to carry the cost of the uneconomic services the Government had decided to

185

maintain? It was a good point, for although the vast majority of closures had been accepted by the Minister, a few had been refused, leaving the railways with an obligation to keep the trains running — something that was not wholly reconcilable with their duty under the 1962 Act to run services at a profit. Stanley Raymond was rapidly becoming unpopular at the Ministry of Transport, and the incumbent Minister, Tom Fraser, not only refused to sanction the application of Social Surplus techniques to railway closures, but he also ignored the innovative proposal to create a Transport Highway Authority.

Meanwhile, Harold Wilson was beginning to lose patience with his lacklustre Minister of Transport. Fraser was proving something of a liability where the public and the railway unions were concerned but, late in 1965 an imminent general election gave Wilson an excuse to reshuffle his cabinet. In December, Fraser was ousted in favour of Barbara Castle, an able politician who proceeded to turn the Ministry of Transport apparatus on its head. In fact Barbara Castle's toughness and attention to detail brought success in an area where all previous ministerial incumbents had failed, for she actually stood up to her civil servants.

Mrs Castle found the motorway construction programme out of control, and her Permanent Secretary, Thomas Padmore, unashamedly biased towards road transport. Despite valiant attempts by the new Minister to have Padmore removed, he clung to his post, later retiring to take up a political job with the RAC.

On April 1, 1966, Labour scored a decisive victory in the election, and Mrs Castle set about a thorough investigation of the country's transport requirements. By April 22, she had turned the tide against railway closures by refusing a package of six, mostly in and around urban areas. Traffic congestion, said the new Minister, was reaching critical levels:

We are already faced with growing traffic congestion in our large city centres, and in my view it would be commercialism gone mad to take decisions which can only add to these problems.

Stanley Raymond was, of course, still waiting to hear who was going to pay, estimating in public that the six lines would require an annual subsidy of almost £250,000...

The answer came in a Government White Paper later in the year. In a flurry of gripping new phrases, such as "infrastructure", and "social and economic criteria", the White Paper, *Transport Policy*, outlined the Labour Government's transport objectives. At last there was a realisation that the railways were unlikely ever to comply with the commercial criteria of the 1962 Transport Act, and the White Paper brought the first mention of the "socially necessary" railway. Commercial viability, the paper claimed, "is important, but secondary".

By and large, it was a well-reasoned document. The road problem, for example, was tackled head on:

The nation has not yet begun to face up to the implications of the motor age. Each of us still believes he can find his own individual means of escape from the accompanying unpleasantness; for example, by finding a house further afield and buying a car... or cars... to enable him and his family to get to it.

According to *Transport Policy*, the nation's transport infrastructure would be modernised, investment carefully planned, and future judgments based upon "social" needs. Once again (though much further down the agenda than in 1945) a Labour government announced its intention to "integrate" public road and rail transport. Past railway closure decisions would not be reversed, though, and in the words of the White Paper, "there is some pruning still to be done", but there was every indication that the wholesale closure programme would be abandoned.

To study the question of railway finance, the Government introduced another selection of choice phrases into the national vocabulary by establishing a system of "Joint Machinery", involving both the Ministry of Transport and the Railways Board. Aptly enough, the Joint Machinery would be controlled by a "Steering Group" under John Morris, the Joint Parliamentary Secretary to the Minister of Transport. The terms of reference sounded perfectly reasonable and were surprisingly free of incomprehensible jargon:

To establish an acceptable basis for costing and to identify those categories of services... which are not covering costs... and to cost in detail the annual loss on each passenger service which is unlikely ever to be viable.

It was by no means the end of the closure process, however, for, after deliberating for nine months, the Government announced its intentions with regard to the Great Central.

While it had been considering the problem, the Railways Board had done its utmost to assist, introducing a timetable so derisory, so ill-considered, and so poorly planned, that it was surprising any passengers continued to use the line at all. The fastest service averaged just 38 mph, and there were gaps of up to five hours between trains.

The suggestion that British Railways never intentionally "ran down" services prior to closure was an outrageous one, for the schedule in the last days of the Great Central was astonishingly poor. It was also astonishingly expensive, for the Board had done nothing to economise on staff, and the handful of local trains that remained were almost exclusively steam-hauled. So lethargic was the schedule in those last gloomy days that, when a diesel multiple unit was occasionally brought in to cover for a missing or failed locomotive, it caused embarrassment by arriving early.

The reason why this travesty of a service had been allowed to drag on for so long was a political one, for the official pronouncement had been delayed by the general election. Thus there could be little doubt about the Minister's decision, for if Barbara Castle had settled on a reprieve she would have been unlikely to wait until three weeks after the election to announce it...

The Great Central was to close: it was the culmination of an agonising decline. Besides the worthless retention of a shuttle service between Rugby and Nottingham, all passenger trains would be withdrawn at an estimated saving of about £900,000 — the largest, and ultimately one of the most hotly contested, savings yet announced. At the TUCC inquiry the previous year, gross expenses had been put at £977,000, with income at about £438,000. Under no system of accountancy did the loss equate to £900,000.

It later emerged that the cost of the closure process itself, in terms of investigation, planning, and the deliberate imposition of loss-making services, had been enormously expensive. And little if any money was actually saved in the years after closure, for most of the staff were moved elsewhere to placate union objections.

Despite all the talk of "social need" and subsidy, Labour continued to implement the Beeching plans. Tom Fraser approved more than a thousand miles for closure in 1965. Barbara Castle went on to agree to a smaller number of **proposals** in 1966, but they were larger, more controversial candidates, and the mileage lost that year actually increased to almost 1,200.

For an aging Professor Hondelink it was the final straw. As consultant to the Great Central Association, he had fought long and hard to save the Great Central and his beloved railway now lay in ruins. At almost 80 years of age, and suffering from advancing ill-health, the professor wrote one of his last campaigning letters to his political friend the Right Honourable Philip Noel-Baker MP:

> I am glad to know that you will continue to battle on for a saner transport policy; you are still in a position of responsibility and authority to do so. I have largely given up the struggle. My rewarding work for the World Bank and the United Nations has until now mostly balanced the disappointment in my endeavours to help stem the deteriorating transport policy at home.

> Since we started nearly 20 years ago, and renewed our efforts about eight years ago to attack the Marples-Beeching planning, all I said and wrote has come true and was completely justified. I have been called a "major thorn in their side" and instructions have gone out not to attempt arguing with me, an outside expert.

In May 1967 the newly electrified Ryde to Shanklin service reopened, further closures were refused, and figures from the Euston to Liverpool and Manchester electrification scheme (completed in April 1966) indicated a remarkable 45 per cent increase in passenger journeys. It appeared as though Barbara Castle really had turned the Beeching tide, but events were rapidly to overtake such an optimistic view.

In an effort to "stabilise" the system, Mrs Castle unveiled the so-called

Network for Development plans in May 1967. They marked the culmination of the joint Railways Board and Ministry of Transport study, although (rather ominously) the Government was already making it clear that it would take the final decisions.

The railway network, standing at 13,200 miles, would be "stabilised" at 11,000 miles, of which just 8,000 miles would be open to passenger traffic. And there was a vague promise that the stabilised network was now firmly based and would remain unaffected by future developments.

At the remunerative end of the scale, the main trunk routes and a few of the secondary lines were to be developed. At the other extreme, certain commuter lines, and a handful of loss-making rural routes (which failed to meet financial criteria but served a "social" function), were to be retained and subsidised.

The real shock came with the list of lines that fitted neither of the above categories and consequently were not to be included in the "basic" network. These lines, neither profitable, nor (in the Government's view) socially necessary, were left in the hands of the British Railways Board. None, it was claimed, were immediately threatened with closure, but the Government had made it clear that none were to have an assured future either. It appeared that many supposedly "safe" secondary lines were to be swept away, as were the majority of the marginal branch lines.

Had the Government agreed to adopt cost/benefit analysis techniques where railway closure proposals were concerned the picture would have been very different, for under such criteria no more than a handful of lines produced a negative benefit. Barbara Castle was convinced that the urban commuter lines performed a useful function, but she had failed to be swayed by the argument that seasonal holiday lines, or cross-country routes serving large rural populations, were essential to the nation's well-being.

The cynically minded pointed out that the new proposals had concentrated resources on urban Labour constituencies while withdrawing facilities from the Tory shires. However, Barbara Castle was fighting her corner from a Ministry with an overwhelming road bias, and attempting to justify her policies before a Cabinet that held similar views. Whatever the true position, a number of lines were sacrificed in the Network For Development plans.

Lines in and around urban areas were left largely intact, as were certain of the loss-making branches in the remote regions — for "social" reasons. It was a brave policy as far as it went, but the result was often to subsidise routes that made heavy losses, while allowing others whose financial state was comparatively healthy, to fade away. The real brunt of the cuts was to be borne by the middle ground — lines that in many cases carried considerable traffic, but were not immediately profitable, and failed to meet the Government's social, economic and commercial criteria for retention.

189

A number of trunk lines were included in the list: the entire Waverley route between Edinburgh and Carlisle, the Settle & Carlisle, the Central Wales line and the Oxford to Cambridge cross-country route (already under stay of execution). Many branch lines were affected as well, including those to Mallaig, Kyle of Lochalsh, Fraserburgh, Peterhead, Pwhelli, Newquay, Falmouth, Ilfracombe, Hunstanton, Sheringham and Swanage.

The Government went to great pains to point out that it had not actually authorised closure of the lines, and that their future was entirely in the hands of the railway management. But it had also made it clear that the lines were not worthy of subsidy, and it knew perfectly well that closure proposals would follow.

It was a skillful political move. Unlike the previous Conservative administration, which had lost public good will by attempting to close every railway that failed to measure up in a commercial sense, the Government placated public criticism by agreeing to subsidise certain railways for social reasons, but the effect was to leave a gaping hole in its railway policy and, ultimately, to precipitate another round of closures.

The plans were to create some strange anomalies. The largest closures, in both route mileage and infrastructure terms, had been of the so-called "duplicate" trunk routes. Most of Devon and North Cornwall had been served by the ex-London & South Western line, reaching deep into Great Western territory via Salisbury, Exeter and Okehampton to Plymouth, with branches throughout Devon and Cornwall. With the railway grouping of 1923, the line fell into the hands of the Southern Railway which enthusiastically improved services to the general detriment of the Great Western.

Had the Great Western and LSWR routes been genuinely duplicate, the case for closure would have been overwhelming, but they were not. Certainly, both started in London and ended in the West Country, but there the similarity ended, for the two lines served very different areas along the way.

In September 1964, the Railways Board had withdrawn the Atlantic Coast Express from the LSWR route — a move that plunged all the associated services into a terminal decline. One by one, the branch lines were closed, until the former trunk route succumbed between Exeter and Plymouth.

It was a fine example of the fallacy of the Beeching doctrine. As a group, the railways of Devon and North Cornwall had been reasonably prosperous, but once the contraction had begun, it was easy to prove that the individual branches were uneconomic. And once the branch lines had been removed, the trunk line itself became vulnerable.

At this point Barbara Castle arrived, wielding her "social criteria". The former LSWR trunk line from Plymouth to Exeter would remain partially open (and heavily subsided) between Plymouth and Bere Alston, to provide a service

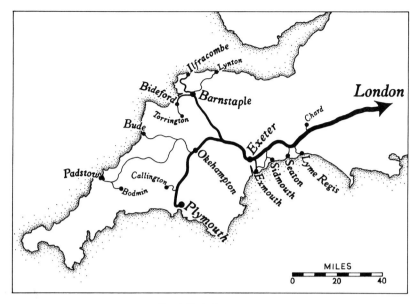

Contributory revenue

The map provides a graphic illustration of the contributory revenue theory. During the Victorian era, the London & South Western Railway Company reached deep into Great Western territory, establishing a network of secondary and branch lines that fed traffic on to the trunk route to London.

Things were rarely as simple as this, in practice, and even here there was a degree of overlap with Great Western lines, which have been omitted for the sake of clarity. Not all the branch lines were owned, or even operated, by the L & SWR, but it soon became clear that the branches were as essential to the health of the trunk line as the trunk line was to the branches.

In the 1960s every single line was considered for closure but, against all the odds, the branches to Barnstaple and Exmouth survived, as the did the trunk line from Exeter towards London. There is now talk of renewed investment, raising the question of why the retrenchment process was taken so far in the first place.

for a handful of residents at Gunnislake on the former Callington branch. This section fitted neatly into the Minister's "social" category, as the line carried commuter traffic and it had proved impossible to provide a reasonable bus service to the village.

The problem lay in the geography of the landscape, for the villages of Gunnislake and Calstock lay in a loop of the river Tamar and were not easily served by road transport. It was hardly railway territory either, but British Railways had suffered the misfortune to inherit a fine viaduct across the river, so it was obliged to continue running trains to Calstock and Gunnislake. It was an expensive operation that showed little in the way of returns.

From Exeter, the line would remain open as far as Okehampton (as even Beeching had recommended that it should), but the crucial stretch between Bere Alston and Okehampton was to close. The result was to leave Tavistock — larger than Okehampton and Gunnislake combined — completely isolated, and remove from the network a useful diversionary route (the main line between Exeter and Plymouth remains susceptible to sea damage).

Areas of north Cornwall were now as far from a railhead as the remotest corners of Wales, with a complete cessation of services to Tavistock, Launceston, Bude, Holsworthy, Camelford, Wadebridge and Padstow. And the express services had also helped to support the branches to Ilfracombe and Bideford in north Devon; and Sidmouth, Seaton and Lyme Regis to the south. One by one these branches also died, endangering the remains of the trunk line between Salisbury and Exeter, which was downgraded to lowly secondary status and put on the doubtful list. Finally, the Exeter to Okehampton stretch, bereft of through traffic, was deemed unworthy of subsidy and lost its passenger services as well.

None of these towns justified a rail link in their own right, but together they had sustained a viable network. Within a few years the whole operation had collapsed, leaving a permanent population in excess of 60,000 people without adequate public transport. And such figures were just the tip of a very large iceberg, for the number of tourists denied use of from the railways and forced onto the roads was considerably higher. All that remained was a short loss-making branch to a single village on the Cornish border. The lesson was a simple one: contraction, once begun in earnest, became a self-fuelling process.

A similar situation would arise should the Settle & Carlisle line close for, according to Network for Development, much of the route would be retained for freight use to serve military sidings at Warcop near Appleby. Only the centre section would close, and with it would go all the through traffic. On the other hand, the policy of subsidising lines for social reasons was supporting some very minor branches, such as those to Bridport in Dorset and Alston in Cumbria. Both ran through thinly populated country, but were retained because inadequate roads precluded the introduction of a replacement bus service. Yet, it should be pointed out, there still remained persuasive social arguments for the retention of lines such as the Alston branch which served what has since become a growing tourist destination. At the time of closure Northumberland County Council, through whose territory most of the line ran, said it would rather spend the money earmarked by the Department of Transport for the necessary road improvements on running the rail service itself. It was denied that opportunity.

By the end of 1967, just 9,882 miles of railway remained open to passenger traffic, and Barbara Castle proudly announced that she had "stopped the Beeching butchery". In reality, the Beeching closure programme had almost reached its logical conclusion... the butchery had only lost momentum because there were few potential victims left.

After publication of Network for Development, all that stood in the way of further closures was the much maligned TUCC inquiry procedure. Fortunately, public opinion had hardened since the Beeching days, and local authorities and pro-rail pressure groups had learnt a great deal. Even the attitude of the TUCCs was gradually beginning to change.

As expected, British Rail wasted no time in introducing closure plans. In late 1967 it made public its intention to close the Swanage branch from September 1968. It had, however, underestimated both the opposition and the logistical difficulties of providing a bus service to cope with the summer traffic. The Swanage branch failed to close in September 1968... it also failed to close the following year. Indeed, so vociferous was the opposition from pressure groups, local MPs, the county council, and various other local authorities, that a public inquiry was called. After hearing evidence that buses would be quite unable to handle the traffic during the summer months, the Department of the Environment's inspector decided that the line should stay open. Unfortunately, his decision was later overturned by the Secretary of State for the Environment and closure came in January 1972.

Meanwhile, Barbara Castle was emerging as one of the ablest ministers ever to tackle the problems of transport. After taking advice from the Joint Steering Group established the previous year, she prepared a formula to head off the railways' financial crisis, while taking a serious look at road problems, particularly where heavy freight vehicles were concerned. In a brave attempt to clarify the road costs debate, she undertook a detailed analysis of the problem, anticipating that major changes could be incorporated into a new Transport Act.

On a simple year-by-year basis, it emerged that road users were paying more in taxes than the Government was spending on road construction and mainte-nance, for in 1965-66 road costs had amounted to £450 million, while tax income stood at £926 million.

If, however, the roads were subjected to the same financial criteria as the railways and other nationalised industries, the annual costs rose significantly, to £625 million. And after making an allowance for "community costs", including accidents to non-road users, airborne pollution and noise, it emerged that road users might well be paying too little. It certainly appeared as though heavy freight vehicles were causing a disproportionate amount of environmental damage, and provision was made in the forthcoming Transport Act to raise an extra £30 million a year in taxes from the road haulage industry. The British Road Federation invested £50,000 in fighting the proposals and it was to prove money well spent.

The Wilson administration was in difficulties, for the technological revolution had failed to go according to plan, the hottest areas proving to be not nearly as white-hot as had been expected. The 1968 budget had been severe, and while the fortunes of the Government teetered on the brink, Wilson moved quickly to placate the road lobby. In April, Barbara Castle was promoted to the Ministry of Labour, while Richard Marsh was brought in to handle transport. The forthcoming Transport Act would be amended by removing the extra charges on heavy road vehicles in favour of a small general increase in fuel taxation. Barbara Castle, the only post-war Minister of Transport to have stood up to the road lobby, had been removed for political reasons.

As expected, railway closure attempts began to concentrate on the lines that had failed to be included on the Network for Development maps. Matters came to a head in July 1968 when the new Transport Minister approved closure of the Waverley route, claiming an annual saving of £700,000. It was an extraordinary figure, for at the TUCC inquiry the Railways Board had claimed a loss of only £256,000. The reason for this strange anomaly was shortly to emerge in the provisions of the 1968 Transport Act.

* * *

After a record 45 sittings at the committee stage, and no fewer than 2,500 amendments, the most radical transport legislation since 1962 became law in October 1968. The effect on the railways was immediate and profound for, as in 1962, the intention was to make the railway system self-supporting. Once again, various capital liabilities were written off, but it was hoped that the long-term objective of commercial viability would be achieved by the provision of grants rather than further cutbacks.

The Railways Board had hoped for a "surplus capacity grant" to cover the cost of maintaining double or quadruple tracks that were not immediately useful, but might, in case of national emergency or severe weather conditions, prove essential. But the Ministry presumably came to the conclusion that surplus railway capacity would never again be needed, for the Act provided instead for the railways to be paid a grant to scrap surplus equipment: a move that was expected to produce an annual saving of around £15 million. The grant arrangements placed considerable pressure on the Railways Board to remove track and equipment as quickly as possible — often before they became due for replacement — yet it was an area where careful study of future trends was of the utmost importance.

In any event, by the time the 1968 Transport Act had been published, there was already plenty of evidence that over-enthusiastic pruning of railway facilities could be counter-productive. Almost the entire 90-mile route of the former LSWR trunk line between Salisbury and Exeter had been reduced to single track in the summer of 1967, with gaps of up to 20 miles between passing loops. The effect, far from saving money, was close to disastrous, for the prospect of even a minor breakdown on long stretches of single-track trunk line was so nerve-shattering that the railway authorities are said to have provided a mechanic on every train — just in case!

Integration of rail and road transport remained elusive, although the 1968 Act made a move in the right direction by establishing Passenger Transport Authorities (initially Conurbation Transport Authorities) in the West Midlands, Merseyside, Greater Manchester and Tyneside. Other PTAs followed in Greater Glasgow, 1973, and in West and South Yorkshire with local government reorganisation in 1975. The authorities, managed by Passenger Transport Executives, would make agreements with British Rail and other transport operators as to the levels of fares and subsidies in their particular regions. Another attempt at integration was incorporated into the Act, but it met with such hysterical abuse from the road lobby and the road transport trade unions, that it was never successfully implemented, and was repealed shortly afterwards by an incoming Conservative Government.

The new measure, known as "quantity licensing", was an echo of the freight vehicle mileage restrictions bound up in the 1947 Act. The operators of the largest road vehicles would be obliged to offer first refusal to the railways on traffic carried over more than 100 miles, or less where the merchandise included coal or minerals. If the railways were unable to match the road operator in terms of price, speed and reliability, the traffic would go by road... but if the railway could offer a better deal, they would be given the business. Besides all manner of difficulties in actually implementing the legislation, the whole affair raised one rather obvious question. If the railways were able to tender at a favourable price, there should have been no need for compulsion, which showed the railway management in a rather bad light, and merely reinforced the widespread view that the railways were just another "lame-duck" nationalised industry.

As expected, the unremunerative or social railways were to be subsidised with the aid of grants. In future, British Rail would put forward grant applications for loss-making services, and the Government would authorise an annual grant (expected to be in the region of £50 million) to make good the deficit.

Perhaps inevitably, there was a catch. There was no specific guarantee that particular services would receive grant aid... not even those that had been earmarked for development in the plans of the previous year. Cash would only be forthcoming for lines that met vague social and strategic criteria set by the Government, and the grant aid arrangements were to be no more than a temporary measure... none would be authorised for more than three years ahead, and most would be subject to renewal annually.

Of even more significance was the system put in place to calculate the grants. Sir William Carrington's proposals, in use since 1962, were thrown out and replaced by a new costing technique, known as the Cooper Brothers formula, after the firm of chartered accountants (whose Henry Benson had served on the Stedeford Committee) that produced it.

There were several significant features of this formula. The Railways Board was to take no account of contributory revenue, true engineering costs would be ignored and replaced by a high "average" figure, and 12.5 per cent would be added to cover administrative expenses, regardless of the true figure. In addition, no account would be taken of freight or other services that might already be sharing certain costs. The new system was to push "paper" losses through the ceiling, with the result that quite insignificant branch lines suddenly appeared to have produced unlikely deficits.

The effects of the Cooper Brothers formula became apparent when Corby Urban District Council applied to British Rail for reinstatement of passenger services on the seven-and-a-half mile line between Kettering and Corby. As the line carried a good deal of freight traffic, the Railways Board agreed to the request, subject to a token annual grant of £10,000. In the meantime, the Cooper Brothers formula arrived, and the Board hastily revised its grant requirement to £45,000, a figure that proved quite unacceptable to the council.

This was the reason for the jump from £256,000 to £700,000 in losses on the Edinburgh to Carlisle line. With the imposition of the Cooper Brothers formula, and Government refusal to pay a subsidy, the line was doomed: it was destined to become the last great railway closure. The £700,000 actually equated to around £7,000 per mile — the expenditure that Beeching had considered necessary to maintain a line **with no income at all**.

The Government had set an important principle. The commercial lines and freight operations were to be viewed as self-supporting, and London would receive a single block grant to cover the cost of commuter and social services. All other services were to receive grants, but only where the Government considered the subsidy to be cost-effective.

The effect of the too generous grant formula was quite beneficial to British Rail, which used the additional income to subsidise losses in other areas. According to one member of the Railways Board, the grant-aided lines had become the railway's "most profitable" services. For the handful of remaining marginal branch lines, however, the grant system was to spell disaster.

Whether by accident or design, the Government had come up with a solution to the uneconomic railway problem, by inflating theoretical costs to such a degree that the lines were easily written off. It would not have mattered in the slightest (apart from adversely effecting the morale of provincial railway staff) as long as all the loss-making services were to remain grant-aided. It rapidly emerged that they were not.

The first block of grants, representing estimated losses under the Cooper Brothers formula, amounted to £62 million. So generous was the grant system that almost every railway service in the country was to receive some degree of financial assistance. The effect on managerial and union morale was far from beneficial, for even a few of the crack inter-city express services appeared to be losing money. But the real problems lay in store for the branch lines.

The Government had decided that a selection of lines would not be eligible for full grant aid — including 130 miles that had been declared worthy of retention under the Network for Development plans just a year before:

Railway Service	Grant claims
Bridgend to Treherbet	£150,000
Bangor to Caernarfon	£60,000
Colchester to Sudbury	£90,000
High Wycombe to Bourne End	£60,000
Colne to Skipton	£110,000
Kidderminster to Stourport via Bewdley	£55,000
Cambridge to St Ives	£120,000
Exeter to Okehampton	£150,000
Kirkham to Fleetwood	£120,000

Some of the grant claims were astonishing. The Exeter to Okehampton line carried considerable freight traffic, yet the passenger service was reckoned to cost £10,200 per mile. Cambridge to St Ives also carried freight, yet it was estimated to be costing £8,100 a mile to maintain the passenger service.

For the Railways Board there was every incentive to err on the high side in making grant applications. If the grant was approved, the money could be used elsewhere and, if it was refused, it had a perfect excuse to close the line, and an apparently overwhelming financial case in favour of such a move.

All the lines that were refused grant aid, or failed to receive a full grant, were put up for immediate closure by the Board, and all but the Sudbury branch subsequently closed. British Rail was later to admit that many decisions taken at the time were in error, particularly the closure of the Caernarfon to Bangor line where contributory revenue had been particularly high, and nearly all was lost after closure.

In addition to the grant package, the 1968 Transport Act wiped out most of the railway's outstanding debts. Not surprisingly, the result of these two moves was to produce a small £15 million profit the following year and a rather smaller surplus of £9.5 million in 1970. It was a totally false situation though, for investment had dropped from a less than satisfactory £121 million in 1965, to a derisory £69 million by 1969.

The new railway system, billed as compact, efficient and modern, was really demoralised, inefficient and chronically short of investment capital. The closure programme was more or less complete, yet even those who had approved of the closure policy admitted the savings had been small. There had been no real administrative savings, and closures had contributed no more than a quarter to the general rise in productivity since the start of the programme, while traffic worth at least £11 million had been lost for good.

That was the situation on the eve of the new decade, as a smug and self-confident western world floated high on an ocean of cheap and plentiful fuel oil. In just three years a cataclysmic shock was to arrive, changing attitudes to the motor car for ever — the 1973 Arab oil embargo.

But in 1970, such a turn of events seemed unthinkable. The rapidly advancing railway crisis was to get a great deal worse before salvation arrived.

8.
The energy crisis
1970-1990

Our Continental friends just do not understand how we could allow our railways to be butchered as they have been in the last 15 years, and with the impending energy crisis we may very well be frantically trying to restore in ten years time facilities which we gaily abandoned ten years ago...

J D Wylde, Transport Co-ordinating Officer for Leicestershire County Council, September 1973

BY *the late 1960s the burgeoning railway preservation movement appeared to offer hope to those who continued to oppose the railway closures. The first priority was to keep track on the ground then, at a later stage, when the preserved line was up and running, it might be possible to restore a proper service. Wages were costing British Rail as much as 60-70 per cent of total operating costs, and it followed that a preserved line, staffed almost entirely by volunteers, could realistically maintain a year-round service where the unwieldy national concern had failed.*

But after several brave attempts, the experiment ultimately proved fruitless, and the railway system continued to contract. Indeed, by early 1973, the financial situation had reached crisis point once again. But just as the Government was considering whether to implement another round of closures, the oil crisis arrived, severely denting the seemingly unassailable position of the road lobby, and permanently altering the balance of transport economics. In the decade that followed, faith in the motor car continued to crumble, and the railways gradually began to take the initiative. In 1983 the rail lobby scored a decisive parliamentary victory with the introduction of the Speller legislation that eased the path towards railway reopenings. By the late 1980s, the long awaited railway renaissance had arrived, and the financial situation looked relatively secure.

* * *

From humble beginnings, with the preservation of the little Talyllyn narrow-gauge line in 1951, and the standard-gauge Bluebell line in 1959, the railway mileage in private ownership had steadily increased. It was not, however, until the successful reopening of the Keighley and Worth Valley and Dart Valley railways in the late 1960s, that the preservation movement began to be taken seriously.

After a fitful start, the pioneer preservation bodies had proved that railway nostalgia was a marketable commodity. But would they be able to put trains back into service on a regular, year-round basis? There were many sceptics, for although some 50 miles of line had been transferred into private hands by 1969, not a single mile had seen the return of a full service, and most lines were open to the public for just two or three months of the year. The sole exception was the narrow-gauge Ravenglass and Eskdale in Cumbria, which operated a single daily train... but the Eskdale line had never been under the control of the Railways Board in the first place. Many potential operators had grandiose plans, and 1969 saw publication of the grandest and most prestigious scheme of all.

The Waverley route between Edinburgh and Carlisle had proved to be the last major railway closure in Great Britain, and it was fitting that the line should also be the test-bed for a new and radical idea: a privately-owned and fully commercial trunk line.

Many had felt the closure had been an act of monumental folly on the part of the authorities, for the Waverley line was actually a few miles shorter than the alternative route via Carstairs, and closure had left a sizeable population without access to rail transport.

Even British Rail was later to admit that closure of the line might have been a mistake, for once electrification had been completed through to Glasgow and Edinburgh in 1973, it became apparent that the Waverley line might have provided a useful feeder for the new electric services.

It was exactly as Professor Hondelink had predicted for, paradoxically, the modernised services had improved the viability of former "duplicate" routes — some finding a new role feeding traffic to the main lines. This possibility seemed to have escaped the architects of the Beeching Reports, and the Network for Development plans. They had chosen to concentrate resources on particular routes and remove the others altogether, but the effect of concentrating investment on primary routes had often been to feed revenue to the secondary lines.

Had the BTC electrified the West Coast Main Line in the early 1960s (as it had intended), the future of the Waverley route might have been assured for, by 1974, the electric trains had cut the journey time from Carlisle to London to four hours or so, and there was suddenly a new potential for a connecting service to Hawick and Galashiels.

Instead, the business traveller from, say, Hawick needing to make a trip to London or Bristol is today less likely to make his or her way to the railhead at Carlisle than to drive a similar distance and fly from Newcastle.

Yet, at the time, many observers had foreseen the possibility for the

Above: "Golden Plover" leaves remote Riccarton Junction (with the Border Union line into the Tyne valley in the right background) on the magnificent Waverley line in September 1964, while, below, the same locomotive is pictured at Galashiels, hauling a special the following year. Colour-Rail. SC207 & 594.

Waverley to feed into the West Coast route. Even in 1969 it had looked as though the 100-odd miles of the Waverley route could be operated as a viable and profitable private concern. Seasonal steam trains would satisfy the tourists and generate income, while a diesel railcar would handle the day-to-day trade and connect with inter-city services at Carlisle.

A group of individuals formed the Border Union Railway Company in February 1969 and began to seek financial support for the scheme. Initially, British Rail was by no means unco-operative, offering to negotiate running rights into both Carlisle and Edinburgh, and suggesting a figure of around £750,000 for the line — a reasonable, if not over generous, price.

The Border Union had prepared an ambitious scheme quite out of keeping with earlier preservation attempts. Most of the line would be reduced to single track, but there was talk of diesel railcars, gas turbine locomotives, low-loader wagons (to pick up road lorries from an M6 railhead) and other more or less commercially viable schemes. The line would be operated on a fully commercial basis, providing work for about 100 ex-BR employees and, unlike the majority of private lines, the North British Railway (as the operating company was to be known) would not be seeking a Light Railway Order. It was, in short, a very professional operation.

Almost immediately there were financial and legal problems as the company became bogged down in negotiations with the Railways Board. The Board demanded £10,000 in legal fees and a non-returnable deposit of £250,000. The Border Union needed more time, for it was awaiting the conclusions of an independent feasibility study. At the last moment, British Rail consented to allow four months grace in exchange for £8,000 per month interest. The Border Union was unable to comply and, by December 1969, negotiations had drawn to a close. Meanwhile, the Ministry of Transport chipped in, reportedly demanding £170,000 should a bridge be required to carry the new M6 motorway over the line.

It was more or less the end of the project. The Border Union responded with a rather weak offer to purchase just the formation and buildings, and later reduced its interest to the section between Hawick and Carlisle. Gradually, the hopes of the Border Union Railway Company faded away and, by April 1970, the scheme was effectively dead.

Despite all the optimistic forecasts, the plan had been too ambitious. No private operator had yet succeeded in purchasing such a large concern, and the general feeling from the private companies was that there was no particular **need** to utilise any great mileage. Car-borne steam enthusiasts were generally satisfied with just a few miles of track... the most successful preserved lines operating over less than ten miles or so. With the exception of the Keighley and Worth Valley, none had yet secured a proper connection to the railway network, and none had introduced a year-round service. With the collapse of the Border Union, it became clear that most preserved railways were to be just that — short stretches of track maintained as working museums, and generally preserved in the heady aspic of a rather vague golden era, set somewhere between the 1930s and the 1950s.

To those who had become involved with the private concerns out of frustration with a Railways Board that seemed bent on self-destruction, the private railways were ultimately to prove a disappointment, for they had neither the cash nor the incentive to operate a full service. Many failed to get off the ground at all.

Several brave schemes were to collapse after facing exorbitant demands for surplus track and equipment. In 1963 the Board had asked £4,800 per mile for the $12^{1}/_{2}$-mile Kingsbridge branch in Devon, but when the preservation attempt failed, the fixtures subsequently realised little more than £1,800 per mile for scrap. The following year the Board demanded a reasonable £4,700 per mile for the Leominster to Presteigne line but, in 1966, almost £11,000 per mile for the little Clevedon branch in Somerset. Against such a figure, the all-in price of about £7,500 per mile for the impressive engineering of the Waverley route looked something of a bargain.

The British Railways Board, firmly under the control of the Ministry of Transport where the sale of surplus equipment was concerned, was never to give an adequate explanation for these high prices. Proof that the value placed on surplus equipment was, indeed, highly inflated, came when a preservation group attempted to purchase the line between Sheringham and Weybourne in Norfolk. British Rail had asked a fairly typical £5,250 per mile for the track, but when the preservation attempt failed, the Board sold the fixtures at an undisclosed price to a Norwich scrap dealer.

The preservation group approached the dealer and found that, not only had he paid rather less than £5,250, but he was more than willing to resell for £3,000 per mile. Since scrap dealers were not widely known as philanthropists, there seemed little doubt that the Board had offered the equipment for scrap at a favourable price. Unfortunately, the dealer found he was bound by contract not to sell the track for "re-use" and, if the society wanted it, it would have to pay the original price.

Many other preservation schemes, for branches including those to Westerham, Hayling Island and Ilfracombe, failed, in part, as a result of the prohibitive purchase costs involved, the Ilfracombe line being valued at no less than £410,000 in 1974. The preservation groups argued that the Board had no right to charge top market values for a line on which the object was to preserve a part of the nation's heritage. The sole aim of the Railways Board (under orders from the Ministry) was to fix the highest possible price to offset mounting deficits.

It had no evidence that the preserved lines would provide a penny in contributory revenue, and it cared even less. It was a situation which has changed little in many respects, with the disposal of assets now an important source of BR revenue. In one instance, the Warcop branch on the Settle-Carlisle line, preservation plans were at stalemate at the time of writing because of Railfreight's wish to see the line sold for its "full commercial value".

Several local authorities, aghast at closure announcements in busy holiday regions, had gone to great lengths to back private ventures. Perhaps typical was the affair surrounding the Paignton to Kingswear branch — a line reportedly carrying between 20,000 and 40,000 passengers a week in the summer, but less than 6,000 in the winter months. The prospective purchaser, the Dart Valley Railway Company, was offering to instigate a year-round service, and an overjoyed local authority offered British Rail £3,625 a month to keep the line ticking over until private operations could commence.

Once the line had been safely transferred into private hands, the winter service to Kingswear lasted just a season and, in October 1973, the company announced the virtual cessation of its winter schedule. According to Alan Sanders, of the Dart Valley Railway, the winter services had "proved a financial burden". Be that as it may, the loss of winter trains to Kingswear marked the end of the privatisation dream, and the county council, which had expected great things of the arrangement, was left to provide a bus service for school children at short notice. And, although there was again talk of a winter railcar in 1991, it was clear that, while the private railway would bring welcome tourist trade in the summer months, a full service appeared to be out of the question.

By this time there were few seaside branch lines left... the handful that remained having outlasted Dr Beeching by a considerable margin. Most had been condemned in 1963, with the assistance of the various distorted figures in the Reshaping Report, but the real situation was rather different, and despite the best efforts of the Board, traffic levels had remained embarrassingly high in many cases.

Devon County Council had helped to save the Kingswear line to take pressure off the Paignton to Kingswear road, while the Skegness service had won a full reprieve for similar reasons. Others, including Mablethorpe, Hunstanton, Ilfracombe and Swanage had succumbed, although the arguments in favour of retaining the branches (during the summer at least) had been overwhelming.

To the various local authorities, the affair must have appeared quite inexplicable. Central government had failed to provide grant aid for their busy, if unremunerative, branch lines, but it had also failed to provide the new roads that might have helped alleviate the worsening traffic situation. Truly, the Cooper Brothers grant formula had worked its wonders in a mysterious way.

TWO DORSET BRANCH LINES: *Above — A loose goods train crosses from the Isle of Portland in the mid-1960s, just before closure. (Patrick Henshaw picture). Below — The Swanage line closed in 1972 but much of the track has since been reinstated by the Swanage Railway Company, as illustrated in the author's picture of Corfe Castle.*

At Swanage, a preservation group circulated a petition in the town and found that 86 per cent of residents were in favour of a restored service. The line had closed in January 1972, and although (or perhaps because) the Swanage Railway Society had offered to purchase the line on the basis of an independent valuation, the Railways Board had torn up the track within a few months.

Undaunted, the Society grew into a powerful and influential body, and in 1974 it issued detailed plans for a proposed year-round "amenity" service to be subsidised by summer steam operations. If nothing else, the plans illustrated the near impossibility of a small private company maintaining a full service. It was estimated that the amenity trains would earn in the region of £34,000 a year, but costs, including those of BR train crews (to pilot trains over the main line between Worgret Junction and Wareham), signalling and maintenance to main line standards, would run to around £82,600. The resulting deficit of £48,700 would be borne by the summer service, leaving an annual profit of just £3,000. It was a distinctly marginal return, whereas a purely seasonal operation would yield a handsome operating profit to fund future developments... The lesson was not lost on other companies.

One of the longest running closure dramas had been acted out on the north Somerset coast, where a branch ran from Taunton to the resorts of Watchet and Minehead. At the closure inquiry in 1968, the local bus company had informed the TUCC that six buses would be required to operate a replacement service in the winter months, which was perfectly reasonable, but that even 20 vehicles might prove inadequate on summer Saturdays. The bus company didn't have the resources to cope with such an influx and, in any event, the long and rather tortuous road link between Taunton and Minehead would have difficulty coping. British Rail, on the other hand, was determined to close the line and, armed with the Cooper Brothers formula, it announced a loss of £141,000 a year.

By January 1971 a compromise had been agreed under which the line would close — a move that left Somerset County Council far from satisfied. The county council agreed to buy the line and lease it back to the West Somerset Railway Company, which would operate a full winter schedule besides the more usual tourist services. In order to get some return on its £245,000 investment, the council would charge an annual rent of £14,000 to the railway company, with the inducement that most of it would be returnable should the company instigate a daily year-round service.

Through no fault of its own, the railway company never fully succeeded. The bus drivers (who were, ironically, mostly NUR men) adopted an intransigent attitude to the scheme, and British Rail found a variety of reasons to refuse running rights into Taunton station. The sight of Sidney Weighell, the then General Secretary of the NUR, arguing **against** a rail reopening did not do a lot for the union's credibility at this time.

As the years passed, the affair was gradually forgotten. The bus company never did require 20 buses, for the former rail traffic either evaporated or took to private transport, the local residents came to accept road congestion as a fact of life, and the West Somerset Railway, after a very rocky start, began to turn in a small profit on its seasonal services. It appeared as though Minehead had left the national railway network for good in 1971.

The net effect of preserving railways had been to increase road traffic, rather than reduce it, for the tourist potential of the lines had exceeded all expectations, but as few of them were connected to the railway network the majority of travellers arrived by road.

Local authorities seeking to preserve their services were having more success by negotiating with British Rail — as the Railway Development Association and the Railway Invigoration Society (which had been working quietly and effectively behind the scenes) had long argued that they should. In June 1971, the line between Peterborough and Spalding reopened with local authority grant aid after being closed to passengers for eight months. It was a unique arrangement that was to provide the impetus for many similar schemes. In December that year, Gipping Rural District Council won a protracted battle for the reopening of Needham Market station in Suffolk, closed since January 1967. Such small victories heralded the start of a trickle of reopenings.

However, the overall picture remained bleak, for the return to power of the Conservatives, following Ted Heath's June 1970 election victory, saw road interests to the fore once again.

The Heath Government attempted to combine the doctrines of the welfare state with the economics of the market place and succeeded in doing neither. Indeed, the major side-effect of this "soft" capitalist approach (later gleefully condemned by Prime Minister Margaret Thatcher as "wet" politics), was an uprising of industrial militancy culminating in the three-day working week and strict power rationing.

Transport policy stagnated during the Heath years. The new Minister for Transport Industries, John Peyton, made it clear that he had little time for loss-making nationalised industries, and for British Rail in particular. His appointment pleased the road lobby immensely and, in April 1971, a meeting of the British Road Federation, the RAC, the Road Haulage Association, the AA and the Freight Transport Association set a target for 3,000 miles of new motorway. Two months later the Government announced a programme that included 2,000 miles of motorway and 1,500 miles of dual-carriageway. It was close enough.

April 1970 saw the demise of the Cambridge to St Ives branch and, later in the month, the Ashford to Hastings line won an eleventh-hour reprieve when a bus licence was temporarily refused pending road improvements. In October, the Railways Board mopped up in much of Lincolnshire, finally closing the lines between Lincoln, Firsby, Louth and Grimsby. The only link with the coast in the south of the county was the line to Skegness via Boston, and it had only survived because the approach roads to the town were already saturated at the height of the summer season. In May the same year, the Board began to run down the Settle & Carlisle by closing all the local stations just in time for the summer season, presumably with the intention of provoking a collapse along Great Central lines.

Beyond the commuter lines in and around London and the major cities, little remained of the "social" railway services, the majority of the survivors being concentrated in thoroughly unremunerative regions such as central Wales and the Highlands of Scotland. To the remotest regions, the railways were an essential lifeline, and to city commuters (where the motor car had made travel equally difficult) the railway was grudgingly accepted as the only means of transport available.

By 1973 the closure process was virtually complete: a system that had once extended to more than 20,000 miles had been cut to 11,300 miles, but in terms of services things were far worse than the figures suggest, for a proportion of the network carried only goods traffic and, of the remainder, many lines had lost all stopping trains.

Some remote services had survived on a thread of political expediency. The Central Wales line reportedly passed through so many marginal parliamentary constituencies that no-one dared to close it. British Rail, which had begun a winding-down operation in the early 1960s, was later told to make a few economies and keep the trains running. Thanks to better timetabling and promotion, receipts had more than doubled by 1972 but, because of the extraordinary logic of the Cooper Brothers grant formula, costs were reported to be £464,000 against income of only £45,000.

The associated Cambrian Coast branch proved similarly charmed, surviving all manner of vicissitudes, including formal notice of closure, and a devastating travel survey conducted in June 1974. The survey, by Professor Graham Rees of the University of Wales, Cardiff, found that only 1.9 per cent of Meirionnydd residents used the line, and just three per cent of visiting tourists arrived on it, while 7.2 per cent came by bus or coach and the vast majority by private car.

Generally speaking, the railways had proved unable to service investment from income despite the grant provisions of the 1968 Transport Act and, by 1972, finances were once again in a critical state. Closure proposals had been prepared for most of the Welsh and Scottish lines, and the Government was looking hard at the general worth of the railway network.

Fortunately for the railways, the road system was creating problems of its own. In 1971, annual expenditure on the British road system had reached £812 million, while tax subsidies for company cars were costing the nation somewhere in the region of £1,000 million a year. Against such astonishing figures, a railway line that served most of Central Wales for well under £500,000 looked something of a bargain. In fact, the British railway system continued to provide remarkable value for money when measured against overseas concerns. In 1971, the German system received a subsidy of £700 million, the French £400 million, and the much vaunted Japanese railways had been subsidised to the tune of £300 million and received an additional £500 million to cover capital expenditure. British Railways made small losses on top of a grant of around £60 million and wound up £150 million in the red, after interest.

In comparative terms, the cost of the railway network was fairly modest, and there was a growing feeling that the motor car might not offer a panacea to all transport problems — indeed, railway closures had thrown such a volume of traffic onto the roads that the Government was finding itself forced into a vicious circle of road spending that promised to far exceed railway losses.

The pendulum had swung so far in favour of road transport that the Government was now obliged to subsidise the road system. If a road improvement scheme was refused, industry replied with the perfectly legitimate objection that output would be affected, for there was virtually no alternative means of distribution. If a new bypass scheme was rejected, the public had a perfectly legitimate grievance that the Government was blighting its community.

The cost of pouring investment into a single mode of transport had been appalling. Congestion alone was calculated to be costing industry somewhere in the region of £700 million a year, and the burgeoning road building programme was having little effect. It began to look as though the policy of judging the railways by economic criteria alone was too restrictive, and that factors such as pollution and road congestion were already altering the balance in favour of rail transport.

In 1972, such arguments were brought sharply into focus with the publication, by the Organisation for Economic Co-operation and Development, of a report entitled *The Motor Car and Natural Resources*.

In Europe, fuel was, by tradition, cheap and plentiful, and pollution of little consequence. But North American experience was telling a different story. The brave new super-highways of the 1960s, that had received such Parliamentary praise in Britain during the railway debates of the Beeching years, were clogged with traffic and the Los Angeles sky wreathed in poisonous smog.

The immediate concern of the OECD was whether the world would actually be able to accommodate the growing volume of road vehicles. By the year 2000, the report predicted, there would be more than 28 million in the UK and 500 million throughout the world. The figures revealed an awful truth: it appeared as though the cities of the world would succumb, one after another, to the nightmare of airborne pollution, and oil (suddenly deemed a finite resource) would run short from the turn of the century, and become a rare commodity by 2075. Car ownership was approaching saturation point, particularly in the USA, and there didn't seem to be any easy solutions:

> ...there is now in the USA a great awareness that the growth of the private car must be curbed; that its price is enormous in terms of congestion, pollution, accidents, the destruction of cities by roadworks and many other social costs; and that future growth should be prevented as far as possible by both restricting the private car and forcing the development of alternative means of transport.

According to the OECD, similar measures would be necessary in Europe within 20 to 30 years. If not the end, it was certainly the beginning of the end for the dreams of the road lobby. By 1972, road transport in the USA was guzzling almost 30 per cent of the country's total energy consumption, and almost everyone had realised that the situation would need to be held in check. Unfortunately the British had blindly followed the Americans in pursuit of an unattainable goal... and the road had led, literally, nowhere.

Road congestion in the States had remained fairly localised, but Britain already had the most crowded roads in the world. On a "vehicles per mile of road" basis, Britain dominated the world congestion league table. Japan (with a large and viable rail network) supported 24 vehicles per mile, the vast highway network of the USA carried 28 vehicles, Germany 55, but the little British Isles supported a total of 15 million vehicles... more than 62 vehicles for every mile of road.

The OECD report had little impact in Britain. In June 1972, the Minister for Transport Industries called for a review of the railways' current position and future prospects.The Railways Board replied in June 1973 by answering the three questions posed by the Minister:

● What has gone wrong in the past?

● Is there a viable rail network?

● Is there a "necessary" rail network?

It was a crisis examination of the most fundamental kind, but under the decisive leadership of Richard Marsh, the former Labour Transport Minister, the Railways Board fought back. "Within the present financial terms of reference," said the Board, "no railway network can be viable." According to Richard Marsh:

> We then told the Government they must accept the fact that there were no benefits from cutting the system and that it must be accepted that the social benefit to the community as a whole by keeping it intact was far greater than the book-keeping loss.

The Board now fully accepted that many of the closures made during the Beeching era had reduced the viability of the lines that remained, and it followed that a smaller network would never be financially viable. Growth, on the other hand, could be achieved, but it would cost £1,787 million in investment over a ten-year period. The Board was unable to define "necessary", as it considered that this was something only the Government could do as part of its overall transport strategy. The Government, however, was still unable to choose a clear option and, faced with a demand for almost £2,000 million from a loss-making nationalised industry, it stalled.

One option would be to continue investing in roads in the vain hope that the increase in road mileage might eventually outpace the growth in the vehicle population. The Government, still undecided as to whether to impose further surgery on the railways, began to think seriously about such a policy. Construction of Ringway One, an inner orbital motorway for London (first advocated by Marples) was considered a distinct possibility, although the road would cost between £600 million and £2,000 million and cut a swathe through residential areas.

Meanwhile, the public was calling for freight traffic to be transferred back to the railways, and the Ministry of Transport responded by reconstituting the figures that had been trotted out during the Beeching era. Putting 50 per cent more traffic on the rails, it was claimed, would reduce congestion by only two per cent. What the Ministry conveniently ignored was that the reduction would be in the heaviest and most damaging long-distance traffic. Increasing the level of rail freight by 50 per cent might well have reduced the number of road **journeys** by only two per cent, but in terms of ton-miles transferred from the roads, the figures would have looked very different. In 1972 the roads carried ten times as much freight as the railways, but in terms of ton-miles the ratio was reduced to less than four. Pro-rail campaigners suggested the railways could easily handle an increase in freight of 100 per cent — a move that would reduce road carriage by almost a third.

Perhaps the arguments proved nothing, other than that figures could be made to prove anything. There was no disputing the accident figures, though, for in a two-year period (1971-72) there had been just five deaths on the railways and more than 15,000 on the roads. In any event, the various arguments for and against road transport were about to be taken out of the Government's hands by factors beyond its control.

By the early 1970s, road transport had attained such a dominant position that no-one could control it. Car production meant employment, as did road-building, policing, and repair services for both vehicles and road users. Yet the cost of motorway maintenance had been woefully underestimated, the environmental effects of the car had not even been properly considered and, above

211

all, the incalculable tragedy of death and injury on the roads continued to mount. As a nation, Britain had clamoured after the new freedom of the motor car and forsaken the freedom to live without noise, pollution, seemingly endless Tarmacadam, death, and destruction. Above all, with the near disintegration of public transport, it appeared as though the nation was about to lose the right to choose.

* * *

In October 1973 — in retaliation for supposed Western backing of Israeli forces in the Yom Kippur war — the Arab oil-exporting states increased prices by 70 per cent and imposed sharp cuts in output. The results of the oil embargo were far-reaching — fuel prices doubled, then quadrupled, leaving the long-standing complacency of Western governments largely shattered. Despite a growing realisation that oil would eventually run out, no-one had seriously considered that the oil producers might hold the wealthy industrialised nations to ransom in the meantime...

Suddenly fuel became a valuable commodity and the private car (as the least efficient end-user of fossil fuels) was to bear the brunt of the crisis. In November 1973, ration books were issued to British motorists (although rationing was never actually implemented) and, on December 5, a blanket 50mph speed restriction was imposed on all British roads. By late December, the country was in the throes of a major crisis: industrial strife brought a return of the three-day week, and high oil prices caused the balance of trade to slide disastrously into the red.

The search began for fuel-efficient transport — something like the railways perhaps. Within six weeks of the crisis the Government had shaken the dust off its railway files and offered the system some hard cash... not quite as much as the Board had wanted, but £891 million was enough to finance a five-year investment programme, and there would be grants to keep operations afloat on a day-to-day basis.

There had never been any doubt that rail was the most efficient mover of people and freight (over long distances at least), but it was really only in Britain that the advantages of a broadly based transport policy had been ignored. Consequently, of all the European industrialised economies, it was Britain's that received the sharpest shock during the fuel crisis. Despite the fact that oil had been discovered in the British sector of the North Sea as early as June 1969, the full extent of the reserves had not been established, nor was it known whether the oil would prove economically recoverable. Road transport relied exclusively on large quantities of imported oil.

Independent transport observers had foreseen the risks of such a policy for many years. All of Britain's major competitors — Germany, France, Italy...

The Isle of Skye is the romantic backdrop as the evening train from Kyle passes Erbusaig Bay on its journey to Inverness, ten years after the line's closure was proposed. In the late 1980s, the line survived a bigger threat when services on both this and the Far North line were forced to terminate at Dingwall when a bridge at Inverness was washed away. British Rail illustrated its commitment to both lines by replacing the bridge swiftly. N E Stead.

even Japan — had made better use of their railways, especially where the carriage of freight was concerned. And now the awful truth was being driven home with a vengeance. The immediate crisis soon passed, to be replaced by a worldwide recession, causing the plans of the oil exporters to backfire. The recession, coupled with increasingly frugal oil consumption and the discovery of fresh supplies (notably in British North Sea waters), had caused the price of oil to drop, but transport economics would never be quite the same again.

Unfortunately, the demoralised and crisis-ridden railways were not in a position to capitalise on the motor car's temporary demise, and such was the inertia behind the retrenchment process that closure plans continued to hit the headlines. In Scotland it was announced that the Dingwall to Kyle of Lochalsh line would close on January 1, 1974 and the Fort William to Oban branch later in the year.

In the event, neither plan came to anything — in the case of the Kyle line, the Edinbugh-based consultants PEIDA, who subsequently were contracted by the local authorities fighting the Settle-Carlisle closure, carried out a broadly based study which showed, among other things, that BR had failed to consider the effect that closure would have on receipts from "rover" tickets. Although the railway system was not yet ready to grasp the nettle and fight back, it became apparent that full recovery was as vital to the health of the nation as it was to each and every railway worker. Gradually, as the realities of the situation sank in, the mood began to swing in favour of rail transport.

In February 1974, the Heath Government finally succumbed to the overwhelming might of the unions. In response to an increasing militancy on the part of the mineworkers that had begun to threaten the very fabric of Britain's parliamentary democracy, the Government called an election, lost, and returned (possibly with a sigh of relief) to the opposition benches. Harold Wilson returned to power as leader of a minority Government, although a further election in October was to give him a distinctly marginal majority of three.

In April, the outgoing Minister for Transport Industries announced a moratorium on railway closures until the end of the year, and the railway press, which had remained strangely acquiescent to the various closure programmes of the preceding 20 years, began to speak out in favour of the railways. According to *Railway Magazine*, some of the economy measures taken by the Railways Board had been counterproductive: removal of points at Windermere, at the end of the one remaining branch to the Lake District, had made it impossible for loco-hauled excursion trains to use the line, and the only remaining section of the Oxford to Cambridge line (between Bedford and Bletchley) was uneconomic and bound to remain so with the severance of the through route. Most damning of all, there had been serious errors in the closure programme... the Cambrian Coast line might have proved more of a success had it stayed open to Caernarfon and Bangor rather than terminating at Pwllheli.

Transport 2000, a new and fairly radical pressure group, unearthed some interesting fuel efficiency statistics, many gleaned from the Department of the Environment's files. An urban traffic study in 1971 had found that the average car travelled around 30 miles on a gallon of fuel, while a two-car diesel multiple unit travelled around four miles to every gallon — something that had been known for many years. What had not been closely studied, was that the average car carried just 1.3 occupants, while the average diesel unit carried 35... the fuel consumption **per passenger** was thus 39 miles per gallon by car and 140 by train. And had all seats been filled (four in the car and 140 in the train), the differential would be even more striking — 120 miles per gallon by car and 600 miles per gallon by train. Taking speed into account, it emerged that the two-car multiple unit was as much as six times as efficient as the car. In fact, these humble diesel units, designed in the early 1950s, appeared to be among the most economical of **all** transport vehicles. This had been the case since the introduction of diesel multiple units in 1954, but it was a fact that had been conveniently ignored.

Such figures added a new dimension to the arguments raised in the Beeching Report ten years before, and aired at regular intervals ever since. In global **environmental** terms (something that Beeching had never been asked to consider), a diesel unit bearing a mere 35 passengers was very efficient — more efficient than a fleet of cars, and far more efficient (with every seat occupied) than a bus, a car, a moped, or any other road vehicle. The advantage of retaining the railways was suddenly very compelling, while the short-term and somewhat arbitrary guidelines of direct profitability receded into the background. The fuel crisis had made the railways essential. British Rail announced that most of the diesel multiple units (now almost 20 years old) would be refurbished to provide another ten years of active life... many of them were to remain in service a good deal longer.

The new Government bowed to the inevitable and granted the railway network a total of £2,130 million, including up to £1,500 million to support the uneconomic services for five years, and a rather more modest sum to cover capital investment. The same Parliamentary Bill introduced incentives to industrial concerns wishing to build private sidings for rail traffic. Commercial objectives were thrown out of the window and, for the following five years, the railways were cushioned with a blanket of state finance. Public expenditure cuts and the ongoing energy crisis had brought about a change in policy — the road-building programme would be reined in and the railway network retained. Most of the remaining branch and secondary services were safe, including six that had come perilously close to closure: the Cambrian Coast, Kyle of Lochalsh to Dingwall, Ashford to Hastings, Bedford to Bletchley, Wimbledon to West Croydon, and Stockport to Stalybridge. Only the Alston and Bridport branches were to close and, although both provided an essential service in remote rural

Left: The Alston branch is now home to the South Tynedale narrow gauge line. Right: Lifting track on the Bridport branch, November 1975. Author's pictures.

areas, the closures did, at least, affect a relatively small number of regular travellers. There were plenty of other closure scares in the mid to late-1970s, but few were successfully implemented.

The downside of the new financial arrangement was an increasing burden of state interference, for all policy objectives would, in future, need to be approved by the Government.

Quietly, and almost imperceptibly, the tide had begun to turn. In 1975 the Central London Polytechnic initiated a Survey and Review of the Exeter to Barnstaple rail service — the only passenger line remaining in north Devon. Although British Rail was claiming a loss of £98,000 a year on the service, the survey discovered something that the Railway Development Association could have told it all along: that the contributory revenue generated by the line might be as high as £700,000, making closure proposals a nonsense.

It was becoming clear that railway subsidies were a far more cost-effective option than bus subsidies, for the new bus services had lost almost all of the traffic that the much maligned railways had built up over a century or so — indeed, rarely did more than 20 per cent of former rail passengers transfer their custom to the replacement buses.

The cost of subsidising "socially necessary" bus services had been transferred from the railways to the National Bus Company under the provisions of the 1968 Transport Act, but few of the services had proved a financial success. As early as 1965, the bus operators had suggested that buses were losing former rail traffic to private transport but, at the time, the loss had been dismissed as part of a general move away from public transport. A decade later, according to David Glassborrow of the National Bus Company, the writing was on the wall:

> Very often these special bus services are very lightly loaded. The fact that any passengers remained on the railway services was almost certainly due to the unsuitability of bus services... In one or two recent cases the average number of passengers was less than one, that is, on some days he got a lift by car one way...

The so-called "bustitution" policy had proved wholly ill-founded, for where the railways had proved more than capable of competing with the private car, buses had failed. Indeed, the railway closures had actually forced many people to buy their own transport, precipitating the near collapse of rural public transport.

By the mid 1970s, the buses were losing business at the rate of about two per cent a year, while the railways continued to maintain their market share. Further proof came in 1975 when the Bridport branch in Dorset was closed, and replaced with a bus service. Within a few weeks, the disappointed bus operators found that traffic had slumped to a quarter of its former level. The operation soon proved uneconomic and the bus was withdrawn, leaving the area almost bereft of public transport. This situation was by no means exceptional — few replacement bus services had retained as much as half of the railway traffic, and most services had faded away very rapidly.

One reason for the failure of bus services was their scheduled speed. Many bus journeys took more than twice as long as the train services had, and the problem was particularly severe in urban areas where congestion caused insoluble difficulties. In Bournemouth, where the average speed of the buses had dropped to about 11mph, the cost of congestion had been estimated at an additional five per cent on gross expenses for every 1mph lost on the schedule. The Greater London Council had come to a similar conclusion — that a 1.5 mph drop in speed (from 11.5 to 10mph), added about 11 per cent to costs. According to the South Western TUCC, more than half of the replacement buses brought in since 1962 had stopped running. Such evidence was to have a profound effect on the attitudes of the Consultative Committees which began to realise that they had been seriously misled:

> **Had it been known between 1962 and 1969 that replacement buses could by Government order be taken off after two years without ministerial approval... it is likely that the Committee would not have been so ready to suggest alternative means of transport, but rather to have informed the Minister that no reliable alternative could be suggested.**

South Western TUCC, 1977

The various committees began to see themselves as transport watchdogs, and as the policy of bustitution had clearly failed, they shifted their attention towards maintaining rail services. In March 1978 the Central Transport Consultative Committee agreed to publish all future reports into prospective rail closures. It was a milestone in public consultation, and proof that the central body was now also on the side of the travelling public.

But if the fuel crisis had lasted such a short time, why had the public mood continued to swing in favour of the railways? To a great extent, the 1973 oil crisis had provoked an awakening: a crystallisation of public opinion in favour of environmentally "clean" public transport, and away from destructive road projects. Environmental views that had seemed "cranky" or anti-social a year or two before, had become acceptable... even fashionable.

As the decade progressed, the forecasts of the OECD began to take shape more or less as predicted — car ownership really was on target to reach saturation level by the year 2000. There were clear indicators that saturation point had already been reached in the major cities, for the number of car registrations in urban areas was growing rather more slowly than elsewhere. Few people had predicted that the process would eventually spread to the smaller cities, and even to Britain's larger towns, but as time passed the reality began to dawn. In any event, motorists had remained penalised in the wake of the fuel crisis, for although speed limits were increased again on motorways and dual carriageways, the 70mph limit was never universally restored.

Road planners began to realise that saturation traffic levels produced some strange effects. Paradoxically, new road construction tended to attract traffic away from public transport, restoring the level of congestion... the loss of traffic from public transport tending to increase fares and reduce the level of service. The result was to leave both public and private transport slower and less convenient.

There were problems in store for the motorway network too. Not only had congestion succeeded in negating many of the advantages of the motorways, but maintenance costs had risen far beyond predictions. Roadworks and slow, dangerous contraflow diversions had become commonplace, for increasingly heavy freight vehicles were causing considerably more damage than had been expected. To make matters worse, pressure from the European Community to bring British regulations into line with those on the Continent was about to unleash onto British roads juggernauts of a size and weight (up to 38 tonnes) that had never been envisaged.

After two decades of prevarication, the Department of Transport grudgingly accepted that the tests carried out by the American Association of State Highway Officials in the late 1950s might be of value. The AASHO had spent $27 million and reached the conclusion that damage caused to a road surface by a given vehicle axle was proportional to the weight of the axle to the power of four.

In other words, where it might be assumed that the wheels of a heavy lorry carrying 10 tons would cause ten times as much damage as the wheels of a lighter vehicle bearing a ton, the actual figure was a thousand times greater. In fact, heavy freight vehicles had wrought havoc on the motorway network, for a 12-ton lorry with two axles was causing as much damage as 160,000 cars. Results soon began to arrive from studies in other countries — a German survey in the early 1980s revealed that freight vehicles might be paying no more than

12.5 per cent of their true cost.

For more than ten years, the Ministry of Transport had poured scorn on the American findings, but the statistical evidence was suddenly overwhelming. After conducting lengthy experiments of their own at the Transport and Road Research laboratory, scientists from the Department of Transport had shown that the American findings were actually rather optimistic where heavy lorries were concerned — a view backed up by practical experience on the M1. Heavy road transport was going to cost rather more than had been envisaged.

The motorways had proved slower, more dangerous, and more expensive to maintain than had been predicted, while the railways were only just finding their feet in an age of rapidly advancing technology. In 1976 (against all the predictions of the Beeching Report) long-distance rail services achieved a permanent advantage over road transport of any kind, and put inter-city rail schedules within reach of the airlines as well.

The 125mph High Speed Train could not have come at a better time for the demoralised and broken British railway industry. Introduced to revenue earning service in the West Country from May 1975, and fully utilised between King's Cross and Edinburgh three years later, the High Speed Trains produced an immediate and outstanding boost to income and railway morale. They were destined to become one of British Rail's greatest success stories.

The turn-round had been painfully slow, but in January 1978 the number of railway stations in Britain began to rise from an all-time low of 2,358. In all, 13 stations reopened that year, with a promise of others to follow. In co-operation with various local authorities the railways began to show a little imagination, stealing back traffic where the impact of the motorcar had been particularly severe. In June 1978, an experimental park-and-ride facility was introduced to carry tourists into the little town of St Ives in Cornwall. It proved successful, and both British Rail and the local authorities were delighted with the scheme. In Birmingham, the National Exhibition Centre was constructed adjacent to Birmingham International Station, opened in 1976. Paradoxically, when the Motor Show was first staged there two years later, 40 per cent of visitors arrived by rail. Another success story came with the "parkway" station concept — out-of-town stations, usually sited near motorway or trunk road interchanges, to appeal to motorists. Unfortunately the parkway stations were, on occasion, used as an excuse for a lack of proper central facilities, as at Mansfield, where a rather optimistic parkway station was constructed nine miles from the town centre. Nevertheless, the stations drew in business, and helped British Rail to capitalise on the success of the new High Speed Trains.

The Passenger Transport Authorities were gradually finding their feet in the urban areas, and there were a number of constructive developments, including new stations and track refurbishment in Birmingham, Liverpool and Manchester.

The Tyne and Wear Metro succeeded where plans in the 70s for the Pic-Vic network in Manchester failed to win Government backing. The Metro involved extensive tunnelling and new bridges, including one across the Tyne. Elsewhere, former BR lines which were first electrified by the NER at the turn of the century but converted to diesel traction in the Beeching years, make up the modern system. Various extensions are underway or contemplated. Picture at Simonside, near Tyne Dock, by N E Stead.

Tyneside went a step further and developed the Tyne & Wear Metro system — a complete rethink of urban rail transport that deserved (but failed for political reasons) to spread to other urban areas.

By the late 1970s, the Railway Board's attitude towards the private railway companies was beginning to change, following a gradual realisation that a once-and-for-all scrap price was nothing compared with the contributory value of reopened branches. It became more accommodating.

In 1979 British Rail ran a series of special trains between Birmingham and Bewdley where visitors were transferred to the Severn Valley Railway and, in 1981, it applied the same thinking to the Nene Valley line near Peterborough. In a more favourable climate, the private sector continued to grow and, by 1981, nearly 200 miles of former state-owned railway had reopened in private hands.

With the influence of the road lobby severely curtailed, the pro-rail groups began to assume a more influential role. In 1978 the Railway Development Association merged with the Railway Invigoration Society to create a larger and more streamlined organisation, the Railway Development Society. Meanwhile Transport 2000 (a group that had begun life in 1972 with one part-time member of staff) took on its first full-time appointee in 1977. Against a road lobby, whose annual turnover ran into hundreds of thousands of pounds, the railway groups were very small indeed, but sophisticated lobbying techniques brought firm results.

During 1979, British Rail carried almost a billion passengers and clocked up 19,900 million passenger-miles — more than in any year since the beginning of the Beeching era in 1963. The following year proved difficult financially, for the railways were hit by a general recession, but the real turning point came in 1981, for at long last the rail lobby scored a parliamentary success.

The pro-rail parliamentary lobby had achieved very little in the lean years, but in May 1981 an apparently insignificant piece of legislation reached its Third Reading in the House of Commons, paving the way for a minor renaissance on the railways. The Transport Act 1962 (amendment) Bill, put forward by Tony Speller, MP for North Devon, gave British Rail the opportunity to reopen railway lines and stations on an "experimental" basis outside the provisions of the 1962 Act. The TUCC closure process had created a positive disincentive to reopen stations, for the Board was loath to restore services where subsequent closure might involve lengthy and expensive investigations, and the risk that closure might not be consented to at all. Under the Speller legislation, a station could be reopened on an experimental basis and only six weeks notice would be required if BR wanted to close it again.

It was ironic that the impetus to reopen branch lines should ultimately have come from legislation that reduced public consultation, but the Bill was to have the desired effect.

Tony Speller had hoped to save the Torrington to Barnstaple freight line which ran past his home. Repeated attempts had been made to reopen the line since 1976, but they all had failed, not because traffic forecasts were particularly pessimistic, but because the Railways Board, steeped in the surreal world of the Cooper Brothers grant formula, had demanded £175,000 to reopen the line, plus a subsidy of £90,000 a year from the county council. The Speller legislation was intended to ease such reopenings by making a limited experiment a feasible proposition.

Once the Bill became law in August 1981, British Rail adopted a more conciliatory attitude to the North Devon line. The capital cost of reopening was now, apparently, just £36,000, giving an all-in cost for a one-year experiment of £120,000 but, by this time, the council had lost interest. The North Devon link road was close to becoming a reality and, under tight new financial strictures, the council felt it had more worthy schemes to support. To reopen the line would have cost a third of the total annual subsidy paid to rural buses in the county.

After closure of the line to freight later in the decade the hopes of Tony Speller and the railway restoration movement in this area were shattered.

For almost two years, the Speller legislation had no tangible effects, but in June 1983 Pinhoe station on the former LSWR trunk line to Exeter, reopened on an experimental basis and, in October that year, another reopening on the same line brought real success. Templecombe station, formerly an interchange with the Somerset & Dorset railway, had closed in 1966, but a concerted local campaign brought experimental reopening and a steady flow of passengers. Within six years, another 48 stations had reopened.

The Conservative Government, led by Margaret Thatcher, arrived in May 1979 and attacked public spending with an almost religious zeal. The cost of subsidising the loss-making railway services had steadily risen, giving rise to real fears that the Thatcher Government might attempt to reduce the burden on the tax-payer by drastic means. In May 1982 the inevitable happened, and the Government set up an inquiry under Sir David Serpell (formerly Ernest Marples's Deputy Permanent Secretary at the Department of Transport, and a member of the Stedeford Committee) "to secure improved financial results in an efficiently run railway in Great Britain over the next 20 years". If the intention had been to instigate a Beeching-style hatchet job, the Government grossly misjudged the mood of the times. The Serpell Report consequently appeared, then disappeared under an onslaught of opposition from all quarters (there was a 25,000-signature petition from the Railway Development Society) most notably from the Central Transport Consultative Committee, which said:

> ...there is a strong case for restoring rail links to some substantial communities now isolated from the rail network... bus replacement after Beeching was a total failure. If buses are to replace rail services in future, the conditions must be carefully worked out and monitored.

The CTCC, having made its views clear on the policy of bustitution, went on to advocate light rail techniques such as radio signalling, lightweight trains, and simplified level-crossings and stations. The consultative committees were still smarting from their involuntary involvement in the Beeching closure programme. They had been seriously misled, and put in the invidious position of agreeing to closures that denied a fair proportion of the public any transport facilities. And as the South Western TUCC succinctly observed, the closures had yielded virtually nothing in the way of economic savings:

> The involvement of this committee in the Beeching closure programme revealed to us that closures such as those envisaged in the Serpell Report do not in the end reduce BR's deficit by a great deal... when a local service is withdrawn people tend to look for a through service either by coach or private car.

The conclusions of the Serpell Report fell on stony ground. In any event, the railway financial position was about to improve beyond all expectations.

In 1982 British railway passenger services were reorganised into three quasi-independent organisations. InterCity would operate the prestige express services, Network Southeast (initially, and rather less inspiringly, known as London & Southeast) the commuter trains in and around the capital, and Provincial the remainder, including a few heavily subsidised rural lines.

If nothing else, the reorganisation allowed a detailed appraisal of the financial value of various services and, for the first time in many years, the railways were given a proper financial strategy to follow. Whether the Thatcher Government had decided to prepare the various railway divisions for private ownership was not immediately apparent, but the effect of investment, manpower efficiency, and improved morale was most beneficial.

In 1983, total external finance was running at around £900 million, InterCity receiving £159 million in grant aid, Network Southeast £282 million, and Provincial £502 million, while Freight made a £27 million loss and Parcels a £10 million profit. The following year, a major strike dented the figures, but thereafter the financial picture steadily improved. By 1986, passenger volumes had returned to the 1979/80 figure of around 19 billion passenger-miles, with an annual growth of about four per cent in every sector. Some Provincial services had seen passenger levels increase by 50 per cent or more, and there had been real success on lines reopened under the Speller legislation, the Bathgate branch in Scotland carrying 500,000 passengers in the first ten months.

By 1986 the burden on the taxpayer had been reduced by a quarter; the Freight division was just managing an operating profit; and InterCity was on target for profitability. The railway Chairman, Robert Reid, proudly announced to his workforce:

In the last three years we have together transformed the railway. Today we need £260 million a year less help from the taxpayer. We have restored passenger volume to its highest level since the start of the decade. We have opened new routes and new stations, and each year new electric services begin operating.

It had, by any standards, been a dramatic turn-round, and the process was set to continue. By 1988 InterCity services had achieved profitability, and Network Southeast passenger levels had grown by 15 per cent in three years. Efficiency had improved to such an extent that, while the number of train miles had increased by 18 per cent, unit costs had dropped by almost a third.

It all sounded too good to be true, and perhaps it was, for when every last drop of efficiency had been squeezed from the organisation, the Government pushed its financial demands further still. Even the commuter services in the South-East would be expected to run at a profit, and the eventual aim was for the whole network to cover costs. With little room for further savings through efficiency alone, the railways began to pare services to the bone by running fewer carriages, and raising fares for five consecutive years at more than the rate of inflation.

The railways had become victims of their own success — squeezed between Government demands for profitability and the demands of an increasing volume of passengers who wanted a reasonable service. By the end of the 1980s train services had become overpriced and overcrowded. Finally, aircraft-style boarding cards were introduced on certain express services. It was all a very long way from the demoralised network of the Beeching era. After 30 years in the wilderness, the age of the train had finally arrived, but not all the passengers were enjoying the experience.

In the Provincial sector, losses continued, although tight financial control, renewed investment, and close tailoring of supply and demand yielded firm results. In 1983 the Government gave the go-ahead for a £1.7 million investment on the East Suffolk line, most of the money going into radio signalling technology and automatic level-crossings. According to Gordon Clarke, the Divisional Manager:

> We wanted to show how cheaply we could run a rural railway... So we put all our forward thinking onto one line.

It was 30 years since the Railway Development Association had first advocated such initiatives, and nearly 20 years since Gerard Fiennes had suggested that the "basic railway" formula might be applied to the East Suffolk line. Finally, in the 1980s, the authorities had begun to act. Radio signalling was introduced on the Kyle of Lochalsh line in the same year and, later, on the Mallaig branch and the Cambrian Coast, while the Central Wales line became a test-bed for a variety of light railway techniques. Slowly but surely, new stations continued to open, and by 1989 the overall total had risen to 2,440, growing at the rate of about 15 a year. The most exciting developments involved the Settle & Carlisle; a trunk line that had survived Beeching, Network for Development, the Cooper Brothers formula, and various closure proposals during the 1980s that would, at best, have seen the line converted into a sort of linear theme park. By 1990 the minor stations had been reopened, a proper timetable restored, and future investment guaranteed. Even the Settle and Carlisle — condemned as a worthless anachronism for almost 30 years — was heading towards profitability.*

The Thatcher Government remained doggedly pro-road in its approach to transport policy, however. In the year 1989-90 rail investment reached an all-time high, with a promise of a further £3.7 billion in the following three years. But not a penny was forthcoming from central government, for the whole

---

* The full story of the battle to save the Settle-Carlisle Railway is told in The Line that Refused to Die by Stan Abbott and Alan Whitehouse, Leading Edge Press & Publishing. See p256.

CONTRASTING RURAL LINES: *Above — A three-car Class 158 Sprinter crosses Dent Head viaduct on the Settle-Carlisle line which has seen extensive investment since it performed probably the greatest Houdini act of all the lines threatened in post-Beeching times. Pete Shaw.*

Below: A "minimalist" approach has ensured the survival of the line from Norwich to Cromer and Sheringham. Contrast the basic facilities at Sheringham with the elaborate provisions which inflated branch line costs in Beeching's day. Author's collection.

The historic meeting of the first InterCity 225s, north and southbound, on the East Coast Main Line, near York, 1991. Press Agency (York).

investment plan was to be self-financing. Meanwhile, the financial noose continued to tighten around the grant-aided lines, when a target grant of just £345 million was set for 1993.

There was to be no external investment cash for the railways, but following forecasts of an 83 to 142 per cent rise in road traffic by the year 2025, the Government announced a £12 billion road programme. In a new decade that promised increases in pollution, congestion... and even the unhealthy prospect of global warming, it was a remarkably short-sighted decision. The £12 billion spending spree would buy a two per cent increase in the road network, while demand was apparently set to increase by anything up to 142 per cent.

To most commentators, though, it was the railways that showed the way to the future. Had Professor Hondelink lived to witness the debates of the 1990s, he would surely have joined the voices raised in unison at the shortsightedness of Government policy. Sadly, the Professor died in 1973, without acknowledgement in his adopted country — despite his work for the Allies and the United Nations. No one fought as long or as hard for the railways as had Professor Hondelink, and no-one foresaw with such accuracy just how efficient they might eventually become. Had the cost-effective operating techniques advocated by the Professor been adopted a little sooner, a greater part of the system might have been saved.

That was the bitter legacy of the Beeching years.

9.
Retrospective

If the history of the nationalised industries has one lesson to teach, it is the damage which ideologically inspired administrative changes can have on their working.

Richard Pryke, 1971*

After 30 years watching closely the inner workings of politics, devising schemes for nationalisation and denationalisation, most civil servants end up with a profound scepticism about any scheme for improvement, and a few develop a hankering to be rid of the whole business of democracy.

Anthony Sampson, 1965*

IT IS, perhaps, all too easy to look back from the viewpoint of the environment-conscious 1990s and state that certain actions taken 20 or 30 years ago were short-sighted and foolish. But the fact remains that, between 1947 and 1973, the British railway system was ravaged. Subsequent events were to prove that the cuts had run too deeply — indeed, most had yielded a gross negative benefit to the community at large, and many had damaged the viability of the Railways Board itself.

Many commentators have judged Dr Beeching's methods advantageous, even essential, to the continuing health of the railway system, and such views must be challenged. Even today, it is occasionally stated that Beeching saved the railway network by axing uneconomic lines, yet the railway closure programme was never expected to eradicate more than a proportion of the deficit. Even Beeching himself estimated an annual saving of only £18 million by eradicating passenger services and a further £11-13 million from line closures, whereas the overall deficit was running at close to £100 million. Clearly, many more pressing problems existed elsewhere on the railway network.

But how, exactly, did the railways get into such a precarious financial position? Without a doubt, the atrocious management decisions of the British Transport Commission, and its confused relationship with the Railway Execu-

---

* *Pryke: Author of* Public Enterprise in Practice; *Sampson: Author of* Anatomy of Britain Today.

tive, did untold harm. And as a monopoly carrier, the Commission developed a complacent attitude towards quality of service that a private concern would surely never have countenanced. Another effect of this monopoly trading position was to leave little incentive to modernise or improve rural rail services, for the Commission found that it was considerably easier to precipitate closure and transfer traffic to the roads. That is not to say, however, that state ownership is necessarily a harmful condition for an industry, for many state-controlled enterprises both in Britain and abroad have proved very successful.

Unfortunately for the railways, state control brought state interference, and it was Government intervention that caused the majority of the network's problems. The 1945 Labour administration saddled the railways with an unwarranted burden of debt to former shareholders, and the same Government went on to limit investment, encouraging the Railway Executive to construct relatively cheap steam locomotives rather than expensive, but much more efficient, new diesels.

Much of the blame must rest with the Conservatives, who manipulated and reorganised the railways to the very edge of extinction. Their 1953 Transport Act proved disastrous: just as the Transport Commission was making a success of the policy of integration, it was forced to tear up its plans and start again. However reasonable the objectives behind the Act, its implementation proved a nightmare, resulting in a tangle of bureaucracy that exceeded anything imposed by the former socialist regime. The Conservative Government then manipulated the rates and fares of the BTC (and other nationalised concerns) in a vain attempt to control inflation — an incredibly foolish policy that set the industry on the road to financial ruin.

Most damning of all, the Conservatives entered into an alliance with the road lobby, the full implications of which are only just becoming widely known. By 1959-60 elements within the Conservative Government had produced a plan in concert with the road lobby to destroy, or at the very least mutilate, the railway network. It was a disgraceful abuse of public trust and confidence.

Leaving aside political interference, the Transport Commission and the Railway Executive must carry a heavy burden of responsibility themselves, for the process of modernising the branch lines was woefully mismanaged. The Motive Power Committee deliberated for three critical years before deciding in favour of limited modernisation; a further six months elapsed before the Lightweight Trains Committee completed its investigation into diesel multiple units; it was another six months before construction was finally announced; and several more years passed before the vehicles entered service in reasonable numbers.

It had taken the Commission almost a decade to negotiate a simple and straightforward step, while the minor passenger services were dying on their feet. Yet the sordid tale of management ineptitude continued, for even after the multiple units had entered service, the Commission was unable to decide whether to invest in the branch lines or close them *en masse*. They were well aware that certain railway lines performed a unique social function, and they knew that a few of these lines were terminally uneconomic, but they appear to have done nothing to initiate a wide-scale public debate on the subject. Had the Commission fought its corner in the 1950s, and gained the support of the public and the local authorities, the story might have ended very differently.

* * *

What, then, might have happened had the big four private companies remained in being? Had they been granted a "fair deal" with respect to the common-carrier legislation, and a substantial sum by way of war reparations, the private companies would have been set on a reasonably secure financial footing. It seems astonishing that the financial base of a private industry might have been more stable than that of a nationalised concern, but this was surely the case. No doubt the years that followed would have brought all manner of financial problems for the private companies... cut-backs, reorganisation, amalgamation, perhaps even bankruptcy, but almost anything would have been better than the Transport Commission's handling of subsequent events.

The private companies would undoubtedly have closed many uneconomic services, but they would also have had a real incentive to attempt economies, adopt new technology, and search for radical means of raising finance. A private company would have moved rapidly to close the hopelessly uneconomic lines, to seek subsidies for marginal examples, and to invest where investment was worthwhile. The market would have brought an incentive to match services to the potential demand, and to reduce costs. Such initiatives were desperately needed in the 1950s, but they were not forthcoming from the state transport concern.

Perhaps the best compromise would have been state ownership of the railway infrastructure, with services left in the hands of private operators. Under such a system, the uneconomic branch line question would have come to a head very much earlier, but so too would a proper public debate on the issue. Enthusiasts or local groups would have found it easier to lease operating rights than to purchase a line outright, and such a system would have brought many more lines into the private sector.

Perhaps the most important point — given the relative importance of the lobby system in British parliamentary affairs — is that a private railway industry would have maintained a powerful and influential parliamentary lobby group. It was as a direct result of the near collapse of the rail lobby in 1947 that the various road groups were able to achieve the sort of power that made the

Marples/Beeching axis possible... or even inevitable.

On one point there is little debate: most of the closures instigated by the Transport Commission during the late 1940s and early 1950s were more or less inevitable, and could even have progressed a little faster. In 1948, informed opinion held the view that up to 30 per cent of railway mileage would sooner or later have to close... and it proved to be a fairly realistic prediction. Even the closures debated at the Isle of Wight inquiry in 1953 were, sadly, hard to contest. It is worth observing, though, that almost all of the quaint and anachronistic Light Railways were worthy of retention as working museums, and several eventually found such salvation.

It might be worth looking at the microcosmic world of the Isle of Wight in more detail. The branch to Ventnor West was typical of many closed in the early 1950s. The line should really never have been built but, given that it was, there was no answer other than closure in the 1950s, and the BTC consequently faced little opposition in putting the service quietly to sleep.

The main subjects of the Isle of Wight inquiry in 1953 were the branches to Bembridge and Freshwater and the Newport-Sandown line. The line to Freshwater ran a considerable distance across the lightly populated west side of the island, and was probably unsustainable under any conditions. The same, reluctant, conclusion must be reached for the Newport-Sandown route... the line was uneconomic and could probably never have been made otherwise. Bembridge, on the other hand, was served by a short branch line within reach of the tourist trade. Traffic was admittedly pretty light, but costs were minimal and could have been reduced still further with a few operating economies.

In conclusion, most of the mileage closed on the Isle of Wight in 1953 would have been unsustainable even in Light Railway terms, although any of the lines might have survived under private ownership operating a seasonal tourist service. That, however, is the limit of the closures that should have been made on the island. The Ryde-Newport-Cowes and Shanklin-Ventnor branches (both condemned by Beeching and closed shortly afterwards) should most certainly have been retained. Both lines were ideal candidates for railbus operation and light railway techniques, and both might have earned considerable extra revenue in later years had the Board capitalised on the nostalgia boom, and operated steam services in the summer months. Such revenue-earning techniques are commonplace today, for the key to operating marginal services is flexibility. As one commentator wryly observed, the hotels and guest houses on the Isle of Wight had long learned to adopt a flexible approach... why could the Railways Board not do the same?

Of course, once the decision had been made to abandon all branch line and stopping trains, the railway management cut investment and left outmoded operating practices in place. Inevitably, they were soon able to claim such

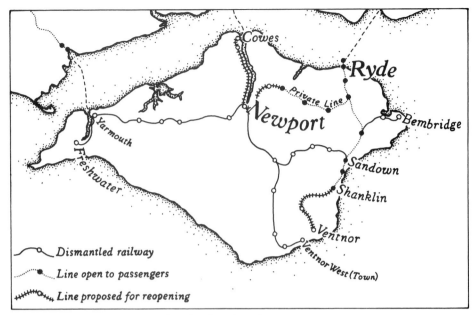

The Isle of Wight railway system

Ex-London Transport stock brought cheap electrification to the rump of the Isle of Wight railways. The picture shows the end of the line at Shanklin in 1990 — beyond the platform, the trackbed to Ventnor has been obliterated. Author's collection.

impressive losses on minor passenger services that the Transport Users' Consultative Committees fell over themselves to advance policies of bustitution. No-one in British Rail was willing to look hard at investment prospects for, from 1960, it was no longer a question of whether to close lines, but simply when.

The next question, must be whether the railway passenger services might have survived in a healthier state had the Beeching Report never been produced in 1963. The answer has to be an unequivocal yes. It was abundantly clear that something needed to be done, but the Beeching policy, whether by accident or design, was utterly to devastate the railways.

Some of the closure and retrenchment proposals were quite reasonable, particularly where freight was concerned. No-one mourned the passing of loose-coupled freight wagons for instance, and the Report contained many other practical and positive proposals. The major fault of the Reshaping Report was to put far too great an emphasis on the losses from stopping and branch line passenger services. Several lines really were terminally uneconomic, but the report predicted that the railways would only achieve profitability by following the American pattern — closing all but the inter-city passenger facilities, and investing predominantly in freight traffic. Yet Britain was very different from the United States. Domestic air travel was never really taken seriously in Britain and, even in 1963, road congestion was more severe than in the States, where the sheer size of the country made possible a network of free-running interstate highways. In addition, Britain's railways were generally capable of carrying denser traffic at higher speeds than their trans-Atlantic counterparts.

In any event, a really close look at North America in 1963 would have revealed the first signs of chaotic city-wide congestion, and the advancing spectre of atmospheric pollution. Yet, despite all the evidence, no-one predicted that, by the early 1980s, British Rail would be pouring resources into a burgeoning passenger sector, while the importance of freight traffic had declined in relative terms.

Once the analytical Dr Beeching had made up his mind to eradicate stopping trains, the figures were massaged in such a way as to present an overwhelming case for closure. Only a decade later did conclusive proof arrive that many of the predictions in the report were ill-founded, although by then it was too late. The result of closing busy passenger facilities served only to cause a loss of confidence with the public (and a loss of morale within the industry) that did untold harm. Yet the programme was essentially unnecessary.

Bearing in mind that about 30 per cent of the network was deemed uneconomic in 1948, and that the BTC subsequently closed around 15 per cent of it before Beeching's arrival, it would be reasonable to conclude that no more than 17 per cent of the mileage remaining in 1963 was fundamentally uneconomic. When Beeching took control, the worst loss-makers were already under review, and many others would have followed. Yet, in the years following the publication of the Beeching Report, another 37 per cent of the railway network was closed. In the author's opinion, at least a third of these should never even have been **contemplated** for closure. These comprised about 1,200 miles of passenger railways (between five and ten per cent of the total network). Appendix 1 lists 94 individual lines, of which a quarter (nearly 200 miles) have already reopened.

If the British Transport Commission had achieved just one thing, it was in conveying the impression that certain closures, hand-in-hand with substantial investment elsewhere, would bring real benefits to the system as a whole. Beeching's closure plans, allied with the near cessation of investment, had the effect of almost destroying the viability of the network. In the final analysis, it is even quite fortunate that the closure of financially viable, or socially necessary, lines ran to no more than 1,200 miles — it could have been even worse.

Had the Transport Commission's more sensible modernisation schemes been allowed to continue alongside a quiet and low key closure programme, the result would have been much more satisfactory. Innovations such as continuous welded rails, electrification, and modern signalling were already reducing operating costs, and had such cost-effective investment continued, the railways would have emerged in a healthier state.

Costs might have been contained had many of the sensible economies proposed in the Reshaping Report been carried out, but progress was alarmingly slow. Even as late as 1968, when most (but by no means all) freight trains were equipped with automatic brakes, the railways employed 7,000 freight guards. Their role was not immediately obvious, yet they remained in service. In 1958, no fewer than eight per cent of the railway workforce had been employed firing and maintaining steam engines... ten years later, after the retirement of the last steam locomotives, most of the firemen still remained.

Despite generous redundancy payments, the railways had failed to shed staff rapidly enough in certain areas, and the vast marshalling yards and heavy industrial workshops remained overmanned and riddled with restrictive practices. They cost a fortune to run, losing tens of millions of pounds against the thousands lost on the branch lines — yet the branch lines were ransacked while much of the heavy industry outlived Dr Beeching. Efficient utilisation of staff and equipment was far behind the best Continental practice, and it was in these areas that the railways should have made a concerted effort to improve matters (although now, perhaps, the pendulum has swung too far in the other direction). The 1962 Transport Act had finally set the railways free from the archaic rates and charges apparatus, but it was another eight years before British Railways began to introduce realistic charges. Not surprisingly, productivity remained largely stagnant throughout the 1950s while most other European railways achieved rapid improvements. It was not until the following decade that productivity on Britain's railways began to catch up, and then only by way of retrenchment and closure. While other railway systems were improving productivity by actively encouraging new traffic, British Rail achieved it through the rather negative process of closing the least profitable services. It was easier to close railways outright than to improve efficiency, and that is exactly what was done.

It might be unfair to place too great an emphasis on the failings of the Reshaping Report. By the time Beeching arrived, government interference and management ineptitude had already brought the railway system to its knees — it was perhaps too late to do anything other than reduce the size of the system as rapidly as possible. In any event, the most serious losses occurred after Beeching's departure. The branches to Swanage, Hunstanton, Okehampton, St Andrews and Bewdley had all been safeguarded in the Reshaping Report, but they were closed under a later, and supposedly more benevolent, regime.

Once confidence in the railways had deteriorated sufficiently, the philosophy of railway closures could have been taken to almost any lengths. As it was, the late 1960s turned into an orgy of destruction, and it was during this era (overseen by Tom Fraser and Barbara Castle at the Ministry of Transport) that the real mistakes were made. The threshold was around 1966. Many of the closures made before that date could be justified, but very few made during and after 1966 should have been allowed. Harold Wilson had promised to mount a thorough investigation into the nation's future transport needs and act accordingly, yet once in power he allowed the closure process to continue unabated.

Perhaps politicians were the wrong people to make such long-term decisions. Few had any real understanding of transport affairs themselves, and they were easily swayed by "experts" at the Ministry of Transport. Some, like Marples, had positive personal and financial incentives to see railways close. It would be wrong to suggest that Marples deliberately made political decisions for personal gain, yet with the best will in the world, he would have been unable to make fair and reasoned judgments on transport affairs, and he should never have been allowed to try. Tom Fraser made little impact at the Ministry of Transport and succeeded in offending both camps in the transport debate. Barbara Castle — although among the finest of all incumbents at the Ministry — was finally removed after challenging the powerful road lobby.

The largest closures, in terms of route mileage and infrastructure, were those of the so-called duplicate trunk routes. Four notable lines were systematically run down and destroyed during this era — the Somerset & Dorset, the Great Central, the Oxford to Cambridge line, and the ex-LSWR trunk route between Exeter and Plymouth. Critically short of investment capital, and providing a service that was inferior even to that of the Edwardian era, all four appeared ripe for closure, yet there seems to have been no proper investigation into their future prospects.

The Government knew very well that Milton Keynes (within easy reach of the Oxford to Cambridge line) was set to grow into a city the size of Southampton within a decade. Indeed towns along the entire route of the line were starting to expand at remarkable speed, and most of the growth was in the exciting new industries that Harold Wilson had promised to encourage. Spectacular growth was also about to hit the area north and west of Bournemouth, but the Government made no attempt to reverse the closure of the Somerset & Dorset, or the Brockenhurst-Ringwood-Poole line. In 1961 the population in the area stood at around 20,000... 20 years later it had passed 83,000 and, by the 1990s, it had become one of the fastest growing urban areas in Europe. Yet it was almost bereft of rail facilities.

Whereas the Brockenhurst to Poole line was closed in its entirety, others were only partially dismantled. The ex-LSWR line between Exeter and Plymouth was cut in two, leaving an 18-mile gap between Okehampton and Bere Alston. The same happened between Oxford and Cambridge, where services were retained on a 16-mile section between Bedford and Bletchley. Further south, seven miles of track were removed between Uckfield and Lewes with similar results. The savings from such closures (in terms of maintenance and upkeep) were paltry, yet the loss of traffic was overwhelming. Of course, the Railways Board had never intended to create such anomalies — the intention had been to close all the above lines in their entirety, but public pressure brought the closure process to a halt before the plans had been fully implemented.

The Great Central falls in a class of its own. Traffic on the line was so heavy that it took several years of deliberate neglect and retrenchment before closure could be achieved. In many ways, the line came more firmly into the "duplicate" category than any other, yet the Great Central literally reached the parts that other trunk lines could not reach: it was a unique transport artery.

There was no easy alternative route for express services from the south-west to the north-east of England, and (constructed partly to the European loading gauge) the line might have found a new lease of life as a dedicated route for Channel Tunnel traffic. In 1966 Harold Wilson was busy finalising negotiations with the French Government over the Channel Tunnel project, yet with the other hand he was extinguishing a ready-made route between London and the very heart of the Midlands — a railway that would have brought Europe within reach of Rugby, Leicester, Derby, Sheffield and Manchester (via the Woodhead tunnel). To the French, who were already planning a network of dedicated high-speed lines, closure of the Great Central must have appeared quite incomprehensible.

One way or another, the railways closed during those years were victims. Victims either of a shameful lack of judgment, or a deliberate attempt to push traffic onto the roads... roads that were soon congested beyond reasonable limits. The Wilson Government was well aware of the areas where growth could be expected. And it knew perfectly well that a Channel Tunnel was a distinct possibility. How then, could it have made such decisions?

The blame must lie with the powerful and ruthless road lobby groups, which succeeded (beyond their own expectations) in convincing the nation that the railways were largely unnecessary. By the mid-1960s the all-pervading influence of the road lobby had reached deep into the corridors of power, affecting decision-making at the very highest level, and making a mockery of the democratic process.

If, then, the downfall of the railways, and the construction of the motorway network, was to some extent engineered by the road lobby, was the explosive growth of road transport really inevitable, as we have long been encouraged to believe? There can be no doubt that a basic motorway network of some description would have been built whatever the political climate, and Britain would have been quite unique amongst industrialised nations had it avoided such a course. But the road-building process went a good deal further than that, and a considerable mileage was constructed to encourage further growth in the road sector, rather than to contain growth that had already taken place. The overwhelming success of the publicity campaigns undertaken by the road lobbyists in the early 1960s can be judged from the fact that it took 20 years to challenge them effectively, and by that time the railways had been firmly displaced.

* * *

Several railway lines survived thanks to determined local campaigns, a very few closure attempts were stopped through the courts, and others were discarded as politically unacceptable. Passenger services were retained to a solitary village in Cornwall, but removed from a town of more than 50,000 inhabitants in Nottinghamshire, where a healthy coal traffic paid every penny of the track costs. While some communities were little affected, others left the system altogether... it was ultimately a rather arbitrary programme.

The result of two decades of vague and random retrenchment was not a viable network, but an assortment of good, bad and indifferent services. In 1948 the Chancellor of the Exchequer had described the newly nationalised railway system as a "poor bag of assets". By 1970 little had changed — the then Chancellor simply found himself holding a smaller bag. It was only with the fortuitous arrival of the oil crisis, and later scares over the environmental impact of road transport, that the process was brought (hopefully) to a belated end.

The brand new Woodhead tunnel in 1953 — it could have formed part of a high speed route from the Channel Tunnel to Manchester. Colour-Rail.

That a note of caution must still be sounded here is due to important considerations at the time of writing: the new roads programme inherited by Malcolm Rifkind from Cecil Parkinson appears unstoppable; one reopened railway (Corby) has closed; railway finances remain vulnerable; newspaper deliveries by rail are a thing of the past; Post Office business is shifting towards road and air; and the closure of BR's Speedlink operation has killed off many private sidings.

Yet, on the other side of the equation, light rail is returning to the streets of Manchester, with other schemes in the pipeline for Sheffield, Birmingham and many other British towns and cities. With it being, surely, only a matter of time before road transport hits the environmental buffers it seems most unlikely at any rate that we shall see a return to large, or even medium scale, network closures.

To sustain the argument that at least a proportion of the closures should never have been permitted, a measure of proof is required. Probably the most damning evidence is that a number of lines (all having remained open to freight traffic in the intervening decades) have subsequently reopened to passenger trains, and most have proved very successful. Even British Rail now openly admits that several other lines would remain in use today had the permanent way not been torn up and destroyed. This is the sad part of the affair, for a bus service can easily be reinstated, a factory rehoused, or even a community rebuilt... but it appears as though a railway — once the formation has been obliterated — is lost for good. It would be agreeable should such a judgment prove ill-founded.

Appendix 1.

Line reopenings

THE list of lines reopened since the renaissance of the railway industry includes a few examples where the population has fallen since the 1960s. However, the figures tend to mask the fact that these, mostly industrial, areas have a very substantial population, even allowing for a fall of 20 per cent or more in the past 20 years.

The question as to whether railway closures might actually have caused a reduction (or even a rise) in population, is a complex one. Closures probably had little negative effect on wealthier communities in the South, but a marked effect in the industrial areas of South Wales, the Midlands and the North, that experienced a simultaneous loss of industry. Loss of population has occurred predominantly where heavy industrial complexes have closed... mainly in the coal mining valleys of South Wales and in the vicinity of former steel towns, such as Consett.

A loss of population does not necessarily mean that a reopened railway service would be any less viable, however, for the old labour-intensive industries have generally been replaced by smaller high technology enterprises employing a wealthier and more mobile workforce. Thus, several lines in depressed regions, which were considered uneconomic during the Beeching era, have successfully reopened.

All the reopened railways listed in TABLE 1(a) are open to regular scheduled services. Those in TABLE 1(b) — mostly privately owned — are open on an occasional or seasonal basis only, but all have secured full interchange facilities with BR main line services and are

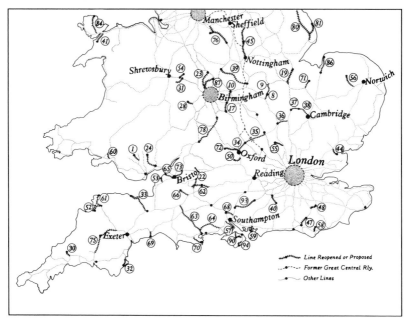

therefore worthy of inclusion.

The list is not exhaustive — it merely identifies the lines which (in the author's opinion) should not have closed, either for strategic reasons, or because they served a large static or seasonal population. Many other private lines deserve a mention, notably the Worth Valley, between Keighley and Oxenhope, the Watercress Line (table 4, 93) and a number of narrow gauge concerns, such as the Ffestiniog, which performs a unique role (on a seasonal basis) in connecting with British Rail at both termini. Several other groups aim to restore a gap in the rail network — none

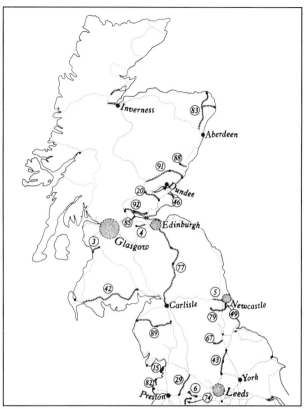

would reach substantial local populations, but all could be expected to perform a useful role by encouraging tourists to visit remote areas by rail, rather than car or coach. Peak Rail is relaying the line from Matlock towards Buxton (table 4, 76), the North Yorkshire Moors Railway runs from Pickering to Grosmont, on the Whitby line, and an extension into Whitby remains a possibility. The Wensleydale Railway Association is investigating the viability of relaying track between a BR freight terminal at Redmire and Garsdale station on the Settle-Carlisle line, a distance of 18 miles.

Key to tables

Spel	*Reopened under the 1981 Speller legislation*
RDS	*Proposal supported by the Railway Development Society*
** %	*Population change of little relevance*
@	*Population figures calculated wholly or partially from 1951 census rather than 1961*
¶	*Population change calculated by comparing 1971 and 1981 census*

Numbers in tables correspond with those on maps.

Table 1(a)

Line	Pop change *** (1961-1981)		Miles	Current position	Primary traffic
1 Aberdare-Abercynon	-19%	RDS	6	Reopened 1989	Commuter
2 Addleston Junc-Byfleet Junc	**%		1/2	Reopened 1986	
3 Barassie-Kilmarnock	**%		13	Reopened 1969	Strategic
4 Bathgate-Edinburgh	+28% @	Spel/RDS	10	Reopened 1986	Commuter
5 Blaydon-Dunston-Newcastle	**%		4	Reopened 1984	
6 Burnley-Todmorden	**%	RDS	10	Reopened 1984	Strategic
6a Drclough Jct-Bradley Jct	**%		5	Reopening 1993	Strategic/ commuter
7 Cardiff City Line	**%	Spel	5	Reopened 1987	Commuter
8 Corby-Kettering [1]	+9%	Spel/RDS	5	Reopened 1987 }	Commuter
9 Corby-Manton Junc	**%		10	Freight Line }	Strategic
10 Coventry-Nuneaton	-15%	Spel/RDS	10	Reopened 1987	Commuter
11 Dalston-Stratford	-13%¶		3	Reopened 1983	Commuter/ Strategic
12 Deansgate-Edgeley Junc	**%		7	Reopened 1989	
13 Derby-Sinfin	**%		2	Reopened 1976	Commuter
14 Glasgow 'Argyle' Line	**%	RDS	5	Reopened 1979	
15 Heysham Harbour-Morecambe	**%	Spel	5	Reopened 1987	Strategic
16 Kensington-Willesden	**%	RDS	3	Reopened 1986	Strategic
17 Leamington Spa-Coventry	**%	RDS	10	Reopened 1977	Strategic
18 Lichfield City-Lichfield TV	**%		1	Reopened 1988	Commuter/ strategic
19 Peterborough-Spalding	-8%		16	Reopened 1971	Commuter/ strategic
20 Perth-Ladybank	**%		19	Reopened 1975	Strategic
21 Rotherham Central Junc-Aldwarke	**%		2	Reopened 1987	Strategic
22 Trowbridge-Chippenham	+46%	Spel/RDS	10	Reopened 1985	Commuter/ strategic
23 Walsall-Hednesford	+27%	Spel/RDS	10	Reopened 1989	Commuter [2]
***					
24 Ebbw Vale-Newport	-25%		20	May reopen	Commuter
25 Newcastle Airpt.-Kenton Bankfoot	**%	RDS	2	Reopened Nov 91	Tyne&Wear Metro
26 Paisley (Canal)-Glasgow	-13%¶	RDS	7	Reopened 1991	Commuter
27 Wakefield-Pontefract	**%	RDS	9	To reopen	Commuter

Total 210 miles

[1] *Services between Kettering and Corby are currently suspended*
[2] *Potentially strategic if reopened through to Rugeley Trent Valley*

Table 1(b)

Line	Pop change *** (1961-1981)		Miles	Current position	Primary traffic
28 Bewdley-Kidderminster [3]	+62%		4	Private line	Commuter/ tourist
29 Blackburn-Hellifield	4%¶	RDS	25	Reopened 1987	Seasonal
30 Bodmin-Bodmin Parkway	+73%	RDS	3	Private line	Tourist/ commuter
31 Coalbrookdale-Telford	**%		5 1/2	Reopened 1987	Seasonal
32 Kingswear-Paignton	-25%		7	Private line	Tourist
33 Minehead-Taunton [3]	+14%		25	Private Line	Tourist

[3] *Part of the Severn Valley Railway, which operates from Bridgnorth to Kidderminster (13$^1/_2$ miles)*
[4] *No connecting trains at present*

Total 69$^1/_2$ miles

A second group includes examples that the the Railway Development Society feels merit serious investigation. The society continues to campaign for new railway construction, as well as the reopening of stations and freight lines to passenger traffic. In all, the society believes that up to 200 miles of new construction should be considered for the future. Notable in this category is a route from Oxford to Cambridge, already reopened between Oxford and Bicester and the subject of a prolonged campaign for restoration onwards to Milton Keynes. To complete the link through to Cambridge via Huntingdon and St Ives would require the reconstruction of 18 miles of line, but the benefits would be outstanding — through services from Bristol, Didcot and Oxford to Milton Keynes and Cambridge, and restored local services between Cambridge and St Ives, where the population has almost quadrupled since the early 1960s. Another spin-off would be a shorter route from Cambridge to Peterborough.

Table 2

Line	Pop change (1961-1981)		Miles	Current position	Primary traffic
34 Oxford-Bicester Town	+107%	Spel	12	Reopened 1988 }	
35 Bicester-Milton Keynes	**%	RDS	23	Freight line }	
36 Bedford-Sandy	**%	RDS	8	Derelict }	
37 Huntingdon-St Ives-Fen Drayton	+277%	RDS	7	Derelict }	
38 Fen Drayton-Cambridge	**%	RDS	14	Freight line }	Strategic/ commuter
39 Burton upon Trent-Leicester	+10%	RDS	32	Freight Line	Strategic/ commuter
40 Cranleigh-Guildford	+72%	RDS	8	Derelict	Commuter
41 Caernarfon-Bangor	+1%	RDS	6	Derelict	Tourist/feeder
42 Dumfries-Stranraer	**%	RDS	55	Derelict	Strategic
43 Harrogate-Ripon-Northallerton	+18%	RDS	22	Derelict	Commuter/ strategic
44 Maldon-Witham	+26%	RDS	7	Derelict	Commuter
45 Mansfield-Nottingham [5]	+30%	RDS	18	Derelict/freight	Commuter
46 St Andrews-Leuchars	+11% @	RDS	5	Derelict	Tourist/ commuter
47 Uckfield-Lewes	**%	RDS	7	Derelict/private }	Strategic
48 Tunbridge Wells-Eridge	**%	RDS	5	Derelict }	Strategic
49 Washington New Town-Pelaw	+147%	RDS	4	Freight [6]	Tyne & Wear Metro

Total 233 miles

[5] *Mansfield to Worksop is also under consideration*
[6] *Some new construction will also be required*

The third group includes lines in areas that have mostly experienced a substantial increase in population since closure, notably the Poole-Ringwood-Brockenhurst line; branches to towns such as Abingdon and Hailsham; and the Swansea arm of the Central Wales line between Hendy Junction and Gowerton (passing through Gorseinon, a town that has grown faster than almost any other in South Wales, and providing a direct link to Swansea for Central Wales traffic). Some are now wholly or partially open in private hands but can not be included in Table 1(b) because they have yet to secure a connection to the railway network.

Some areas have not experienced particularly rapid growth, but other factors, such as tourism, industry, or heavy commuter traffic, have tilted the balance in favour of rail transport since closure. A few lines have remained open for freight use in the intervening years, and although this does not reduce reopening to a formality, it does make such a possibility rather more likely. Other routes, such as those to Bideford, Portishead and Abingdon have only lost freight services very recently, and could have track restored with comparative ease. Sadly, several examples, such as the Brockenhurst to Poole line, are probably lost for ever and are included for academic interest only.

There is every likelihood that most of these railways, had they survived (and received suitable investment), would be marginal or profitable today... certainly none would have increased the railway operating deficit by more than a token amount.

Table 3

Line	Pop change (1961-1981)		Miles	Current position	Primary traffic
50 Abingdon-Radley	+81%		2	Derelict	Commuter
51 Avonmouth-Filton	**%	RDS	6	Freight line	Avon Metro
52 Bideford-Barnstaple	+28%	RDS	9	Derelict	Tourist/feeder
53 Clevedon-Yatton	+47%		4	Derelict	Commuter
54 Donnington-Wellington	[7]		3	Freight line	Commuter
55 Dunstable-Luton	+72%	RDS	4	Freight line	Commuter
56 East Dereham-Wymondham	+54%	RDS	12	Freight line	Commuter #
57 Fawley-Southampton	+63%	RDS	13	Freight line	Commuter
58 Hailsham-Polegate	+175%	RDS	3	Derelict	Commuter
59 Havant-Hayling Island	+39%		4	Derelict	Commuter
60 Hendy Junc-Gowerton	+385%		5	Derelict	Strategic/commuter
61 Ilfracombe-Barnstaple	+51%		14	Derelict	Tourist
62 Patney-Devizes-Holt [8]	+40%		13	Derelict	Commuter/strategic
63 Poole-Templecombe or Bruton	+176%	RDS	31/39	Derelict	Strategic/commuter
64 Poole-Wimborne-Brockenhurst	+305%		26	Derelict	Commuter
65 Portishead-Bristol	+89%		11	Derelict	Avon Metro
66 Radstock-Frome [9]	+29%		8	Derelict	Local #
67 Richmond-Eryholme Junc	+8%		11	Derelict	Commuter/tourist
68 Romsey-Eastleigh	**%	RDS	7	Freight line	Commuter/strategic
69 Seaton-Seaton Junction	+71%		4	Private/derelict	Tourist
70 Swanage-Wareham [10]	+13%	RDS	10	Private line	Commuter/tourist
71 Wisbech-March	+31%	RDS	8	Freight line	Commuter
72 Witney-Oxford	+48%		12	Derelict	Commuter
73 Yate-Mangotsfield-Bristol	+79% [11]		11	Derelict	Commuter

Total 238.5 miles

[7] *Donnington and Wellington are now suburbs of Telford. Donnington has grown by at least 100-200%*

[8] *The Railway Development Society believes that a Devizes Parkway station on the nearby Reading to Taunton line would be a more realistic option*

[9] *Reopening has been proposed in private hands*

[10] *The Purbeck Railway Company intends to secure a connection with BR in the near future*

[11] *The population of Yate has grown by more than 300 per cent. A station has recently reopened in the town; services operating to Bristol via Bristol Parkway rather than Mangotsfield*

Prospective private operator

For a variety of reasons, the final examples are less likely to see services restored, but there are sound strategic, commercial or social reasons why they should have been retained. Many are now partially restored in private hands operating a successful seasonal service.

Other lines are included, not so much because passenger traffic was ever particularly heavy (or could be expected to be so in the future) but because they continue to earn a living from freight traffic. Where freight pays a proportion of the track costs, the expense of providing a railbus service would be much reduced. The former freight line between Washington New Town and Consett would have served a population of more than 40,000 had it survived... future developments may well tip the balance in favour of restoration.

A few examples in this group are trunk lines that left a large gap in the railway network after closure, such as Exeter-Bere Alston, the Waverley route between Edinburgh and Carlisle, and the Cheltenham to Stratford-upon-Avon line. Few have seen a substantial growth in population, but all pass through tourist areas, and population trends can be unpredictable. The village of Bishops Cleave, near Cheltenham, has more than doubled in size since closure of the Cheltenham to Stratford line, with a current population in excess of 8,000, and mounting road congestion in the area has put loss of railway services into question.

Many would argue that at least part of the Great Central should also be included. Several serious proposals have been put forward in recent years, including relaying the line from the present railhead at Calvert in Buckinghamshire northwards beyond Rugby, and perhaps even as far as Leicester. A new viaduct would be needed, together with many other engineering works, but if the economic and environmental balance continues to tilt in favour of railway restoration anything is possible. For this reason, the lines listed below — mostly considered "dead" just a decade ago (and long since obliterated for at least part of their length) — may well be worthy of consideration in the future.

Table 4

Line	Pop change (1961-1981)		Miles	Current position	Primary traffic
74 Bacup-Rawtenstall-Bury	-12%		13	Private/derelict	Commuter
75 Bere Alston-Exeter	+27%¶		46	Derelict/freight	Strategic/ tourist
76 Buxton-Matlock	**%	RDS	20	Private/derelict	Tourist/ # strategic
77 Carlisle-Hawick-Edinburgh	+21%¶ [12]		98	Derelict	Tourist/ strategic
78 Cheltenham-Stratford upon Avon	**%		30¹/₂	Derelict/private	Tourist/ strategic
79 Consett-Washington New Town	-52%		16	Cycleway	Commuter
80 Firsby-Louth-Grimsby } [13]	** %	RDS	33	Derelict	Local
81 Willoughby-Mablethorpe }	+35%		9	Derelict	Tourist
82 Fleetwood-Poulton	-2%		6	Derelict/freight	Commuter
83 Fraserburgh/Peterhead-Aberdeen	+26% @		60	Derelict	Tourist/ commuter

Line	Pop change *** (1961-1981)		Miles	Current position	Primary traffic
84 Gaernwen-Amlwch	-15%		$17^1/_2$	Freight Line	Local
85 Grangemouth-Falkirk	-11%¶			Freight	Commuter
86 Hunstanton-King's Lynn	**%		15	Derelect	Tourist
87 Lichfield-Brownhills-Walsall	-38%	RDS	$10^1/_2$	Derelict/freight	Commuter
88 Montrose-Brechin	15%¶		$9^1/_2$	Derelict/private	Tourist
89 Penrith-Keswick-Workington	23%¶		40	Derelict	Tourist
90 Ryde-Newport-Cowes	-2%		14	Derelict/private	Tourist
91 Stanley Junc-Forfar-Arbroath	17%¶		40	Derelict	Tourist/commuter
92 Stirling-Alloa-Dunfermline	87%¶		$20^1/_2$	Freight/derelict	Strategic/commuter
93 Winchester-Alton [14]	**%		19	Private/derelict	Strategic/commuter
94 Ventnor-Shanklin	-20% @		4	Derelict	Tourist

[13] *The Railway Development Society has long supported reopening between Louth and Grimsby and the Grimsby-Louth Railway Preservation Society aims to relay as much as possible north of Louth.*

[14] *Open in private hands between Alton and New Alresford*

[12] *Excluding towns within commuting distance of Edinburgh (such as Bonnyrigg) which have seen explosive growth in population in recent years.*

FOOTNOTE: At the time of writing, a great many towns and cities were the subject of schemes evaluating the potential for the introduction of light rail transit systems. Many of these, particularly those proposed for the West Midlands, would use former rail alignments. With a few exceptions, these have fallen outside the scope of this appendix.

An excursion train at Consett in 1979 — both the steelworks and the railway have now gone, the disappearance of the latter in the late 1980s representing a missed opportunity. Neville Stead.

Appendix 2.
The case for reopening

The overwhelming question is one of finance. Thanks to the increasing burden of road congestion, and a more businesslike attitude on the part of British Rail, railway finances are healthier now than they have been for many years. But the Government has continued to squeeze the railways to the point where investment might, once again, be put at risk. The Thatcherite vision of a profitable private railway network is probably attainable, but at what cost?

The railways are currently finding new traffic; not because the public are keen to take advantage of railway fares and quality of service, but because Britain's roads are chronically congested, particularly in and around London. Network Southeast might, conceivably, in times of economic boom, push fares higher around the capital, to the point where commuter services were operating at a surplus but, environmentally and socially, such a vision is not an attractive one.

In order to provide a genuine alternative to road transport, rather than just a service for captive and unwilling commuters, fares must be kept down to a reasonable level. Under present conditions this could never be achieved, although it must be said that the Thatcherite ethos of efficiency and cost-effective operation have had, in some ways, a positive effect on the railways.

As monopoly carriers, the railways were more than capable of generating a healthy profit on their operations... under the present rules they are not. We already owe the railways a great deal for their role in safeguarding the environment, and they are capable of doing a great deal more in the years ahead by containing the growth in road traffic. To achieve this, something must be done to adjust the relationship between road and rail finance.

As we have seen, the arguments for and against a more radical solution to road/rail finance have ebbed and flowed for many years. One possible answer, regarded by many as the best compromise, would be to leave the railway infrastructure in state hands and privatise the movement operations. This would put the railways on a more or less equal footing with road transport, the operators paying a licence fee for the use of a state-owned infrastructure. A less radical solution might involve an adjustment to the relative cost of road and rail transport, for the railways problem stems from a continuing bias towards road transport.

The owner of a road vehicle pays a fixed annual licence fee, and a certain amount of taxation on the fuel he uses. In other words, the motorist (and the coach and HGV operator) pays an annual down-payment towards road "track" costs, and the remainder as and when he pays for movement costs by purchasing fuel. His natural inclination is to use the vehicle as frequently as possible in order to take advantage of the track costs he has already paid.

The rail traveller, on the other hand, pays for rail track costs (and movement costs) every time he travels by train. Thus, the public perceive rail travel to be expensive, and motor transport to be relatively cheap... little more than the cost of fuel on a day-to-day basis. The effect is to limit rail travel and to increase road congestion.

Disregarding the various arguments as to whether motorists actually pay enough to cover policing, hospital cover, and all the other hidden road transport costs, a few measures could be taken to alter the balance in favour of rail transport.

If the Government was to pay a proportion of railway track costs from central funds there would be more incentive for travellers to use the railways. If, at the same time, the road fund licence was reduced or abolished, and taxation on petrol and diesel fuel increased, the cost of motoring would remain unchanged, but the perceived cost would increase. The railway traveller would pay a smaller proportion of rail track costs, while the road user would pay in relation to mileage travelled.

If the sum paid to cover the railway track costs was directly linked to the mileage open to regular passenger traffic, the railways would be encouraged to reopen more lines and further alleviate road congestion. Even the small private railway companies could be treated in the same manner — any that chose to provide a full passenger service would receive track costs from the Government in recognition of their role in reducing road congestion.

Such a payment would not be a general subsidy, but a fixed sum based upon railway passenger mileage, leaving the railway system of the future with every incentive to operate efficiently. Some might argue that measures to assist the railways would have little impact on road congestion, but it would be a start — a small beginning that might well show a positive return. There is no possibility that the railways will ever again come to dominate transport in this country in the way they did 100 years ago. The motor car is here to stay, and understandably so, but the all-pervading influence and domination of the car over our society must be curbed and a healthier transport balance attained.

British governments of all political shades have made a single cardinal error since the war by taking little action to curb the demand for motor transport. No-one could have prevented the boom in car-ownership, and in view of the positive attributes of the car — the freedom and flexibility that it provides — it is right that none has done so. But much could have been done to limit the impact of the motor car age, and from this viewpoint all governments must bear equal responsibility.

For more than 40 years the railways have staggered beneath the demoralising weight of a subsidy, but since losing monopoly status they have not been, and could not be expected to be, self-supporting. That is perhaps the real lesson from the Beeching years — that no railway system, however small, is likely to be directly self financing under present conditions. The cuts were virtually worthless in financial terms, and very expensive by any other criteria.

No-one has yet calculated the true cost of railway closures in terms of human life. The Friends of the Earth have calculated that the number of people killed on British roads since the war now exceeds the number who died fighting it. Of the present annual total of around 5,000 road deaths, a fair and measurable proportion have died because there were no alternative transport facilities available. It would even be possible to calculate the number who have died as a direct result of railway closures: those who bought and continued to use a car where public transport had ceased to exist. The environmental cost can be calculated too, as can the cost of policing, hospital care, road building, road maintenance and so on. Perhaps it is better to leave the figures alone, for the truth might be difficult to face.

For the moment it is essential to keep the formation of closed railway lines intact, and legislation such as Robert Adley's Railway Re-openings (Tribunal) Bill will assist in this direction. The environmental and social benefits of rail travel are overwhelming. The case for a fairer system of payment for both the road and rail infrastructures is equally overwhelming. Half a century of history has taught us that, if nothing else.

Appendix 3
Survey of small European towns (10,000-15,000 population) July 1991

Sample size	Passenger rail station	Integrated rail/bus service	No proper facilities
Britain			
88	52% *1	2%	46%
France			
29	24% *2	69%	7%
Germany *3			
55	82%	16%	2%

*1 4% of these have re-opened since the Beeching years, and a further 18% would reopen if the suggestions tabulated in Appendix 1 were carried out.

*2 nearly all have track in place for freight or through passenger services

*3 Former Federal Republic only

Three very different approaches to public transport. Obviously there are many factors that might restrict the validity of such a comparison. However, having started with a denser network, Britain might be expected to have retained a comparatively large number of stations, and in France (and to a lesser extent, in Germany) the towns tend to be more thinly spread — a factor that might be expected to count against efficient public transport.

Thanks to Britain's poor record in such matters, the opposite is true. The German network is close to the ideal: 82 per cent of small towns have railway stations of their own, the remainder being served by integrated buses connecting with rail services at the nearest station. In France, many local rail services have been abandoned, but almost every town is served either by rail, or rail and connecting bus, and the vast majority of towns are on existing lines used for freight or through passenger services. Few local stations have actually been demolished, indeed many remain open and staffed for the convenience of bus passengers, and the collection and delivery of goods and parcels.

In Britain, where the integration of bus and rail services has never been satisfactorily accomplished the picture is comparatively bleak. About half the towns are served by rail, but only a tiny proportion of the remainder have had axed rail services replaced by comparable bus services; that is buses that British Rail recognises (and advertises as connecting with trains at the nearest rail-head).

Random sample of 254 towns and villages throughout England and Wales:

Population:	500-1,500	1,500-5,000	5,000-20,000	20,000-60,000
Passenger railway service in 1948				
	62%	86%	98%	100%
Passenger railway service in 1984				
	16%	32%	59%	84%
Potential for reinstated service				
	45%	51%	77%	96%
Sample Size				
	58	90	81	25

Bibliography

Nationalisation Bill 1947 *HMSO*

The Report from the Select Committee on Nationalised Industries 1960 *HMSO*

The Somerset & Dorset Railway The Branch Line Re-invigoration Society 1962

The Reshaping of British Railways BRB 1963 *HMSO*

The Railways & the Nation A J Pearson 1964 *Allen & Unwin*

Anatomy of Britain Today Anthony Sampson 1965 *Hodder & Stoughton*

The Organisation of British Railways Michael Bonavia 1971 *Ian Allen*

Public Enterprise in Practice Richard Pryke 1971 *MacGibbon & Kee*

The Railwaymen NUR

Transport Disintegrated Roger Calvert 1973 *R Calvert*

Rail 150 Ed Jack Simmons 1975 *Methuen*

Economics & Transport Policy K M Gwilliam & P J Mackie 1975 *Allen & Unwin*

Transport policy (Vol 2) 1976 *HMSO*

Transport Bill 1967 *HMSO*

Railway Policy 1967 *HMSO*

The Kennet & Avon Canal Kenneth Clew

The Social Consequences of Railway Closures Mayer Hillman & Anne Whalley 1980

BR: The First 25 Years Michael Bonavia

My Years with Churchill Norman Macgowan

The Tunnel; the Channel & Beyond Ed Bronwen Jones 1987 *Ellis Horwood*

Rural Transport: What Future Now? Rural District Councils Association

Chronicle of the 20th Century 1988 *Longman*

Accounting for life Henry Benson, Baron 1989 *Kogan Page*

Beeching — Champion of the Railways? R H N Hardy 1989 *Ian Allan*

Wheels within Wheels Mick Hamer 1987 *Routledge & Kegan Paul*

Various editions of **Hansard**

Various **TUCC Annual Reports**

Various **CTCC Annual Reports**

I Tried to Run a Railway Gerard Fiennes

The Birth of British Railways Michael Bonavia 1979 *Allen & Unwin*

Railway Policy Between the Wars Michael Bonavia 1981 *Manchester University Press*

Fiennes on Rails Gerard Fiennes 1986 *David & Charles*

BR Diary 1958-1967 John Glover 1987 *Ian Allen*

BR Diary 1968-1977 Chris Heaps 1988 *Ian Allen*

Glossary of terms

Branchline Committee: Formed by the Railway Executive in 1950 to establish which railway lines were suitable candidates for closure. Later replaced by the Unremunerative Railway Services Committee.

Branch Line Re-invigoration Society: Formed as the Society for the Re-invigoration of Unremunerative Branch Lines in the United Kingdom (or SRUBLUK) in 1954, the Society was later renamed the Railway Invigoration Society and merged with the RDA in 1978 to form the Railway Development Society.

BRF: British Road Federation — road lobby group formed in the 1930s.

BTC: British Transport Commission — formed under the 1947 Transport Act to co-ordinate and integrate public transport in the British Isles. Under the 1953 Transport Act the BTC also took over the day-to-day management of the railways and other transport concerns. Abolished in 1962.

CTCC: Central Transport Consultative Committee. Formed under the 1947 Transport Act to liaise between the Local Transport Users Consultative Committees and the British Transport Commission.

DMU: Diesel Multiple Unit. A group of diesel rail-cars connected to form a single unit - usually comprising a power car (with driver's compartment) at either end, and a single unpowered car in between. Such 3-car units could be joined to produce multiple units of six, nine or more vehicles.

Lightweight Trains Committee: Formed by the Railway Executive in 1951 to investigate the suitability of rail-cars and rail-buses for marginal services.

NCIT: National Council on Inland Transport. A rail lobby group, formed in 1962.

Push-pull unit: A small steam locomotive coupled to one or more carriages, with facilities for remote operation from a small driver's compartment at the rear to allow for reverse operation.

Rail-bus: Originally a road bus converted to run on rails (and usually a four wheeled, uni-directional, vehicle), but the term was later applied to more specialised light-weight vehicles designed specifically for railway operations.

Rail-car: A single, powered, railway carriage, usually with a driver's compartment at either end, a road bus-type diesel engine beneath the body, and two bogies, each with four wheels. A larger and more powerful cousin of the rail-bus.

Rail-motor: A small steam locomotive permanently articulated to a railway carriage. Remote controls at the rear allowed for reverse operation.

Railway Executive: Created under the provisions of the 1947 Transport Act, the Railway Executive effectively managed the railways under the guidance of the British Transport Commission. The Railway Executive was abolished under the 1953 Transport Act (together with the Executives empowered to manage other forms of public transport), and control of the railways was passed to the BTC.

RDA: Railway Development Association. A rail lobby group formed in 1951 for the purpose of fighting branch-line (and in later years, secondary and trunk line) railway closures. Merged with the Railway Invigoration Society in 1978 to form the Railway Development Society.

Index

References in the appendices are excluded

Aberdeen 184
Abergavenny 141
A C Cars 101, 102
accidents 18, 126, 131, 137
  road 30, 117, 131, 151, 194, 210, 211
Adley, Robert 128
A E C Company 61
Aickman, Robert 59, 88
air transport 11, 28, 143, 145, 147, 154,
155, 185, 219, 232, 237
Aire and Calder canal 107
Albu, Mr. 126
Aldeburgh 177
Alston 192, 193, 215
American Association of State
Highway Officials 218
Amlwych 76
Annemasse - Geneva line 60
Appleby 192
Area Boards 71, 73, 115, 116
Arlott, John 71
Ashford 207, 215
ASLEF 138, 140
Atlantic Coast Express 21, 190
Attlee, Clement 34, 94
Automobile Association (AA) 23, 207
Aylesbury 19, 165, 166

Baldwin, Archer 88, 89, 92, 98, 99
Baldwin, Stanley 94
Ballater 96, 183, 184
Ballinamore 51
Banbury 103, 104, 166, 167
Bangor 76, 197, 198, 214
Barnes, Rt Hon Alfred 35, 49
Barnsley 105
Barnstaple 168, 215, 221
Bath 19, 148, 181, 182, 183
Bathgate 223
battery-powered transport 96, 183, 184
Bedford 93, 178, 214, 215, 235
  Duke of 48
Beeching, Dr. 7, 8, 10, 11, 16, 85, 116,
121, 122, 128, 130, 131, 134, 136-144,
145-170, 172, 174-177, 186, 189, 190,
192, 193, 196, 200, 204, 209, 211, 215,
219-222, 224-227, 230, 232, 233, 234
Belfast 53
Bembridge 66, 67, 68, 69, 70, 230
Benn, Anthony Wedgewood 174
Benson, Lord Henry 122, 128, 196
Bere Alston 83, 190, 192, 235
Berwick 43
Betjeman, Sir John 80
Besford viaduct 165
Bevan, Aneurin 94
Bewdley 197, 220, 234
Bideford 192
Billacombe station 48
Birmingham 35, 61, 65, 96, 104, 114,
119, 120, 152, 166, 171, 219, 220, 237
  International Station 219
  New Street Station 104

Blandford 181, 182
Blee, David 104
Bletchley 178, 214, 215, 235
Bluebell Line 49, 199
Bodiam 46
Border Union Line 201, 202, 203
Boston 61, 167, 208
Botterill, William 177
Bourne End 197
Bournemouth 148, 166, 181, 182, 183,
217, 235
Bowes Committee 107, 108
Bradford 61, 76, 96, 105
  Earl of 48
Brading 66, 68, 69, 70
Branch Line
  Committee 47-50, 55, 57, 62, 63, 66,
67, 69, 70, 77, 80, 81, 82, 84
  Re-invigoration Society 183
  SEE ALSO Closure of Branch Lines
Subcommittee
Bridgend 197
Bridport 192, 215, 216
Bright, F.W. 66, 68
Brighton 26, 49
Bristol 19, 35, 62, 143, 152, 200
  Commercial Vehicles railbus 93
  /Eastern Coachworks 101
British European Airways 154
British Industries 104
British Railways Board 132-134, 139,
140, 142, 143, 146, 148-151, 153, 156-
164, 166-168, 174-176, 178-180, 182,
185, 186, 189, 190, 194-197, 200, 202-
204, 207, 210, 211, 212
British Railways Plan for Modernisa-
tion and Re-equipment 78
British Road Federation 23, 30, 35, 45,
79, 194, 207
British Road Services 101
British Transport Commission 34, 38-
42, 44, 46, 47, 49, 50, 53-59, 62-75, 77-
79, 81, 82, 85-92, 94-98, 100, 101, 104-
116, 119 -123, 125-127, 129-134, 136-
138, 142, 143, 147, 150, 177, 183, 200,
227-230, 232, 233
British Transport Stock 44, 113, 119,
132
British Waterways Board 108
Brockenhurst 182, 235
Brown, Colonel Clifton 35
Bruton 183
Buckfastleigh 83
Buckingham 103, 104
Bude 192
Bufton, W.E. 77
Burgin, Leslie 30
Butler "Rab" 167
Buxton 158, 160

Cadbury, Sir Egbert 47
Caernarfon 197, 198, 214
Callington branch 192

Calstock 192
Calvert, Roger 157-160, 162, 163, 178,
179, 185
Cambrian Coast Line 208, 214, 215,
224
Cambridge 177, 178, 190, 197, 207,
214, 234, 235
Camelford 192
canal 14, 17, 20, 24, 107, 108, 109,
185
  companies 43
  shareholders 44
  SEE ALSO Inland Waterways...
car 11, 30, 82, 86, 117, 121, 152-154,
156, 163, 187, 198, 199, 208, 209, 212-
214, 216, 219, 222
  manufacturers 10
  production 28, 211
  ownership 210, 217
  SEE ALSO company cars
Cardiff 35, 152, 178, 208
Carlisle 12, 35, 62, 111, 148, 177, 190,
196, 200, 202
  SEE ALSO Settle-Carlisle Line
Carrington, Sir William 133-137, 196
Carstairs 12, 200
Castle, Barbara 128, 171, 186-190,
193, 194, 234
Castle Bromwich 104
Central Transport Consultative
Committee 40, 58, 81, 82, 84, 85, 88,
89, 96, 101, 124, 133, 137, 158, 217,
222
  SEE ALSO Transport Users Consulta-
tive Committee,
Chamber of Commerce
  Birmingham Junior 65, 76
  Newport 66
Champion, A.J. 87
Channel Tunnel 19, 166, 235, 236, 237
Charleston Line 17
Chester 77
Churchill, Winston 22, 34, 35, 37, 55,
56, 57, 79, 122
Cinderford 87
Cirencester 102, 168
civil aviation industry 36
Clacton 79
Clark, E. Kitson 27
Clarke, Gordon 224
Clevedon branch 203
Closure of Branch Lines Subcommittee
137
Clydach 141
coal 14-16, 27, 37, 54, 58, 67, 110,
115, 118, 165, 195, 236
  industry 36, 38, 58
  strike 23
coaches 17, 82, 175, 208, 222
  operators 114
  SEE ALSO bus
Cockley Brake Junction 103

Colchester 197
Colne 197
Commercial Motor, The 110
commuter services 147, 152, 158, 189, 192, 196, 208, 223
company cars 209
Comrie 150, 151
Confederation of Shipbuilding and Engineering Unions 140
congestion SEE road congestion
Conservative government 31, 57, 58, 64, 94, 97, 109, 172, 190, 195, 222, 228
party 34, 110, 125, 127, 143
Conservatives 35, 37, 55, 56, 58, 59, 65, 74, 79, 95, 128, 138, 144, 164, 207, 228
container traffic 147
contributory revenue 20, 21, 22, 67, 114, 134, 150, 151, 152, 163, 191, 196, 198, 204, 216
Cooper Brothers 122
formula 196, 197, 204, 206, 208, 221, 224
Corby 196, 237
Corfe Castle 205
Cornish Riviera 75
Cornwall 114, 190, 192, 219, 236
Coronation Scot 66
Corwen 77
cost/benefit analysis 184, 186, 189
Coulsdon 26
Council on Tribunals 157
Country Landowners Association 175
County Donegal Railways SEE Donegal Railways, County
Courtaulds 122
Cowes 66, 71, 179, 180, 230
Craigendoran 93
Crewe 127
Cromer 225
Croydon 215
Cumberland 77, 168
Cumbria 96, 147, 192, 200
Cumbrian Scheme 76

Daily Mail 177
Dalton, Dr. Hugh 41
Darlington 13-17, 20
Dart Valley Line 83, 199
Dartford 26
Dartmoor 80-83
decentralisation 74, 122
denationalisation 58, 65, 71, 227
Denbigh 77, 78
Dent Head 225
Department of Environment 193, 214
Department of Transport 10, 98, 193, 218, 219, 222
SEE ALSO Ministry of Transport
Derby 177, 235
Derbyshire 87
Development of the Major Trunk Routes 174
Devon 48, 80, 114, 147, 152, 190, 192, 203, 204, 216, 221
Devon Line, North 221

diesel
multiple units 51, 53, 56-63, 65, 66, 75, 76, 85, 87, 90, 94, 96, 99, 100, 101, 104-106, 112, 114, 122, 147, 149, 150, 179, 183, 187, 214, 215, 228, 229
SEE ALSO railbus; railcar
services 26-28, 32, 33, 42, 46, 50, 54, 55, 61, 62, 65, 70, 76- 79, 82, 85-87, 91, 96, 100, 105, 119, 164, 177, 179, 220, 228
dieselisation 79, 168
Dingwall 64, 213, 215
Docks and Inland Waterways Executive Committee 40
DonauwÖrth 101
Doncaster 43, 78
Donegal Railways, County 50, 51, 92
Doody, E.J. 34
Dorset 43, 148, 181, 182, 192, 216
Dublin 53
Dudley 29
Dumfries 172
Dunkirk 33
Dunnett, Sir James 126
Dutch Railways 42

East Anglia 62, 85, 120
East Coast Main Line 12, 78, 105, 155, 226
East Grinstead 49
East Kent Light Railway 43
East Suffolk Line 178, 179, 224
Easton and Church Hope Railway Company 43
Eastern Area Board 97
Eastern Coaches 93
Eastern Region 43, 85, 115, 178
Eden, Anthony 79, 106
Edinburgh 12, 21, 32, 62, 65, 148, 152, 190, 196, 200, 214, 219
Edmonton 126
electric traction 27, 32, 33, 42, 46, 78, 105, 154, 223
vehicle, battery SEE battery powered transport
electrification 26, 27, 42, 46, 49, 65, 78, 79, 100, 105, 106,111, 112, 114, 116, 127, 129, 130, 154, 180, 181, 188, 200, 230, 233
Elizabethan 65
environmental damage 151, 194, 211
SEE ALSO pollution
Erbusaig Bay 213
Eskdale Line 200
Europe 30, 32, 46, 100, 182, 209, 210, 235
European
Community 218
loading gauge 19, 164, 235
railways 92, 234
Euston 78, 100, 111, 112, 116, 127-130, 188
Executive Committees 40, 41, 56
SEE ALSO Docks and Inland Waterways; London Transport; Road transport; Railway
Exeter 105, 168, 190, 192, 195, 197,

216, 222, 234, 235
express trains 32, 42, 56, 60, 61, 75, 153, 161, 166, 192, 235
SEE ALSO Elizabethan; inter-city; High Speed Train
Eye 178

Faith, Nicholas 7
Falmouth 190
Far North Line 213
Faversham 70
Felixtowe 79
Ferndown 182
Fiennes, Gerard 142, 143, 161, 162, 178, 179, 224
Fife 177
Fintown 51
Firsby 167, 168, 208
Fisher, Mr. 77
Fleetwood 197
Foley, T.C. 158
Fort Augustus 83
Fort William 64, 213
Four Oaks 119
France 53, 59, 75, 212
Fraser, Tom 171, 177, 178, 180, 181, 186, 188, 234
Fraserburgh 190
freight 13, 16, 19, 23, 78, 79, 109, 111, 115, 117, 147, 149, 174, 177, 192, 212, 213, 221, 222
services 27, 38, 64, 124, 145, 146, 161, 196
traffic 30, 45, 50, 77, 79, 143, 146, 150, 151, 161, 162, 166, 197, 237
vehicle mileage restriction 195
vehicles, heavy 71, 176, 193, 194, 218
SEE ALSO lorry; juggernaut; road haulage
Freight Sector 223
Freight Transport Association 207
French railways 17, 60, 61, 209
Freshwater 66, 68, 70, 230
Gaitskell, Hugh 110, 138
Galashiels 200, 201
Garnock, Viscount 82
Garrod, Trevor 10
gas turbine locomotives 202
Geddes, Sir Eric 23, 24, 26
Committee 176
Geneva 60
Germany 30, 35, 59, 75, 209, 210, 212
Gipping Rural District Council 207
Gladstone Act 18
Glasgow 152, 154, 174, 195, 200
Glassborrow, David 216
Glastonbury 181
Gleneagles 150
Gloucester 87, 101
goods transport SEE freight
grant aid to railways 194-198, 204, 207, 215, 226
SEE ALSO subsidies
Great Central 11, 19, 25, 111, 148, 161, 164-167, 180, 187, 188, 208, 234,

235
Great Central Association 188
Great Central trans-Pennine route 27
Great Central London Extension 19
Great Eastern 25
Great Glen 83
Great Isle of Wight Train Robbery 66, 69
Great Malvern to Hereford Line 31
Great Northern 11, 25
, Ireland 53
Great Western 19-21, 25, 27, 29, 31, 37, 43, 44, 50, 59, 61, 75, 101, 125, 166, 190
Greater London Council 217
Greece 53
Green, Sidney 140
Grimsby 61, 167, 208
Guildford 26
Guillebaud Committee 118, 124
Gunnislake 83, 192

Halifax 61
Hampshire 62
 Magazine 71
hardship 133, 135, 157, 158, 166, 185
Hardy, Richard 7
Harrogate 96, 105
Harwich 79
Harvey, Major G.B. 81
Hastings 207, 215
Hathaway, R.F. 55
haulage SEE freight; road haulage
Hawick 200, 202
Hay, John 116, 118, 124, 125, 128
Hayling Island 49, 203
Headcorn 84
Heath, Ted 207, 214
Heathrow 155
Hereford 31
Hertford 91
Hetton 53
High Speed train 154, 155, 219
High Wycombe 197
Highlands region 138, 147, 152
Hill, J.E.B. 94
Hill Stanley 67, 68
Hitler, Adolf 7, 30, 77
Holland 54, 99
Holsworthy 192
Home, Sir Alec Douglas 167
Hondelink, Professor 54, 55, 72-74, 106, 109, 136, 146, 148, 157, 163, 179, 188, 200, 226
Hopkins, C.P. 68, 69, 70
Horncastle 81
horse-drawn trains 13, 14, 15, 16, 41, 118
House of Commons 31, 34, 35, 36,50, 58, 79, 87, 94, 123, 221
House of Lords 13, 31, 130, 158
Hudson, George 87
Hull 35, 162, 180
Hunstanton 85, 190, 204, 234
Hurcombe, Sir Cyril 40, 46, 47, 57
ICI 122, 131, 176

Illfracombe 190, 192, 203, 204
Independent, The 7
inland waterways 36, 38, 40, 107, 108, 185
 SEE ALSO canals
Inland Waterways Association 59
Inland Waterways Redevelopment Advisory Committee 107
Institute of Chartered Accountants 133
Institute of Directors 144
Institute of Civil Engineers 20
inter-city services 142, 168, 197, 202, 219, 226, 232
Intercity 223
Inver 52
Inverness 83, 213
Ipswich 79, 178
Ireland 50, 51, 53, 98
Isle of Man Railways 52
Isle of Portland 205
Isle of Skye 213
Isle of Wight 55, 57, 58, 66, 67-71, 94, 99, 162, 179, 180, 230, 231
Italy 30, 212
Ivybridge station 83

Japan 209, 210, 213
Jenkins, Sir Gilmore 106
"Joint Machinery" 187
Joint Steering Group 193
Jones, T.W. 145
juggernauts 218
Junction Road Halt 46

Kearton, Lord 122, 128
Keighley and Worth Valley Railway 199, 202
Kemble 101
Kennet and Avon Canal 20, 108
Kent 70
Kent and East Sussex Light Railway 43, 46, 47, 59, 84
Kenworthy, Edward 66
Kettering 196
Keyse, Stanley 171
Kidderminster 197
Killibegs 52
King's Cross 78, 219
Kingsbridge branch 203
Kingsmoor Yard 177
Kingswear 204
Kirkham 197
Knaresborough 105
Kyle of Lochalsh 22, 64, 190, 212, 214, 215, 224

Labour 34, 41, 94, 95, 122, 124, 127, 128, 176, 186
 government 36, 37, 50, 55, 56, 81, 172, 175, 176, 178, 186-188, 229
 party 34-37, 39, 49, 58, 141, 145, 164, 170, 171
Lake District 61, 76, 214
Lancashire 48, 138
Launceston 192
Ledbury 31
Leeds 35, 61, 76, 78, 96, 105, 152,

174
Leicester 165, 235
Leicestershire County Council 199
Leitrim 99
Lenox-Boyd, Mr. 58
Leominster 88, 203
Lewes 49, 185, 235
Lewes, Captain 49
Liberal party 34, 178
Lichfield 88, 96, 104
light rail parliamentary lobby 98
Light Railway Transport League 59
Light Railways 19, 20, 43, 46, 53, 76, 84, 89, 90, 92, 96, 99, 147, 179, 224, 230, 237
 Act 19, 89, 90
 Order 90, 202
Lightweight Trains Committee 56, 59-63, 76, 228
Lincoln 167, 208
Lincolnshire 19, 61, 62, 85, 122, 147, 148, 152, 167, 207
Lincolnshire Road Car Company 62
"liner train" concept 147, 176
Liskeard 162
Liverpool 16, 79, 100, 111, 112, 116, 128-130, 152, 188, 219
Liverpool Street 27, 49, 79
Llangynog 84
Lloyd, Brigadier T.I. 175
Lloyd George 23
local authorities 107, 108, 148, 193, 204, 207, 214, 219, 229
Locomotive and Allied Manufacturers' Association 124
Locomotive Journal 34
London 19, 33, 59, 67, 138, 147, 152, 165, 168, 174, 178, 196
 -Birmingham 114
 -Brighton 26
 "bypass" 177
 -Cardiff 35
 -Carlisle 35, 200
 -Edinburgh 66
 -Manchester 129, 154
 -Midlands 235
 -Newcastle 32
 -Sheffield 148, 164, 166
 -West Country 21, 190
London Council, Greater SEE Greater London Council
London General Omnibus Company 23
London Midland Region 43, 104, 105, 115, 142, 143, 156
London Midland and Scottish 25, 26, 28, 32, 42, 43, 138
London and North Eastern 25-27, 29, 31, 32, 42, 43, 49, 138
London and North Western 26
London and South Western 26, 190, 195, 222, 234, 235
London Passenger Transport Board 44
London Transport Executive Committee 40
lorry 25, 37, 44, 51, 65, 72, 73, 101, 117, 171, 202, 218, 219

SEE ALSO freight vehicles, heavy; juggernaut; road haulage
Los Angeles 209
Lyme Regis 192
Lyon 17
Mablethorpe 85, 167, 204
Macmillan, Harold 31, 99, 106, 107, 110, 118, 125
Macdonald, Ramsay 81
Macdonald, Sir Peter 57
Maclay, John 57
Mallaig 64, 190, 224
Manchester 16, 27, 42, 79, 100, 111, 112, 116, 127-130, 152, 154, 158, 174, 188, 219, 235, 237
, Greater 195
Manchester, Sheffield and Lincolnshire Railway 19
Manorhamilton 99
Mansfield 182, 219
Marples, Ernest 110, 115-118, 120, 122, 123, 125-131, 133, 136, 140, 157, 167, 179, 188, 211, 222, 230, 234
Mrs. 126
Marsh, Richard 194, 210
Marylebone 65, 165
Meadows 6 cylinder engine 93
Meirionnydd 145, 208
Meldon quarry 83
Mendip Hills 181
Merseyside 195
Merstone Junction 66
Merthyr 141
Metro-Cammell 105
Midland and Great Northern Joint line 122
Midland Railway 11, 18, 25, 26, 93, 166
Midsomer-Norton 181, 182
Midville 168
Milne, Sir James 37
Milton-Keynes 178, 235
Minehead 206, 207
Minister for Aviation and Supply 124
Minister of Transport 23, 24, 30, 49, 58, 94-96, 98, 110, 113, 116, 122-124, 126-128, 132-134, 140, 158-160, 167, 171, 172, 175, 177, 178, 183, 186, 187, 192, 194, 210, 217
SEE ALSO Rt.Hon.Alfred Barnes; Leslie Burgin; Barbara Castle; Tom Fraser; Eric Geddes; Lenox-Boyd; Ernest Marples; Richard Marsh; Harold Watkinson
Minister for Transport Industries 207, 210, 214
SEE ALSO John Peyton
Minister of War Transport 35
SEE ALSO Alfred Barnes
"Ministry of Roads" 126
Ministry of Transport 9, 10, 23, 30, 35, 40, 65, 70, 72, 79, 87, 88, 95, 97, 98, 105, 106, 109-112, 116, 121, 122, 124-129, 134, 142, 175, 176, 178, 179, 185-187, 189, 194, 202, 203, 211, 219, 234
SEE ALSO Department of Transport

Missenden, Sir Eustace 37, 41, 53
Mis-shaping of British Railways...Retort, The 141
Modern Tramway, The 59
modernisation 87, 88, 96, 97, 99-101, 105, 106, 109-113, 116-118, 122, 127-130, 132, 136, 139, 142, 143, 154, 164, 228
Modernisation
Committee 75, 78, 106
Plan 105, 147
Mold 77
Molson, Hugh 94, 97
Monmouth 84
Montgomeryshire 43
Morgan, Professor Victor 178
Morris, John 187
Motive Power Committee, Railway 46, 49, 50, 56, 59, 76, 228,
motor car SEE car
Motor Car and Natural Resources, The 209
Motor Show 219
motorway 65, 79, 106, 109, 114, 117, 120, 122, 175, 184, 202, 207, 211, 217-219, 236
construction 30, 35, 36, 87, 106, 112, 176, 185, 186
maintenance 211, 218
Munro, Alison 97

National Bus Company 216
National Council on Inland Transport 117, 157-160, 167, 178, 185
National Trust 108
National Union of Railwaymen 71, 95, 109, 137-141, 206
nationalisation 11, 17, 18, 22, 23, 34-56, 57, 59, 67, 75, 84, 88, 90, 95, 99, 113, 115, 125, 136-138, 227
Needham Market station 207
Nene Valley Line 220
Network for Development 171, 189, 192-194, 197, 200, 224
Network South East 223
New Zealand state rail system 157
Newby, Don 178
Newcastle 12, 32, 152, 174, 200
Newmarket 177
Newport 66, 68, 70, 71, 179, 180, 230
Newquay 190
Newton Abbot 85
Niendorf 60
Noel-Baker, Francis 124, 128
Noel-Baker, Philip 136, 188
Norfolk 94, 122, 203
North Berwick 21
North Britisb Company 21
North British Railway 202
North Devon Line 221
North Eastern Railway 26
North Eastern Region 43, 115, 220
Northampton 93
Northern Ireland 172
Northumberland 192
Norwich 225
Nottingham 11, 19, 165, 166, 188

Nottinghamshire 182, 236
Oban 213
objectors SEE protesters
oil 10, 27, 198, 210, 213
crisis 11, 30, 198, 199, 212, 217, 236
Okehampton 83, 190, 192, 197, 234, 235
Orkney 22
Organisation for Economic Co-operation and Development 209, 210, 217
Orpington 26
Oswestry 162
Oxford 177, 178, 190, 214, 234, 235
Oxted 185

Paddington 85, 143
Padmore, Thomas 186
Padstow 192
Paignton 204
park and ride 219
Park Royal Vehicles 93, 101
Parkinson, Cecil 237
"parkway" station concept 219
Parliamentary Select Committee on Nationalised Industries 112, 113, 115, 122, 123, 126, 127, 128
Parliamentary Train 18
Passenger Transport Authorities 195, 219
Passenger Transport Executive 195
Pearson, A.J. 64, 142, 156
pedestrians 121
PEIDA 214
Peyton, John 207
Peterborough 167, 178, 207, 220
Peterhead 190
Pickersgill, Richard 14
Pinhoe 222
Plodder Lane station 48
Plymouth 83, 152, 190, 192, 234, 235
pollution 117, 194, 209, 210, 212, 226, 232
Pontypool Road 84
Poole 182, 235
Portal, Lord 37
Portland station 80
Portsmouth 26, 78
Post Office 237
"preferential charges" legislation 32
Presteigne 203
Preston 157
Bypass 106, 107
Princes Risborough 65, 76
Princetown 80, 81, 82
Proposals for Inland Waterways 107
Prosser, Owen 10, 46, 59, 75, 81, 94
protesters 58, 66, 67, 70, 81, 84, 131, 133, 135, 158-160, 170, 172, 184, 185
Provincial sector 223, 224
Pryke, Richard 227
Public Records Office 9, 10
public transport 38, 41, 101, 124, 152, 156, 175, 192, 212, 216, 217, 218
Pwllheli 190, 214
Pye, Colonel John 120

"**quantity** licensing" 195

RAC 23, 186, 207
Radstock 182
rail lobby 99, 116, 123, 129, 145, 146,
149, 151, 157, 199, 221, 229
rail unions SEE trade unions, rail
railbus 9, 50, 51, 59-61, 75, 78, 87, 90-
93, 96, 98, 99, 101, 102, 104-106, 147,
150, 151, 168, 230
  SEE ALSO railcar
railcar 27, 29, 50-53, 59-63, 65, 76, 90,
91, 94, 96, 101-104, 168, 169, 202, 204
  SEE ALSO railbus
Railfreight 204
railway
  companies 11, 16-18, 20, 21, 23-25,
27, 28, 30-33, 36, 37, 40, 41, 43, 46, 48,
71, 73, 74, 83, 90, 131, 138, 206, 220,
229
  SEE ALSO Great Central; Great
Northern; Great Western; London,
Midland and Scottish; London and
North Eastern; London and
  North Western; Midland Railway;
North Eastern
  investment programme 212
  nostalgia 200, 230
  preservation movement 199, 200,
203, 204, 206
  reopening 207, 219, 221, 222, 224,
237
Railway Conversion League 121, 124
Railway Development Association 10,
59, 63, 66, 75, 77, 78, 80, 81, 82, 88,
89, 94, 98, 101, 104, 122, 179, 207,
216, 220, 224
  SEE ALSO Railway Development
Society
Railway Development Society 8, 10,
59, 221, 222
  SEE ALSO Railway Development
Association
Railway Executive Committee 22, 33,
40
  SEE ALSO Railway Executive
Railway Executive 34, 37, 40, 41, 45-
47, 49, 50, 54, 55, 57, 58, 61-74, 132,
227, 228
Railway Gazette 142
Railway Invigoration Society 183, 207,
220
Railway Magazine 53, 214
Railway Motive Powere Committee
SEE Motive Power Committee,
  Railway
Railway Rates Tribunal 24, 32, 39
Railwaymen, The 109
Railways 55
Railways Act 24, 28
Railways, Light SEE Light Railways
Ravenglass 200
Raymond, Stanley 185, 186
Reading 78
redundancies 139-141
Rees, Professor Graham 208
Reid, Robert 223
Renfrewshire 57

Report on Diesel and Electric
Traction, and the Passenger services
of the Future 105
Reshaping of British Railways -
Report 141, 144-149, 150-170, 172,
174, 177, 204, 232, 233, 234
Retford 61
Rhyl 77
Riccarton Junction 201
Rifkind, Malcolm 237
"Ringway One" 211
Ringwood 182, 235
road
  accidents SEE accidents
  congestion 82, 117, 119, 127, 137,
152, 154, 156, 183, 186, 207, 209-211,
217, 218, 226, 232
  construction 30, 117, 127, 156, 193,
209, 211, 215, 218, 236
  firms 109, 126
  haulage 13, 28, 35, 36, 44, 45, 56,
58, 65, 72, 101, 109, 110, 113, 125,
127, 194
  campaign 124
  lobby 64
  operators 41, 57, 59, 73, 109, 114,
132, 195
  improvements 70, 112, 183, 193,
207, 209
  lobby 7, 23, 28, 30, 65, 87, 88, 95,
109, 110, 117, 121, 125,126, 171, 175,
176, 178, 194, 195, 199, 207, 210,
220, 221, 228, 234, 236
  programme 125, 178, 183, 226, 237
  taxes 193
  transport 28, 30, 34, 38, 45, 65, 78,
86, 90, 101, 106, 109, 117, 118, 120,
126, 145, 149, 150, 154, 185-187, 192,
209, 211, 219, 237
  SEE ALSO motorway
Road Federation, British SEE British
Road Federation
Road Haulage Association 109, 110,
120, 124, 125, 207
Road Haulage Executive 50
Road Transport Executive Committee
40, 41
Roads Campaign Council 87
Roads Study Group 87
Robertsbridge 46
Robertson, General Sir Brian 72, 100,
121, 130
Rolvenden 47
Royal Ordnance Factories 124
Royal train 9
Royal Mail, parcels traffic 174
Rugby 165, 180, 188, 235
Russia 23
Ruthin 77
Rural Transport Improvement Bill 88-
90, 92, 94, 95, 108, 109, 150
Ryde 55, 71, 179, 180, 188, 230
St. Albans 151
St. Andrews 234
St. Erth 162
St. Helens 69

St. Ives 162, 197, 207, 219
St. Pancras 42
Salehurst 46
Salisbury 190, 192, 195
Sampson, Anthony 227
Sandown 55, 66, 70, 71, 230
Saner, Colonel J.A. 20
Scarborough 162, 172, 173
Scotland 32, 40, 43, 83, 96, 105, 114,
120, 138, 147, 150, 154, 155, 156, 183,
208, 213, 223
Scottish lines 26, 64, 138, 154
Scottish Region 43, 115, 13, 183, 184
  seasonal traffic 134, 147, 152, 153,
167, 189, 193, 202, 206, 207, 208
Seaton 192
Select Committee on Nationalised
Industries SEE Parliamentary
  Select Committee
Sentinel Company 27, 29
Serpell Report 222
Serpell, Sir David 222
Settle and Carlisle Line 111, 148, 190,
192, 204, 208, 214, 224, 225
Severn Canal 107
Severn Railway Bridge 131
Severn Valley Railway 220
Shanklin 179, 180, 188, 230, 231
Shell 131
Sheffield 19, 27, 42, 148, 152, 164,
166, 235, 237
Shenfield 49
Shepton Mallet 182
Sheringham 190, 203, 225
Shirley, Philip 131
Shropshire and Montgomeryshire light
railway 43
Sidmouth 192
Silkin, Lord 17
Silkin, QC Hon. Sam 158, 160
Silloth 96, 168, 169, 170
Silver Jubilee 32
Simonside 220
Skegness 61, 85, 148, 167, 168, 204,
208
Skipton 197
Slesser, Sir Henry 81, 82
Sligo 98, 99
Snow, Julian 88
Snowdon Mountain Railway 148
social factors in rail closure 152, 184,
186-190, 192, 195, 196, 208, 210, 216,
229
Society of Motor Manufacturers and
Traders 23, 35, 87
Solway Firth 169
Somerset 203, 206
  Railway, West SEE West Somerset
Railway
Somerset and Dorset Line 148, 167,
180-183, 222, 234, 235
South Shields 36
South Tynedale narrow gauge line 215
Southampton 22, 152, 235
Southern Region 43, 71, 78, 105, 115
Southern Railway 21, 26, 31, 37, 41,

43, 44, 190
Southport 157
Spalding 207
Special Roads Act 1949 35
Speedlink 237
Speller legislation 199, 221, 222, 223
Speller, Tony 221, 222
Spier, Rupert 76
Stalybridge 215
steam trains and services 14-16, 27, 34, 41, 42, 46, 50, 53, 54, 58-61, 67, 75, 76, 78, 85, 87, 90, 96, 98, 100, 102, 105, 109, 150, 169, 177, 182, 187, 202, 206, 228, 230, 233
Stedeford Committee 122-130, 196, 222
Stedeford, Sir Ivan 122, 125, 127
Stephens, Colonel 84, 179
Stephenson, George 14, 16, 87
Stephenson, Robert 16
Stevenson, Melford 66-71
Stockport 215
Stockton and Darlington Railway 13-17, 20
Stonham, Lord 136, 157, 167
stopping services 21, 27, 61, 75, 76, 78, 85, 90, 98, 106, 113, 144, 145, 147, 208, 230, 232
Stourport 197
Strange, Lord 13
Stranorlar 51
Stranraer 172, 173
Stratford on Avon canal 108
subsidies 124, 189, 190, 192, 195, 196, 209, 216, 222
   SEE ALSO grant
Sudbury 197
Suffolk 207
Suffolk Line, East SEE East Suffolk Line
Sunderland 53
Sussex Light Railway, West SEE West Sussex Light Railway
Sutton 26
Sutton Park station 171
Swanage 49, 182, 190, 193, 204, 206, 234
Swanage Railway Company 205
Swanage Railway Society 206
Swindon 101, 128, 177

Talyllyn narrow gauge line 199
Tamar river 192
Taunton 168, 206
Tavistock 192
tax subsidies for company cars 209
Templecombe 222
Tenterden 84
Tetbury 102, 168
Thatcher, Margaret 207, 222, 223,224
Thornton New Yard 177
Thurso 22
Times, The 64, 120, 174
Tiverton 168
Torrington 221
Totnes 83
tourism 12, 81

tourist 156, 158, 192, 193, 202, 204, 206, 207, 208, 219, 230,
Towcester 103
trade union 58, 62, 95, 116, 123, 137-141, 148, 174, 186, 188, 197, 214
   road transport 176, 195
   SEE ALSO ASLEF; National Union of Railwaymen
Trade Union Congress 99, 140, 175
trams 24
   SEE ALSO Light Railway
tramway 13, 14
Transport Act 193, 194
   1921 23
   1947 38-40, 50, 54-57, 71, 89, 109, 113, 195
   1953 64, 71-73, 228
   1962 82, 108, 132, 137, 157-159, 163, 172, 174, 186, 221, 233
   1968 171, 194, 195, 208, 216
Transport Bill 64, 71
Transport Commission SEE British Transport Commission
Transport, Department of SEE Department of Transport
"Transport Highway Authority" 185, 186
Transport, Minister of SEE Minister of Transport
Transport, Ministry of SEE Ministry of Transport
Transport Policy 186, 187
Transport and Road Research Laboratory 219
Transport Tribunal 39, 40, 72, 89, 90, 113
Transport Users Consultative Committee 39, 40, 47, 64, 66, 67, 70, 82, 88-90, 97, 131-136, 148, 157-160, 163-168, 178, 179, 185, 188, 193, 194, 206, 217, 221, 222, 232
   East Midlands 81, 167
   South East 67
   South West 80, 81, 217, 222
   SEE ALSO Central Transport Consultative Committee
Transport 2000 214, 221
Treasury 30, 105, 106, 111, 112, 122, 124, 126, 132
Treherbert 197
Tribunals and Inquiries Act 1958 157
Trouble House Halt 168
Tube Investments 122
Tunbridge Wells 185
Tyne 201, 220
Tyne and Wear Metro 26, 220
Tyneside 26, 195, 220

Uckfield 235
Ulster Transport Authority 98
Unilever 131
union SEE trade union
United States of America 46, 92, 154, 209, 210, 232
unremunerative railway grant 171
Unremunerative Railway Committee 47

Uttoxeter 92

Ventnor 66, 71, 179, 180, 230, 231
Wadebridge 192
Waggon und Maschinenbau 101
Wagon Repairing Association 124
Wakes Bus Company 181
Wales 19, 40, 49, 114, 120, 138, 147, 152, 155, 156, 175, 192, 208
   Line, Central 185, 190, 208, 209,224
   North 77
   South 139, 140, 141
Walker, Professor Gilbert 120
Walker, Sir Herbert 26
Walsall 61
Warcop 192, 204
Ware 93
Wareham 206
Warrington 35
Watchet 206
Watford 151
Watkin, Sir Edward 19, 165, 166
Watkinson, Harold 98, 99
Waverly line 12, 62, 148, 190, 194, 200, 201, 202, 203
Weighell, Sidney 206
West Coast line 12, 79, 105, 200, 202
West Highland line 93
West Midlands Railway Passenger Transport Scheme 65
West Moors 182
West Somerset Railway 206, 207
West Sussex Light Railway 91
Westerham 203
Western Region 43, 50, 53, 76, 82, 85, 101, 102, 115, 142, 143, 161
Westminster Bank Review 120
Weybourne 203
Weymouth 80, 105
Whitby 172, 173
Whitwill, Colonel Mark 81
Wickham 91, 93, 101
Williams, Leslie 131
Willoughby 167
Wilson, Harold 11, 145, 164, 167, 171-173, 175-177, 186, 194, 214, 234-236
Wilson, Sir Reginald 85, 97, 104
Wiltshire 168
Wimbledon 215
Wimborne 182
Wincanton 182
Windermere 214
Winter Executive Committee 45
Woodford Halse 166, 167
Woodhead tunnel 235, 237
Worgret Junction 206
World's Carriers, The 120
Worshipful Company of Carmen 120
Wylde, J.D. 199

Yarm branch 16
Yealmton 48
Yelverton 80
Yeovil 168
York 78, 92, 142
Yorkshire 61, 85, 195